SAVE BY ROY

Also by Terry Frei

Horns, Hogs, and Nixon Coming (nonfiction)
Third Down and a War to Go (nonfiction)
'77: Denver, the Broncos, and a Coming of Age (nonfiction)
The Witch's Season (fiction)
Playing Piano in a Brothel (nonfiction)
Olympic Affair (fiction)
March 1939: Before the Madness (nonfiction)

Also by Adrian Dater

Blood Feud: Detroit Red Wings vs. Colorado Avalanche
The Good, the Bad, and the Ugly: Denver Broncos
Then Morton Said to Elway: The Best Denver Broncos Stories Ever Told (with Craig Morton)
100 Things Rockies Fans Should Know & Do Before They Die

SAVE BY ROY

Patrick Roy and the Return of the Colorado Avalanche

Terry Frei and Adrian Dater

TAYLOR TRADE PUBLISHING
Lanham • Boulder • New York • London

Published by Taylor Trade Publishing
An imprint of The Rowman & Littlefield Publishing Group, Inc.
4501 Forbes Boulevard, Suite 200, Lanham, Maryland 20706
www.rowman.com

Unit A, Whitacre Mews, 26-34 Stannery Street, London SE11 4AB, United Kingdom

Distributed by NATIONAL BOOK NETWORK

British Library Cataloguing in Publication Information Available

Library of Congress Cataloging-in-Publication Data Available

ISBN 978-1-63076-000-7 (pbk. : alk. paper)
ISBN 978-1-63076-001-4 (electronic)

∞ ™ The paper used in this publication meets the minimum requirements of American National Standard for Information Sciences Permanence of Paper for Printed Library Materials, ANSI/NISO Z39.48-1992.

Printed in the United States of America

CONTENTS

COLORADO AVALANCHE, 2013–14 ROSTER

Colorado Avalanche, 2013–14 Roster*

		Height	Weight (lbs)	Birth Date (age on opening night)	Birthplace
Goaltenders					
1	Semyon Varlamov	6'2"	209	April 27, 1988 (25)	Samara, Russia
20	Reto Berra	6'4"	194	January 3, 1987 (26)	Bulach, Switzerland
30	Sami Aittokallio	6'1"	174	August 6, 1992 (21)	Tampere, Finland
35	Jean-Sebastien Giguere	6'1"	202	May 16, 1977 (36)	Montreal
Defensemen					
2	Nick Holden	6'4"	207	May 15, 1987 (26)	St. Albert, Alberta
3	Karl Stollery	5'11"	180	November 21, 1987 (25)	Camrose, Alberta
4	Tyson Barrie	5'10"	190	July 26, 1991 (22)	Victoria, British Columbia
5	Nate Guenin	6'3"	207	December 10, 1982 (30)	Aliquippa, Pennsylvania
6	Erik Johnson	6'4"	232	March 21, 1988 (25)	Bloomington, Minnesota
8	Jan Hejda	6'4"	237	June 18, 1978 (35)	Prague
16	Cory Sarich	6'4"	207	August 16, 1978 (35)	Saskatoon, Saskatchewan
22	Matt Hunwick	5'11"	190	May 21, 1985 (28)	Warren, Michigan
44	Ryan Wilson	6'1"	207	February 3, 1987 (26)	Windsor, Ontario
46	Stefan Elliott	6'1"	190	January 30, 1991 (22)	Vancouver
61	Andre Benoit	5'11"	191	January 6, 1984 (29)	St. Albert, Ontario

Forwards

#	Name	Height	Weight	Birthdate (Age)	Birthplace
7	John Mitchell	6'1"	204	January 22, 1985 (28)	Oakville, Ontario
9	Matt Duchene	5'11"	200	January 16, 1991 (22)	Haliburton, Ontario
11	Jamie McGinn	6'1"	210	August 5, 1988 (25)	Fergus, Ontario
14	David Van der Gulik	5'10"	173	April 20, 1983 (30)	Abbotsford, British Columbia
15	P. A. Parenteau	6'0"	193	March 24, 1983 (30)	Hull, Quebec
17	Steve Downie	5'11"	191	April 3, 1987 (26)	Newmarket, Ontario
24	Marc-Andre Cliche	6'0"	202	March 23, 1987 (26)	Rouyn-Noranda, Quebec
25	Maxime Talbot	5'11"	190	February 11, 1984 (29)	Lemoyne, Quebec
26	Paul Stastny	6'0"	205	December 27, 1985 (27)	Quebec City
28	Paul Carey	6'0"	175	September 24, 1988 (25)	Boston
29	Nathan MacKinnon	6'0"	182	September 1, 1995 (18)	Halifax, Nova Scotia
38	Joey Hishon	5'10"	170	October 21, 1991 (22)	Stratford, Ontario
40	Alex Tanguay	6'1"	194	November 21, 1979 (33)	Ste-Justine, Quebec
42	Brad Malone	6'2"	207	May 20, 1989 (24)	Miramichi, New Brunswick
55	Cody McLeod	6'2"	210	June 26, 1984 (29)	Binscarth, Manitoba
58	Patrick Bordeleau	6'6"	225	March 23, 1986 (27)	Montreal
90	Ryan O'Reilly	6'0"	200	February 7, 1991 (22)	Clinton, Ontario
92	Gabriel Landeskog	6'1"	204	November 23, 1992 (20)	Stockholm

*All players who appeared in at least one game for Colorado.

OFF THE RECORD . . .

Adrian Dater and I have written about the Colorado Avalanche for the *Denver Post* virtually since the National Hockey League franchise's sale and move from Quebec City to Denver in the summer of 1995. Adrian stepped up from covering the International Hockey League's Denver Grizzlies, and I began my second stint at the paper that December both as the NHL writer and as a generalist reporter and columnist. It was a return to hockey for me; many years earlier, as a *very* young reporter, I had covered the NHL's Colorado Rockies for the *Post* in the team's final five seasons in Denver before, following years of trials and tribulations, the team was sold and moved to New Jersey to become the Devils. It was a great way to gain "beat" experience before I covered other sports, including the NBA, NFL, Major League Baseball, and major college sports at the *Post*, the *Oregonian*, and *Sporting News*.

In the years since the Avalanche's arrival in 1995, our roles have evolved as the newspaper business and the *Post* sports department situation changed considerably. Adrian has remained full-time on the hockey beat. I have become even more of a generalist writer/commentator as the newspaper stepped away from in-house coverage of the league at-large. (For example, and understandably, no more trips to Pittsburgh for features on Sidney Crosby or traveling to cover playoff series not involving the Avalanche.) During the time frame of this book, as both a newspaper writer and a part-time radio talk-show host, I covered and talked about every other major-league team in Denver, college sports, and much more, and I enjoy the non-specialized role. Yet, I found myself still drawn to attending Avalanche games and writing about the team and the league for the paper when it was feasible.

Individually, Adrian and I both have written previous books for Taylor Trade Publishing and editorial director Rick Rinehart. Adrian's *Blood Feud* is the definitive work about the once-notorious Avalanche-Red Wings rivalry. Among the handful I've done for Taylor Trade is *Playing Piano in a Brothel*, which includes an extensive "Pucks" section about covering the Rockies, Avalanche, and the NHL.

While waiting for the February 2014 publication of my seventh book, Taylor Trade's *March 1939: Before the Madness*, I began talking with Rick about next doing something on Roy and the Avalanche. Soon, Rick, Adrian, and I agreed collaboration was the way to go. The fact that I no longer am assigned nearly full-time to hockey in my newspaper job enabled me to conduct interviews and attend many practices and games on my own time. I did write many commentaries on the Avalanche for the *Post* and covered a few games, too, giving Adrian and Mike Chambers a break. Adrian's work as the "beat" man was the basis of much that appears here, too, and he wrote many passages as reflective, interpretive reaction to the material that has been in his newspaper stories. Of course, much also was gleaned from "official" availabilities and locker-room situations.

So that you know: Adrian and I argue. For many years, we have argued, and argued about almost everything. Including hockey. Many of our conversations, in fact, have paid homage to Dan Aykroyd and Jane Curtin's famous exchanges on *Saturday Night Live* and included the catchphrase: "Jane, you ignorant slut . . ." or equivalents. When other folks have said, "But you guys argue all the time," we generally have responded, "Yeah . . . so?"

We are opinionated, interpretive, and even passionate in telling the story, and we wrote this—appropriately, because this was hockey—mostly on the fly, starting immediately after agreeing to do this book. *Save by Roy* certainly draws on our access and experiences as members of the "mainstream" media, but it is an independent work produced outside the usual constraints, involving both space and style, of newspaper work. We're not going to bog this down with footnotes that specify which one of us has written each passage or conducted each interview. As you'll see, when it seemed especially appropriate or the best way to tell the story, we've dropped in more personal *"From the Note-*

book of . . ." passages. In the rest of the manuscript, though, we didn't debate and produce "compromise" material we both agree with. Discerning readers might even be able to find contradictory opinions, but we're going to live with that. We're not afraid to stand behind our own views and certainly will answer questions about who said what, but the most accurate assumption you can make as a reader as you move along is that although Adrian and I don't necessarily agree with every word the other has written, we'll stand behind this as a collaborative effort.

Terry Frei, Denver, Colorado

Doing my best Aykroyd impression: Terry, you ignorant slut.

Adrian Dater, Thornton, Colorado

Part I

Resurfacing

COACH ROY

The scene at Denver's Pepsi Center on May 28, 2013, was reminiscent of the opening of the Nancy Dowd-written *Slap Shot*, which shows Charlestown Chiefs goalie Denis Lemieux and sportscaster Jim Carr, bad wig and all, waiting for a cue from the director to begin speaking in the live local television show segment.

Avalanche senior vice president of communications Jean Martineau, with the franchise since its days in Quebec City, stood at a podium in a restaurant on the arena's club level. He alerted members of the media and the other attendees—including several Avalanche players—that the news conference wouldn't begin until the opening of a specific time window for the television broadcasts going around the world on the NHL Network and other sports cable outlets.

To Martineau's right, Josh Kroenke, Joe Sakic, and Patrick Roy waited, too.

At a news conference in the same room two weeks earlier, on May 10, the Avalanche had officially announced two major moves:

- Kroenke, the son of team owner Stan Kroenke, was succeeding Pierre Lacroix as team president. Stan Kroenke's sports empire by then also included the NFL's St. Louis Rams; the London-based Arsenal of soccer's English Premier League; the NBA's Denver Nuggets, the Colorado Mammoth of the National Lacrosse League, and the Colorado Rapids of Major League Soccer; and the Pepsi Center and soccer's Dick's Sporting Goods Park just outside of Denver. Josh had been the Nuggets' president for the

previous three years. Now he was going to run the Avalanche, too,
and Lacroix was taking a step deeper into retirement while remaining with the organization as an "adviser."

- Sakic, the former superstar center and team captain who had
  been serving what amounted to a high-profile internship in the
  front office since 2010, was promoted to executive vice president
  of hockey operations, leapfrogging general manager Greg Sherman.

The May 28 news conference was called to officially discuss the next
move, an even flashier one.

Roy, the greatest goaltender in NHL history and instrumental in
Avalanche Stanley Cup victories in 1996 and 2001, was back after a ten-
year absence—rejoining the team as head coach and vice president of
hockey operations.

When Pierre Lacroix offered Roy a chance to return to the team in
2009, Lacroix said that one of the many reasons why Roy declined was a
belief that he had unfinished business remaining in his role as co-owner, GM, and head coach of major junior hockey's Quebec Remparts in
Quebec City, his hometown.

This time, in 2013, Roy said yes. This was big news, locally and even
internationally. Several reporters, print and broadcast, had made the
trip down from Canada to cover the proceedings.

Finally, Martineau greeted the truly international audience, and the
news conference began.

After Martineau introduced the three men on the dais, Kroenke, a
former University of Missouri basketball player still young enough to be
an NHL defenseman, and athletic enough to have been a decent one if
he had been channeled into skates, brought up the recruiting trip he
and Sakic made to Roy's second home in Florida. "I instantly felt his
passion for the game and his desire to be involved with our franchise
and all aspects of the operations," Kroenke said.

Then it was Sakic's turn. "When I took this job," he said, "and I knew
I had to find a coach, Patrick was always my top candidate."

Next, Roy noted that the news conference was taking place in the
same room where he had announced his retirement ten years earlier, to
the day. "To all Avalanche fans," he said, "rest assured I will bring the

same passion to my new role with the team that I did when I was a player."

In the question and answer portion, Roy said that he would have taken the job minus the vice president of hockey operations title; that was the one comment that triggered skepticism. Understandably, he had wanted a voice in forging the roster he would coach.

"I honestly am not here because I am the VP of hockey, but I am happy that Joe gave me that opportunity," he said.

Roy was asked if he had felt angst over the Avalanche's slide after he turned down the coaching job in 2009.

"I'm sure deep inside it probably played a role," he said. "First of all, if the team had been successful, there probably would have never been a coach change and a lot of change in management as well. I think it's the perfect time. In 2009 also, I would say that maybe I was not quite ready for it yet. I was afraid in 2009 that maybe I missed one of the best opportunities of my life, but today here I am in 2013, and the same opportunity is there, and I have the opportunity to work with great people. I am not saying they weren't great people then, but right now it's a really good situation, it's a nice challenge, and I'm just glad to be a part of it."

As the formal part of the session wound down, Roy heard a question he had known would be coming in some form. What about the fact that the great players who get into coaching don't have a great track record?

"You know what? I am not nervous about that," he said. "I was surprised that no one asked me a question about experience and stuff like that, and to be honest with you, I checked one very interesting stat: 100 percent of the coaches who are coaching now in the NHL were rookies at one time in their career. Also, I think my number one quality is that I'm not afraid to put in the time, and I believe that when you work hard and put in the time, nothing will go wrong."

What that meant, of course, was that Roy had that zinger all prepared and ready to go—and his first slick move on the job was to find a way to use it.

Even that seemed a significant change from previous standard operating procedure for the Avalanche front office, which often involved an atmosphere in which joking could seem as appropriate as giggling during a strict Baptist church service.

For the Avalanche, the times, they were a-changing.

✿ ✿ ✿

The Avalanche franchise's past didn't need to be disowned, of course. The NHL team claimed Denver's first major-league championship in 1996, at the end of the franchise's first season in town following the sale and move of the Nordiques from Quebec City after a lockout-shortened 1995 season. The snide remarks about the long-suffering Colorado hockey fans having to wait several months for a Stanley Cup celebration were understandable. But they ignored the reality that Denver's hockey tradition is extensive, including the University of Denver Pioneers, minor-league pro hockey, the short-lived Denver Spurs of the World Hockey Association, and the NHL's Colorado Rockies. Even those bizarre Rockies days had their moments of compelling entertainment, with a series of ownerships, seemingly relentless financial crises and rumors of demise, and a handful of high-profile figures. Those included Don Cherry, who coached the Rockies for one season before being fired and subsequently becoming an iconic figure as the star of "Coach's Corner" on *Hockey Night in Canada*; and high-profile players Lanny McDonald, Barry Beck, Chico Resch, and Wilf Paiement.

The Nuggets' corporate ownership, COMSAT, acquired the young and promising Nordiques almost by accident. Quebec had won the Northeast Division the previous season but lost in the first round of the playoffs to the Rangers. The COMSAT czars were angling for an NHL franchise to begin play when a new Denver arena was built and opened. They agreed to be "used" as a leverage ploy in the Nordiques' quest to get a new arena in Quebec City. Instead, the company ended up with the Nordiques-turned-Avalanche, playing in the inadequate McNichols Arena. Lacroix, the GM, and coaches Marc Crawford, Joel Quenneville,[1] and Jacques Martin all came with the team to Denver. Of course, so did the promising roster, including Sakic, Peter Forsberg, and Adam Foote.

Two months into that first season, the Avalanche acquired the final piece of the puzzle—the goaltender named Roy, exiled from Montreal,

---

1. Quenneville had played for the Rockies from 1979 to 1982. During Cherry's single season behind the bench, Quenneville came to Colorado from Toronto with Lanny McDonald, in the December 1979 trade for Wilf Paiement and Pat Hickey.

where he had been instrumental in the Canadiens' 1986 and 1993 Stanley Cup victories.

The Canadiens had gone 18–23–7 in the '95 lockout season, and Roy chafed. The backstory to the deal didn't come out until later, when former Montreal GM Serge Savard revealed that when the Canadiens lost their first four games to open the 1995–96 season, he began talking about a possible deal with Lacroix, who had been a longtime agent and had Roy as his client before switching sides of the table. They actually agreed in principle to a trade that would send Roy to Colorado for winger Owen Nolan, goaltender Stephane Fiset, and a draft pick. Instead of confirming the deal, on October 16 Savard had to tell Lacroix he had just been fired. Rejean Houle took over as GM; and, with coach Jacques Demers also fired, Mario Tremblay—who had no coaching experience—became the Canadiens' coach. The deal was scuttled, and Roy stayed with the Canadiens. Ten days later, Colorado traded Nolan to San Jose for defenseman Sandis Ozolinsh.

Montreal played well under Tremblay at first, but Roy had an acidic relationship with his new coach. They had been teammates for Roy's first full season in the league, 1985–86, the one that culminated with Roy's coming-out party in the playoffs and another Stanley Cup championship for the Canadiens, with Roy winning the Conn Smythe Trophy as the postseason MVP. Later a broadcaster, Tremblay belittled Roy's early struggles in English. After Tremblay became coach, they repeatedly clashed.

Roy went off after Tremblay left him in for nine Detroit goals on December 2, violating the game's protocol. After finally being pulled in the 11–1 loss, Roy strode down the bench and told team president Ronald Corey, seated next to it, that he had played his final game for the Canadiens. It was hyperbole in the heat of the moment, but the damage was done. The Canadiens and many in the Montreal media were affronted. Houle's hand was forced, and he began talking with Lacroix. On December 6, Roy and right wing Mike Keane came to the Avalanche for wingers Andrei Kovalenko and Martin Rucinsky, and goalie Jocelyn Thibault, who was Fiset's backup but considered a better long-range prospect.

"It was clear from the organization that they had made their decision," Roy said a week later, reflecting in a lengthy interview on his first road trip with the Avalanche. "I said, 'OK, I'll accept my mistake.' I agree I was the one who made that thing happen on that Saturday, and both parties agreed it was in the best interests of us that we go different directions. I understand that you can't put ten years aside and give it a little tap and it's all gone. I lived through lots of good things in Montreal, but, again, it's a turn I accept. This will be a very nice experience for us."

Playing the remainder of his career with Colorado, he got to hold the Stanley Cup aloft twice more, in 1996 and 2001, under coaches Crawford and Bob Hartley, respectively. As with most great teams, the major disappointment was that the loaded Avalanche didn't win *more* championships, as they made it to and lost in the Western Conference finals in 1997 and 2002 (to Detroit), plus 1999 and 2000 (to Dallas), with three of the four series ending in Game 7 defeats. Roy was part of the Avalanche becoming a hot ticket with automatic sellouts and—this line is stolen from Avalanche television analyst Peter McNab—a virtual Hall of Fame roll call when the team bus unloaded. At the height of the run, it could be Roy; Sakic and Forsberg, the centers who each won the Hart Trophy as the league's most valuable player; winger Milan Hejduk, the league's leading goal scorer in 2003; plus defensemen Ray Bourque, Rob Blake, and Adam Foote. It was a good time to be a hockey fan in Denver—or to become one.

Lacroix pulled off many deals that were instrumental in the glory years, and he never had the financial carte blanche his detractors tried to portray him as having. In fact, his major accomplishment might have been keeping the franchise at least semi-on course and competitive through bizarre ownership changes, including two sales that fell through, before Stan Kroenke took over the Nuggets and Avalanche in 2000.

Along the way, Roy became the NHL's all-time winning goalie, surpassing Terry Sawchuk, and was at the forefront of the Detroit-Colorado rivalry[2] with rare goalie fights with the Red Wings' Mike Vernon and Chris Osgood in the most acrimonious games. The wins record meant so much to him because, to his credit, he viewed winning as the ultimate measure of goaltending greatness. Of his 551 career regular-season victories, 261 came with Colorado. Of his 151 playoff wins, 80 came with the Avalanche.

---

2. As detailed in *Blood Feud*.

By the end of his career in Colorado, he was playing for his third head coach, Tony Granato. Officially, Crawford resigned; but essentially, he was forced out after the Avalanche blew a 3–1 series lead and lost in the first round of the 1998 playoffs to Edmonton. His successor, Hartley, was fired 31 games into the 2002–03 season. A 10–8–9–4 (*hike!*) start had Lacroix concerned that the franchise's streak of consecutive division championships was in danger of ending that season at eight, which tied the league record. The untested Granato, the American-born former winger, was promoted from assistant to head coach. It "worked" in the sense that the Avalanche won that unprecedented ninth consecutive division title, clinching it on the final day of the regular season, but the relentless quest for something so relatively minor drained them and left them vulnerable in the playoffs. Andrew Brunette's overtime goal in Game 7 of the first round in Denver gave Minnesota an upset come-from-behind series win over the Avalanche. Roy had decided during the season that he was going to retire, and he stuck to it. He went home to Quebec City, where he already owned a one-third share of the Remparts, and he started out as the franchise's co-owner and general manager.

FROM THE NOTEBOOK OF TERRY FREI

In the first three years of Roy's retirement, I traveled to see him twice— first in Quebec City as he settled in back in his hometown and was in his early days of running the Remparts, then in Toronto when he was inducted into the Hockey Hall of Fame.

In Quebec in October 2003, I was struck by the seamlessness of his transition to life as a major junior hockey co-owner and executive. During Remparts games, he and his wife, Michele, sat at a corner of the lower bowl, with their backs to the concourse. He spent part of his time signing autographs, but mostly he seemed to be a familiar face returning home. His arena office was fitting for an executive, but I admit it seemed strange to see him at a desk. "It was important for me to remain involved in hockey," he told me there. "I needed to do something. When I was thinking about retirement, I didn't just want to retire. I wanted to have something in front of me before I made my decision. The last couple of years, I was pretty sure this is what I wanted to do."

There was indeed a huge picture of Roy playing for Colorado in the Remparts' equipment room. Yet, it didn't show him making a huge save or even holding the Stanley Cup. Blood was streaming down Roy's face as a linesman escorted him off the ice in Detroit after his March 26, 1997, bout with Vernon. He maintained that he was cut when, rushing to teammate Claude Lemieux's aid after Detroit winger Darren McCarty[3] jumped him, Roy ran into Brendan Shanahan and fell to the ice. The point was, Roy wanted his players to see him as a warrior, not just a goaltender.

In November 2006, he and Dick Duff, the late Herb Brooks, and Harley Hotchkiss were that year's Hall of Fame inductees. By then, Roy also was the Remparts' coach after taking over for Eric Lavigne. I spoke with him several times during the several days of events tied to the induction ceremony. At a Fan Forum at the Hall of Fame headquarters on the day before the ceremony, most of those who waited in line and succeeded in gaining entrance in the small NHLPA Zone had come to see Roy. I was among a handful of media types also allowed in. After Roy made a point of saying that he had made his peace with the Montreal organization, a fan asked him if he could envision himself ever coaching the Canadiens someday.

"I know I could change my mind," Roy said, "but I don't see myself at the NHL level. We need people who want to coach at the junior level. You need people who accept that, who will want to be part of the sixteen- to twenty-year-olds and help them fulfill their goals. There are coaches in my league a lot better than me. Their dream is to coach in the NHL, and I wish it will happen for them, more than me."

The next night, in the Hall of Fame rotunda, he gave most of his induction speech in French. "Today, when I look back, I feel very fortunate to have played in the best possible conditions on teams such as the Canadiens and Avalanche," Roy said. "I sure do remember the pain, the sacrifices, the discipline and the efforts. But I also remember the partnership, friendship, and, mostly, this awesome effort of being part of a team." He thanked many of his former teammates and others by name and then switched to English to express gratitude to Adam Foote, then in the second season of his exile to Columbus. He said Foote was "my

3.   McCarty was "avenging" the hit Lemieux laid on Red Wings center Kris Draper from behind in Game 6 of the Western Conference finals—a hit that caused Draper to smash into the boards and suffer a broken jaw and severe facial injuries.

*friend, my roommate during eight years, and probably my best English
teacher." At that point, Roy smiled and teased himself. "I should have
played more years, I guess." His three children—Jonathan, Frederick,
and Jana—were in the audience, and he thanked them too, and indirect-
ly acknowledged Michele, by then his ex-wife. Referring to her as the
children's mother, he thanked her "for giving me the freedom to guide
my career."*

*I spoke with him after the ceremony. He said he had been more
nervous than he appeared, and said he was grateful that he hadn't had
to pick which of his two NHL teams he was representing when inducted. "They're both really special to me," he said. "The years at Montreal and my years at Colorado have been outstanding. I played for
great teams and had great teammates and great friendships."*

*He also said he was proud of his role in the popularization of the
NHL and hockey in Denver.*

*"The people in Denver showed they deserved to have a team, and
they've been extremely supportive of the Avalanche," he said. "They
never let us down. They were there for us every night."*

❖ ❖ ❖

Minus Roy, life had gone on for the Avalanche. In fact, Colorado's high-
profile, two-man "package" signings of Paul Kariya and Teemu Selanne
to one-year deals as unrestricted free agents for the 2003–04 season
raised a reasonable question: Did Roy retire too soon? It turned out,
though, that Kariya was listless, and Selanne was playing on a knee that
subsequently would require complete reconstruction to enable him to
extend his career for another ten years. In the 2004 playoffs, the Avalanche advanced to the conference semifinals and fell to San Jose in six
games. Soon, Lacroix announced that he had hired Quenneville, who
had a successful run as head coach of the St. Louis Blues, as Colorado's
new coach. Granato, the good soldier, accepted a demotion to assistant
coach.

Quenneville would have a long wait to step back behind the Colorado bench because of the labor dispute that led to the cancellation of the
2004–05 season. When the NHL emerged from its yearlong absence, a
hard cap of just $39 million was established, and the Avs were unable to
re-sign Foote, the heart-and-soul defenseman, and, even more shock-

ingly, Peter Forsberg. The fans were aghast, but there was just no room to get them in under the cap as unrestricted free agents.

The Avalanche traded Roy's Swiss successor as the number one goalie, David Aebischer, to Montreal late in the 2005–06 season for Jose Theodore in a deal that summoned comparisons to the Roy trade. Theodore was a former Hart Trophy winner and had worn out his welcome with the Canadiens. Colorado beat Dallas and then was swept by Anaheim in the conference semifinals.

In the summer of 2006, Lacroix relinquished the general manager's title. Although he remained team president, the move was billed as a semiretirement for Lacroix, who had been having health issues. A Lacroix protégé, Francois Giguere, was the new GM.

HOCKEY'S DENVER LIMBO

For the next seven years, one of the mysteries involving Patrick Roy's former team was just how much Pierre Lacroix remained involved in the decision making and the course of the franchise. Lacroix still often represented the Avalanche at such functions as the NHL's board of governors meetings, though at the end Josh Kroenke was listed as the team's governor and Lacroix an alternate.

The Avalanche's home sellout streak ended at 487 games on October 17, 2006. The official attendance of 17,681 for that Blackhawks-Avalanche game was only 326 short of capacity at the Pepsi Center. Actually, at many home games during the streak there probably were at least that many unsold seats but means were found to officially "sell" them. Admitting that the streak was over acknowledged that it soon would be impossible to claim that every ticket was sold. It was becoming apparent that season tickets weren't necessary to get into the arena or to have decent seats; and once fans realized they could pick and choose, that's what many did.

After Lacroix stepped down as GM, the Avalanche's win-at-all-costs culture seemed to morph into relative fiscal restraint, but the implementation of the NHL's hard salary cap in 2005 was a major reason for that. As the cap became larger in subsequent years, though, there could be some flexibility. With Giguere as the GM, Colorado signed big-name free agents Ryan Smyth and Scott Hannan in 2007. Giguere also persuaded Peter Forsberg to return to Colorado and swung a deal to get Adam Foote back from Columbus in 2008.

Quenneville coached the Avalanche to three consecutive 95-point seasons. That was good enough to make the playoffs in 2006, when the Avalanche beat Dallas in the first round and then fell to Anaheim in the Western Conference semifinals; and in 2008, when Colorado beat the Minnesota Wild in the first round before being swept by the Red Wings in the conference semifinals.

Lacroix's semiretirement was acknowledged when he was inducted into the Colorado Sports Hall of Fame in April 2008, but he clearly was involved in the discussions about whether Quenneville would return as coach for a fourth season. Quenneville left the impression that he believed Giguere and the Avalanche front office were unrealistic about the young talent then in the organization and on the NHL roster, and that offended management. So he was gone, and the truly weird part followed.

Granato was re-elevated to head coach, which proved to be a disastrous choice. His second stint lasted only one season. The Avalanche posted only 69 points in 2008–09, finishing 28th in the NHL, despite a payroll in the NHL's upper third. During the season, Lacroix sounded out Roy about a possible return to the organization, whether as an executive or as coach, or both, and they agreed they would talk more when the season was over. The day after the season ended, Lacroix stepped in and fired Giguere. In meeting with the team staff, he declared that he had exciting plans for getting the organization back on track—and would move on them while recuperating from previously scheduled knee replacement surgery. It got messy when Lacroix suffered unforeseeable post-surgery complications and was very ill. Roy came to Denver, anyway, for exploratory talks about becoming the coach and perhaps also having a front-office title, and it all became public when he was spotted having dinner at John Elway's restaurant in the Cherry Creek area, near Lacroix's Denver home.

Roy wanted in the range of $12 million over four years to make the jump; the Avalanche only offered $7 million. Roy's hard-line stance reflected his ongoing desire to coach his sons, Jonathan and Frederick, with the Remparts. Eventually Roy called Lacroix and turned down the chance to return, and the official storyline (essentially true) was that he had done so for family reasons. Lacroix was genuinely hurt that his former client and goaltender hadn't jumped at the chance to work with him again.

Granato, who had two years remaining on his contract, likely was destined to be fired, anyway, but the public nature of the negotiations with Roy clinched it. The Avalanche, still officially without a general manager, fired Granato and replaced him with Joe Sacco, the former NHL journeyman center coaching the Avalanche's Cleveland-based American Hockey League affiliate, the Lake Erie Monsters. A few days later, Greg Sherman was elevated to GM, a move that raised eyebrows because of the noticeable lack of hockey in his background. Sherman was a former baseball player at Cherry Creek High School in the Denver suburbs and a graduate of the University of San Diego who had never played hockey. With accounting in his background and on his résumé, he had joined the Pepsi Center sports empire in 1996. Before he got married and as he began working his way up, he shared an apartment across from the Tamarac Square Mall with a Nuggets video man/assistant coach named Mike Brown—the same Mike Brown who would go on to coach the Cleveland Cavaliers (twice) and the Los Angeles Lakers. Lacroix was impressed with Sherman's energy and brought him more into the hockey side of the operation as a numbers cruncher and detail man. His elevation to GM, although surprising, was part of a progression.

As the Avalanche payroll ranking slid in the next few seasons, the word "rebuilding" became the unofficial organizational motto.

Sacco lasted four seasons, an eternity in a league that treats coaches with the respect of disposable razors. The Avalanche made the playoffs only once in his four seasons, losing to San Jose in six games in an entertaining first-round series in 2010. When Colorado was awful in Sacco's fourth year, getting 39 points in the lockout-shortened 48-game season, his exit was inevitable.

Long before 2013, it was apparent that the Avalanche were[1] dysfunctional in the front office, too. One problem was that nobody knew who really was in charge. Another problem was that *because* nobody knew who really was in charge, it created a culture of unaccountability and passing the buck. Even if this was supposed to be semiretirement for Lacroix, his health problems prevented him from enjoying it much. His issues included a spine tumor and five surgeries in a 33-month

---

1. Sorry, grammarians, we're not going to automatically consider "Avalanche" singular here in deciding between it/they and was/were. Each reference will be subject to an "ear" test.

period. He wasn't much involved in the day-to-day operation, but Stan Kroenke was comfortable with Lacroix still being the titular head of the organization as Josh Kroenke watched and learned. Lacroix later insisted that mainly he had been an on-call adviser from the moment he stepped down as GM, and that nothing much changed in the next seven years, though technically he was the one reporting to Stan Kroenke as, first, Francois Giguere, and then Sherman were said to be running the front office. Regardless, though, his GM successors operated as if it weren't possible to change much of the organizational atmosphere, strategies, or philosophy.

Learning about both the GM's and president's jobs by watching and consulting with Lacroix was a sensible strategy, of course. When Lacroix was in charge and engaged, Avalanche fans always knew their GM was going for the Stanley Cup, even if it meant having to give up future assets.

After becoming GM, Sherman never once pretended to be a hockey "expert." He said he relied on the hockey staff, including Lacroix's son, Eric, a former NHL winger, and former goaltender Craig Billington, whose career included a stint as Roy's backup with the Avalanche. Whether the Colorado regression was Sherman's "fault" was a difficult question to debate because it never was clear just how much freedom he had, and the Avalanche's slide also semi-obscured the fact that some of the moves made when he was in charge turned out well. For example, the signings of free agent forwards P. A. Parenteau, from the New York Islanders, and John Mitchell, from the New York Rangers, in the summer of 2012 proved to be sound. The jury still was out on the 2011 acquisition of goalie Semyon Varlamov from Washington, for first- and second-round draft choices. And although initially Sherman's dealing of defenseman Kevin Shattenkirk, rugged forward Chris Stewart, and a draft choice to St. Louis in 2011 for Erik Johnson, Jay McClement, and a first-round pick was roundly panned, two years later the deal didn't look quite as bad and still was a work in progress.

It didn't help Sherman's image that fans almost never saw or heard from him. More important than his public visibility, though, was Sherman's image within the league. A few prominent agents complained of rarely being able to get Sherman on the phone to talk contracts, and Sherman seemed uncomfortable with or even incapable of schmoozing with other GMs and participating in other rituals that often are part of deal making in the NHL.

Although a decent, friendly man, Eric Lacroix was burdened by a "Daddy's boy" image around the league. His eight-season NHL career included a stint with the Avalanche, but when it became apparent that players were uneasy or worse about having the GM's son in the dressing room, Eric himself requested a trade and was sent back to Los Angeles for a second run with the Kings. (Even his detractors among his teammates generally liked him.) Following his retirement, he worked for a time with the Avalanche before becoming part owner of a Central Hockey League expansion franchise in Prescott, Arizona, but eventually sold his interest and went back with the Colorado front office. By the beginning of the 2012–13 season, he was assistant GM, nudging aside the popular and respected Billington, who became vice president of player personnel, a job with a title that sounded more impressive than the work—strenuous travel throughout North America to check up on organizational prospects. Billington had done that sort of job before, and most thought he had moved beyond that. Unsurprisingly, Billington almost left the organization.

While all this was going on, the Avalanche indeed had an image problem—and the image was that ownership didn't much care about hockey. The "rebuilding" process eventually left Colorado with a young roster and one of the lowest payrolls in the NHL. The suspicion was that the ownership didn't just accept that: it encouraged it while continuing to consider the Avalanche an adjunct to the Nuggets. The one thing you knew was that even *if* ownership was mandating a lowered payroll, neither Pierre Lacroix nor Sherman was going to indulge in leaking and whining about it.

Stan Kroenke's shadow rarely darkened the halls around the Pepsi Center on Avalanche game days. Chances were much greater fans would see the owner shown at courtside at a Nuggets game, or in a luxury box in St. Louis watching the Rams, or across the Atlantic taking in an Arsenal match. To many frustrated hockey fans, the "A" on the Avalanche sweaters stood for "Afterthought" in the owner's portfolio.

At the time, Josh Kroenke was the Nuggets president and increasingly the watchdog of his father's Denver sports operation. There was confusion because for a time, media reports were that when Stan Kroenke took full ownership control of the Rams, because of NFL

cross-ownership rules, he would have to transfer official ownership of
the Denver sports empire to Josh. But that later was deemed unnecessary, and Stan Kroenke remained official owner of the Denver teams.

Part of the delay in Josh taking over as Avalanche president, adding
that to his Nuggets duties, was that he knew what he didn't know about
hockey. But after Josh became president in May 2013 and Joe Sakic
became the lead hockey executive, they agreed to go after Roy. Again.
Meantime, Josh Kroenke surprised many with his hard-boiled decision
to clear out the Lacroixs, father and son. By the summer, in fact, Eric
would resign suddenly. He was said to be going in another direction
with his life.

With Pierre Lacroix stepping even more into retirement and becoming an "adviser" alone, the atmosphere within the organization changed.
Gone was some of the culture of fear and paranoia that had pervaded
the Pepsi Center for several years. Employees no longer seemed to be
looking over their shoulder over everything they said, worrying that it
might get back to the Lacroixs.

Pierre Lacroix's attitude about the media wasn't toxic as much as it
was dismissive—he didn't believe in either romancing or using media
members—but he also had a very long memory about any perceived
slights. The few in the media who felt as if they had gotten to know him
found him to be engaging and sincere, when he wanted to display that.
Many rankled at his policy of mandating secrecy about the organization's inner workings and that no one around him, even his coaches, say
much that was substantive or interesting. An organization full of intriguing personalities had surprisingly little public personality, even during the glory years. Part of that was hockey's traditional cliché-spouting,
which even led to Sakic being labeled "Quoteless Joe" as a player—and
being proud of it. To be fair, the Avalanche players were typical hockey
guys, generally cooperative with the media; even during Lacroix's reign,
the team public relations personnel had more influence over their
players than did any other team PR staff in town. Jean Martineau and
his aides could, and often did, find players and tell them to get back in
the dressing room and talk with a specific reporter or reporters. At
times, though, the Avalanche also seemed to make an art of being
cooperative yet guarded and, well, boring. Some of that was Lacroix's
influence. Lacroix's approach had an upside for the media, though: He
didn't play favorites or leak information to specific reporters who be-

came housemen as part of the deal. That seedy arrangement, which amounted to favorite writers being spoon-fed "scoops" in exchange for being compliant shills, was common in Denver sports during much of Lacroix's tenure, especially with the Broncos in the late 1990s and during one period with the Nuggets.

Lacroix's contract negotiating style—just this side of "take it or leave it"—seemed to carry on with Giguere (with one notable exception: an infamous five-year, $33-million extension for center Paul Stastny) and, especially, Sherman. The Avalanche let productive players either walk for nothing or be traded away shortly after any kind of contract impasse. That long list included goalie Craig Anderson, traded not even a year after practically carrying the Avalanche to the playoffs on his back in 2010. In 2013, the Avalanche nearly let young, promising center Ryan O'Reilly get away over money. O'Reilly was asking for between $5 million and $6 million annually, far more than he was "worth" at that stage of his career under the NHL's—and especially the Avalanche's—wait-your-turn protocols. The Avalanche refused to budge off their offer of $3.5 million. Consequently, they lost the services of O'Reilly for the first part of the lockout-delayed and shortened season, and nearly lost him outright when the Calgary Flames swooped in and forced their hand with a two-year, $10-million offer that included a $2.5 million signing bonus up front and a salary the following season of $6.5 million. Colorado's intransigent management style, in the end, cost it more money than it would have had to pay originally just to keep him. That style also alienated fans and created tensions in the locker room when O'Reilly came back.

Young Avalanche star Matt Duchene, who went to Colorado on the third overall choice of the 2009 draft, or thirty picks ahead of O'Reilly, had much bigger scoring years under his belt. O'Reilly had a strong all-around game; he even had his advocates for being a better player at that point, although they tended to get carried away and parrot what others said because it was such a fashionable stand to take. Regardless, it was stunning that Duchene was getting less money than O'Reilly and had bought into the wait-your-turn ideology that O'Reilly's camp had ignored. Duchene took a two-year, $7-million deal prior to the season. It would be a while before the tension between the two thawed.

✿ ✿ ✿

Even before Roy signed on, a revolutionary change in the "Avalanche Way" was in motion, with Josh Kroenke overseeing the change of tone. Sakic and, eventually, Roy were not only fine with it; they argued for it. All agreed to overhaul the Avalanche's culture and image, not only with players and employees, but also with the media and fans.

On the day Kroenke and Sakic were named at a press conference to their new roles, Kroenke promised a new era of "outreach" to the fans. He got started right away, drawing up plans for a gigantic new scoreboard to replace the big-box TV-sized one and green-lighted an ambitious advertising campaign that would soon see Denver blanketed with billboards featuring Avalanche players. Previously, even when the Avalanche had a handful of the top stars in the game, the advertising campaigns were generic, based on a "the-team's-the-thing" concept.

Then came their biggest job: finding a new coach. Sakic immediately thought of his old friend and teammate, Roy; and after getting a favorable response in a preliminary phone call to Roy, Kroenke and Sakic hopped on a commercial flight to South Florida to romance the Hall of Fame former goalie. Their goal was to convince Roy that now was the time to make the jump to the NHL, and they began with a round of golf at Roy's home course in Jupiter, the Bear's Club. To their relief, both men quickly realized their sales job wouldn't need to be too tough. Roy finally was ready to put Quebec City behind him again for another trip to Denver.

As they neared an agreement, Roy, like Lieutenant Columbo, tossed out "one more thing." He said that, oh, by the way, he'd had a lot of front-office experience in Quebec. He didn't demand a title, but he more or less made it clear that he would consider it public confirmation of what they had discussed. He again reminded Sakic and Kroenke that he'd had years of daily front-office experience in Quebec and that "maybe it could be of use to you, too, in Denver."

The add-on title of VP of hockey operations would be the absolute clincher and bring this more in line with Roy's talks with Lacroix in 2009. After thinking it over together on the plane ride back, Sakic and Kroenke agreed: Why not? It would become a familiar saying around the organization before long.

FROM THE NOTEBOOK OF ADRIAN DATER

The Avalanche's pursuit of Roy again was no secret, but the first word of an agreement was indirect and even farcical—when Patrick's brother, Stephane, said on his Facebook page on May 20: "For all my friends I'd like you to know before the official news spreads that my older brother will be the new coach of the Colorado Avalanche."

Alerted to the posting, at 9:31 Mountain Time that night and facing deadline, I called Stephane to confirm that the posting was genuine.

He was coy at first, and then confirmed it was his.

"They're discussing the final details of an arrangement," Stephane said. "Colorado is going to be very happy. Patrick is looking for a new challenge."

As I noted the time and knew I needed to get off the line and begin writing a story, essentially asking him to assure me he knew this was true, that he wasn't just guessing or wasn't jumping the gun. He again said it was true. "People in Quebec will be sad again that my brother is leaving for Denver," he said. "But he has always loved Denver, too, and wants the new challenge of going back to his old team."

So I wrote the story for the paper the next morning, saying his brother said Patrick Roy indeed would be the next coach of the Avalanche. Knowing the hockey world and the Avalanche, though, I was wary of the possibility Stephane might take grief for his disclosure and backtrack. So I wasn't shocked the next day when he did just that, even telling a Montreal television station that the quotes in my story had been "exaggerated" and "sensationalized." Stephane also took down the Facebook posting.

The Avalanche denied that a deal was in place, and it probably was semantically justified. But I had written the story straight, that his brother had said Patrick would be the coach. That was true, and, of course, it would turn out to be right.

I didn't take what happened personally, and I thought to myself: Well, one thing we know . . . life with Patrick Roy as the coach isn't going to be dull.

❖ ❖ ❖

The official announcement of Roy's hiring came on Thursday, May 23, 2013, with the kicker that because of the upcoming Memorial Day weekend, the news conference wouldn't be held until the next Tuesday.

The Avalanche's new era was well under way. They were digging out of a hole, but there was potential for a quick recovery. It was incorrect to say that the Avalanche had become irrelevant and forgotten, as some in the Denver media claimed. Actually, the hockey fan base, nurtured during the franchise glory years, was larger than ever, reflected in part by the boom in youth hockey and other participation in the sport. Attendance didn't reflect that. High regular ticket prices, televised home games, and disaffection combined to keep thousands of seats empty on hockey nights at the Pepsi Center. The Avalanche's average home attendance in the five previous seasons in the 18,007-seat Pepsi Center had ranged from a low of 13,947 in 2009–10 to a high of 15,498 in 2011–12. In all five seasons, the Avalanche—with the 1995–2006 sellout run seemingly forgotten—ranked in the bottom eight in attendance in the NHL.

Yet when Roy rejoined the Avalanche, a multitude of Colorado fans still were out there. They had to be coaxed into coming back.

MOVING FORWARD

After taking the job(s), Patrick Roy assigned himself two immediate tasks: one, hire a staff he would feel comfortable working with; and, two, call every player to establish a dialogue and find out what they thought the team needed to succeed.

Roy's first assistant coaching hire was Andre "The Bear" Tourigny, a longtime head coach with Rouyn-Noranda of the Quebec Major Junior Hockey League (QMJHL). It wasn't hard to figure out that Tourigny was one of the excellent major junior coaches Roy had been talking about at the Hall of Fame. Known for his keen defensive mind, Tourigny had only two losing seasons out of ten in coaching the Huskies, and his team had many spirited battles against Roy's Remparts. Roy believed Tourigny was the best coach he faced in the league known as the "Q," and convinced him to leave his comfortable job with Rouyn-Noranda to handle the Avalanche defensemen.

Roy also recruited Mario Duhamel to serve as his video coach. That choice seemed curious because Duhamel had already been a head coach for several years with Drummondville, also in the QMJHL. How many head coaches go from head coach to the rather menial job of slicing and dicing video? Not many. But Roy said he wanted his video man to have coaching experience "because they are going to know what to look for; they're going to spot things right away that the normal video guy won't." He retained assistant Tim Army from the previous staff, in part because of his positive relationships with the Avalanche's young forwards during the trying times under Joe Sacco.

Adam Foote, who had remained in Denver after his retirement with his family and spent much of his time coaching his sons' teams and becoming immersed in the Colorado youth hockey scene, agreed to join Roy's staff as a defense development consultant. Basically, that meant he would be at home practices whenever possible but wouldn't go on the road.

Roy had only one person in mind to be his goalie coach: Francois Allaire. Allaire was a legend, making his name as Roy's first goalie coach with the Canadiens in 1986. In Roy's first training camp with the Habs, another legend, Jacques Plante, was Montreal's goalie consultant, and he worked with the recently drafted rookie. Among other things, Plante was famous for being the first goalie to regularly wear a mask and popularize the face-saving practice in the NHL.

Right away, Roy did not see eye to eye with Plante's methods. Plante advised a stand-up approach to the position, whereas Roy was intrigued by the butterfly technique. It was popularized by goaltending great Glenn Hall, but even Hall hadn't been a complete devotee of the approach. For many years, the butterfly was used more as part of a hybrid technique by only a few goalies, but Roy was interested in using it all the time. Plante would have none of that revolutionary strategy, and essentially told the Canadiens staff: *I can't work with this kid. He'll never amount to anything.*

When Plante grew tired of the consultant job and quit, the Canadiens became intrigued by the young Allaire, who never played in the NHL but had spent the previous few years studying new methods of playing the position. Allaire believed in the butterfly approach, but also incorporated what were then considered radical new techniques. One was for goalies to have extremely sharp skates, to better push off and plant the feet in moving side to side. To that point, most goalies were advised to keep their skates very dull, to better slide around the crease on the knees and generally "swim" in the net easier. Generally, Allaire's methodology could be summed up as "push and plant." A goalie successful in the Allaire way of netminding had to have strong hip muscles, because he demanded that a goalie must continually reposition himself to every movement of the puck. Also, the old "stack-the-pads" technique, where goalies would lie on their sides with the pads turned horizontal, was a staple of old-time goaltending. Allaire believed it ineffective. He would be proven correct in the evolving NHL.

In Roy, Allaire found a kindred spirit, a youngster whose desire for knowledge about the position equaled his own. "I was hungry to learn and soak up as much as I could, and he loved to teach. It was, to me, a perfect fit," Roy recalled. Together, they formed something of an ongoing laboratory in the crease for experimentation of new methods. Allaire preached constant movement to the puck, always facing it squarely. The goalies of old would often simply hug a back post and only move at the last second when a shot came their way. Allaire wanted goalies to mirror every movement of the puck and sometimes come out from the crease to better cut down on a shooter's angles. A goalie making himself look "bigger" in the net by coming out more was unusual in the old days of hockey.

Another of his later protégés was Jean-Sebastien Giguere,[1] whose career had been a roller-coaster ride before he was traded to Anaheim in 2000 and got his career righted after working more with Allaire, who was on the Ducks' payroll. By 2013, Giguere was Colorado's backup goalie, in the twilight of his career, and Allaire and his methods were considered archaic in some quarters of the NHL. After serving a couple of years in Toronto, Allaire and the Maple Leafs essentially fired each other. Former Toronto GM Brian Burke, who worked with Allaire for a stretch in Anaheim, including the Ducks' 2007 Stanley Cup-winning team, publicly questioned whether Allaire's methods were useful any longer. Roy still was a believer, and he phoned Allaire to gauge his interest. After a bit of contractual maneuvering, Allaire agreed to join the staff of his former Montreal pupil. Quite naturally, many had wondered whether Roy would serve as his own goalie coach, but he emphasized from the start that he wasn't going to do that, and hiring Allaire underscored it.

"One of my trademarks is I try to make sure guys are feeling good and keep it simple, create good routine, make sure the guy is happy coming to the rink," Allaire said after he was hired. "Then, after that, look at the tape and then find their best strength and build around it."[2]

Roy and Allaire agreed on a unique arrangement, too. Allaire wouldn't be with the team full-time, but he would periodically join the Avalanche to work and talk with the goaltenders, and also plot out a

---

1. The goaltender is not related to the former Avalanche general manager.
2. An initial interview after his hiring was an exception for Allaire. From then on, he politely declined to speak to the media.

likely workload schedule for the near future. Roy would have input, of course, and the power to change the rotation while adjusting to what happened. For the most part, Allaire's plan of which goalie would play in which games was going to be written in ink.

With his staff in place, Roy then methodically called the Avalanche players. Some of the conversations were brief. Some were long, such as the one he had with center Paul Stastny. Stastny was one of the team's most frustrated players, having played on teams that missed the playoffs three straight years and in five of the previous seven. Like many of his teammates, Stastny believed Joe Sacco's strategies didn't effectively use the roster's youthful and talented forwards. Sacco played for disciplinarian Jack Parker at Boston University and seemed to adhere to the philosophy that players were to do what they were told—that included playing the mandated conservative game—and keep their opinions to themselves. That's fine if the players believe in the system, but under Sacco the key players didn't. They increasingly tuned him out. When Roy announced to the players in those phone calls and in later communications that he had a more open-door policy, asking for player feedback and really listening to their suggestions, for most of them it was almost as if a dark cloud was lifted from their moods. Of course, this was all theory. Almost all coaches proclaim at the outset that their doors will be open, and they'll accept and even welcome feedback. The true test of Roy's openness would come once training camp started, then during the high-pressure times in the regular season. But this was coming from a Hall of Fame goalie who, as near as the players could tell, intended to follow through.

"The players need to be comfortable with their system. The system is for the players," Roy said. "I'm here to be their partner. In order to be their partner, I have to listen to what they have to say."

Roy's first calls went to the players he was pretty sure were remaining with the Avalanche. In the 2013 season that got Sacco fired, the Avalanche's 16–25–7 record and 39 points were the second-worst in the league, ahead of only the Florida Panthers. Colorado had a young core, including Duchene; Ryan O'Reilly; winger Gabriel Landeskog, the young Swede Colorado took with the second overall choice in 2011; and Stastny, in the middle ground in terms of age at 27.

Stastny's talk with Roy? "It was a lot better than I thought it would be, to be honest," the center said. "I thought it might just be kind of formal, just basic, but we went into the details of a lot of things, about things he wants from me and from our team. Things that play to our strength, to what we do best."

❊ ❊ ❊

High draft choices are the major benefit to being rotten, and the Avalanche had reaped the benefits following their most dreadful seasons. When Roy was hired, he already knew the Avalanche would have the top overall choice—unless they traded it—in the June 30 draft after winning the draft lottery on April 29 and leapfrogging the Panthers.

For months, the consensus was that Colorado would use the first pick to claim defenseman Seth Jones, an American playing for the Portland Winterhawks of major junior's Western Hockey League (WHL). At his introductory news conference, when Roy was asked about the upcoming draft, he praised three prospects—Jones and two Halifax Mooseheads forwards, center Nathan MacKinnon and winger Jonathan Drouin. Roy had seen the two Mooseheads play often. Most took it that Roy wasn't tipping the organization's hand, and that Jones still was the likely choice.

FROM THE NOTEBOOK OF ADRIAN DATER

In the spring of 2013, if there was one thing I felt confident about, it was that the Avalanche would draft Seth Jones. I convinced my boss to shell out good money so I could fly up to Portland to see him. The son of former Denver Nuggets player Popeye Jones, Seth spent eight years of his childhood learning hockey in the suburban Denver youth system. Popeye even had consulted Joe Sakic, confessing that his son liked hockey and asking what Seth should do to get better. Sakic emphasized working on skating, something that seems obvious but sometimes is overlooked amid other aspects of the game. Seth had gone from the Denver programs to Dallas, another youth hockey hotbed, and then to the National Team Development program in Ann Arbor before joining the Winterhawks.

Now he was 18, and as a hockey prospect, he would be a crossover marketer's dream as an Avalanche draftee. Not only would his African

American heritage (though his mother, Amy, is white) be a great story as a number one draft pick; Jones would be returning to the Avs a defensive savior.

At six foot four, with his great skating ability, Jones still was tops on most scouting lists by late in the season when I went up to see him in the WHL playoffs against the Edmonton Oil Kings.

"As an 18-year-old, obviously you've got to think about your future and where you're going to be for a long time," Jones told me. "I still have a lot of good friends in Denver that I've had my entire life. I'm very familiar with the city, and should I get drafted there I'd be very happy to go back there."

The first hint that I might not be profiling the eventual Avalanche pick came when I ran into Avalanche chief amateur scout Rick Pracey inside Portland's Memorial Coliseum before one game. Pracey was walking with Avalanche pro scout Brad Smith, and although I knew they wouldn't say much on the record, I kind of expected both men to grab me by the arm and say "You bet we are!" when I suggested it was a given that the Avalanche would be drafting Jones first. Instead, both were very complimentary of Jones, but there wasn't the wild enthusiasm I had expected.

The Winterhawks won the WHL title and advanced to the four-team Memorial Cup, the championship tournament for the three major junior leagues playing under the Canadian Hockey League umbrella. There, Nathan MacKinnon was MVP of the tournament for the Cup-winning Mooseheads, the QMJHL champions. Yet Jones played well, too, and many pundits—including me—still assumed he would be the Avalanche's pick at the draft. The Avs badly needed help on defense, after all, and he was a kid many were comparing to Chris Pronger. Those guys just don't come around too often.

Then came something of a bombshell on June 18. Sakic did something he doesn't normally do: He gave me a scoop. On the record, he told me, "If we do pick first, we're leaning more toward one of those three forwards."

He meant MacKinnon and his Mooseheads linemate, Drouin; and Aleksander Barkov, a Finnish center.

Many around the league were skeptical of Sakic's words. He was trying to leverage the top pick for a proven player from either Florida or Tampa Bay and move down a pick or two, many thought. But it was no *bluff, and in hindsight the fact that Sakic revealed the team's draft plans ahead of time made sense.*

The kinds of stories many others and I had already done were conditioning fans to expect Jones to be the top guy. Sakic was savvy enough to know that if the Avs didn't pick Jones, the stories in the paper the next day would be more about that instead of who they did pick.

By draft day, based on more info obtained from my dogged shoe-leather reporting work around the Marriott Marquis the night before (OK, it was at the bar), it became clear that MacKinnon was going to be the pick.

And that made sense. Time and again, history showed it was safer to take a number one center with the top pick than a D-man, who tended to take longer to develop. A top center is usually more of a sure thing than a defenseman.

Given Sakic's words in my stories, the Avalanche's first pick didn't surprise anyone. Not everyone agreed with the pick, but nobody was shocked.

THE KID

NO. 29, NATHAN MacKINNON, 6'0", 182 LBS., BORN SEPTEMBER 1, 1995, HALIFAX, NOVA SCOTIA

It's a reach to say that both Sidney Crosby and MacKinnon are from Cole Harbour, Nova Scotia, but that became part of the narrative, anyway, as the 2013 draft approached. Nova Scotia no longer has incorporated cities, and communities in the Halifax area—including Cole Harbour—were merged into a single Halifax Regional Municipality. So Cole Harbour is more a home area than a hometown, but who's quibbling? MacKinnon was raised in the Bel Ayr neighborhood and played in the Cole Harbour Bel Ayr Minor Hockey Association programs. He was in awe of Crosby every step of the way.

"At age two, he took right away to skating," his father, Graham, who works for Canadian National Railway, recalled as draft day approached. "I had trouble keeping up with him, no joke. We never pushed hockey on him at all. He just took to it right away, fell in love with it, and hasn't stopped. When he was nine or ten, I'd sometimes say to him, 'You know, not everyone makes it in hockey,' and he'd just get mad. He'd say, 'I'm playing hockey, I'm playing hockey. I don't have a Plan B, I just have a Plan A.'"

When Nathan was about seven, his father had a personalized hockey card made for him, with a blank spot on the back where information could be added. Young Nathan wrote in that he wanted to play, first, major junior for the hometown Halifax Mooseheads and then *with* Joe

Sakic on the Avalanche. He got Crosby's autograph many times and had posters and pictures of Crosby playing at virtually every level and with Team Canada.

After his eye-opening two seasons as a 12- and 13-year-old in Bantam AAA with the Cole Harbour Red Wings, MacKinnon did what Crosby had done in 2002, leaving home to attend Shattuck-St. Mary's School in Faribault, Minnesota. "I think he took the best options, and those options were available to me as well," MacKinnon recalled. "I actually went a year earlier than he did to Shattuck. He played midget at 14 at home and then went to Shattuck at 15. I went to Shattuck at 14 and never played midget at home. But it was pretty much the same thing."

MacKinnon stayed at Shattuck-St. Mary's two years, playing for the school's Bantam AAA and Midget AAA teams, scoring a combined 99 goals in 98 games over the two seasons. "I loved it," he said. "My first year was grade nine. Living in a dorm with a roommate was different. Looking back it was a ton of fun. The best part was that everybody was together all the time. You lived with your friends, you ate with them, you went to school with them, you played hockey with them, and I got pretty close to them."

He then was eligible for the QMJHL's draft and was at a crossroads. Playing in the United States Hockey League would enable him to preserve his eligibility to receive a scholarship to play in an NCAA program. Or he could go to the QMJHL and major junior, where the stipends players receive cause the NCAA to consider them professionals and ineligible to play U.S. college hockey. He still was only 15 at the time, but prominent player agent Pat Brisson already was his "adviser." Showily emphasizing his leverage, MacKinnon skated with the Omaha Lancers of the United States Hockey League (USHL) on the QMJHL draft day. The Lancers earlier had taken MacKinnon in the USHL draft.

Next, MacKinnon went to Baie-Comeau in the QMJHL draft. That city, about 250 miles northeast of Quebec City, is primarily French speaking, and the team was terrible. "They knew that the 'Q' was my first option," MacKinnon said. "If Baie-Comeau wasn't going to trade me, I was going to go to Omaha. The owner is a good friend of my agent, and it would have been a good situation for me. The Q would have been the best, but the USHL would have been good as well. It would have been a good organization to go to. I was in Omaha, skating with the team, so I was serious about it. I had a blast there, and I liked the city. I was all set to go there. I figured Baie-Comeau would trade me eventually, that it would be in everyone's interests. If it would have been the next summer, I would have played a year in Omaha."

If he had stayed in Omaha for two seasons, he would have kept open the option of NCAA hockey—beginning in, yes, the 2013–14 season. "I'd be in my first year in college this season," he said with a smile, "and I'd rather be in the NHL than college, that's for sure." He had visited Minnesota-Duluth and liked it, and his guess is he probably would have ended up there if he'd ended playing in the USHL two years and then gone in the 2013 draft. Because initial eligibility is based solely on age, he would have been in the '13 draft pool regardless. But he acknowledged that going straight from the USHL, a notch below major junior in terms of across-the-board talent, to the NHL is virtually unprecedented, and he would have needed at least a year of college hockey as an intermediate step. (Paul Stastny, for example, played in the USHL and then two seasons at the University of Denver.)

The MacKinnons had let it be known they would prefer that Baie-Comeau trade his rights to his hometown Halifax Mooseheads, but at least two other QMJHL teams would have been acceptable—the Saint John (New Brunswick) Seadogs and Patrick Roy's Quebec Remparts. "It would have been funny if I'd played there and we came together here," MacKinnon said. "But Patrick told me Baie-Comeau wouldn't have traded me to Quebec."

Roy said he asked Brisson if MacKinnon would be interested in possibly playing for Quebec. "He said yes, and from there, I approached Baie-Comeau."

How close did Roy come to acquiring MacKinnon's rights back then?

"Not close at all," Roy recalled. "I inquired, I checked, but I knew he was going to play [major junior] only two years. To pay as much as it would have been was too expensive. It would have been a lot of draft picks. I would have had to give too much in assets. We were in the process of rebuilding. There was no need for us to pay that much for Nate. It would have been nice to have Nate, but we would have had no defense, and it would be a tough trade to make. Halifax was in a better position, and it worked well for them, and it worked well for Nate because he was playing in his hometown. I knew he was going to be very special."

The Mooseheads acquired MacKinnon's rights on July 11, 2011, giving up two players and three first-round draft choices. MacKinnon was an immediate hit, getting his first hat trick against Roy's Remparts. He played *for* Roy and the QMJHL All-Stars in the Subway Super Series against Team Russia. "I enjoyed that," Roy said. "He was asking me questions, what do you think of this, what do you think of that. We've talked about that, and it makes him laugh more than me."

In the playoffs of his rookie QMJHL season, MacKinnon helped the Mooseheads rally from a 3–0 series deficit against Roy's Remparts to advance. In his two seasons with the Mooseheads, MacKinnon had 63 goals in 102 regular-season games and 24 in 34 playoff games. His draft stock fluctuated during the 2012–13 season, and he slid from the top of most lists and fell below Seth Jones when he had an unimpressive showing in the World Junior Championships and coped with a knee issue cleaned up in a minor procedure at the Steadman Hawkins Clinic in Vail. But he closed with a rush, and the exclamation point came when he had a hat trick as the Mooseheads defeated Jones and Portland in the Memorial Cup championship game. The International Scouting Service put him back ahead of Jones on the draft list, whereas the NHL's Central Scouting bureau still had Jones at the top.

✿ ✿ ✿

On a swelteringly hot day two days before the draft, the NHL organized a media luncheon along the Hudson River involving the likely top draft picks. MacKinnon said that when he met with Sakic and Roy, he wasn't assured the Avalanche would take him—just that they were leaning that way. "It's pretty cool to hear that they might want me, especially from two Hall of Famers like Joe and Patrick," he said.

On June 30 at the Prudential Center in Newark, the Avalanche indeed drafted MacKinnon. Sakic made the announcement at the podium, and the reaction at the team's official watch party for fans at Chopper's Sports Grill[1] in the Cherry Creek area was mostly positive—

---

1. "Chopper" was Bob "Chopper" Travaglini, the legendary Runyonesque former trainer of the Denver Nuggets. The "Chopper Circle" address of the Pepsi Center also honors him.

again, mostly because the organization had prepared everyone for passing on Jones.

MacKinnon hugged his dad; his mom, Kathy, who worked in the Halifax municipality's recreation department; and his sister, Sarah, an Acadia University student; and then went up to the stage in the arena, shook hands with and hugged the Avalanche delegation. He pulled on a number 13 Avalanche jersey with his name on it, and posed for pictures with his arms around Roy on one side and Sakic on the other. Then he went to be interviewed by James Duthie on the TSN[2] draft broadcast. Sakic was sitting next to him. "I'm so excited, and hopefully, I'm just getting started," MacKinnon said. "This is unbelievable to be a part of the Colorado Avalanche, and I can't wait to get to training camp."

The Avalanche brought MacKinnon to Denver the next day. "You're so jacked up after getting drafted, and I was there for six, seven hours after doing media and pictures and things like that," he said. "I'm pretty tired, but I still have some adrenaline going, for sure. I'm having a great time. . . . My friends and family all came to the hotel after, and we all hung out for a while. I got some sleep on the plane."

MacKinnon was only seven years old when Roy retired. And even when he was drafted, he didn't look old enough to have a driver's license. "I remember lots from watching Colorado as a kid," he said. "They were deep in the playoffs most of those years, and I got to see them lots. And obviously, yeah, there was a little rivalry there with Quebec and Halifax. That's behind us now, obviously. We played him in the playoffs my first year, and we really studied the way his team plays. I'm not sure if he'll still use the same systems or not, but I'm definitely familiar with those. Regardless, I think it's going to be a pretty smooth transition, and he's a great coach. His track record speaks for itself."

FROM THE NOTEBOOK OF TERRY FREI

I was at Chopper's on draft day and noticed the fans' acceptance and even enthusiasm for the selection of MacKinnon. Yes, among the crowd were those who made time to watch the Memorial Cup and even considered themselves hockey draftniks, but for the most part the reaction

---

2. Canada's version of ESPN.

involved showing trust in the organization . . . or the men now making the decisions.

I didn't claim to have extensively scouted the players involved, and I also admit I was affected because I found the Jones story to be so intriguing. During my eight years in Portland, I wrote many columns about the Winterhawks—probably more than I should have. Even when I was a football writer at the Sporting News, *I talked my bosses into allowing me to go to Kamloops, British Columbia, to do a story on the WHL's Kamloop Blazers and the major junior experience. (At the time, they had a line of Shane Doan, Jarome Iginla, and Darcy Tucker.) Years later, my hockey-knowledgeable friends in Portland raved about Jones's ability, maturity, and poise, and were dumbfounded that Colorado was even considering taking anyone else.*

So as I wrote the column offering my opinion, I confessed in it that it involved a gut feeling, not a carefully researched and scouted view. Over the years, I had written many stories documenting the reality that it generally takes longer for elite defensemen to develop than forwards, often using Chris Pronger as the showcase example. So that concept wasn't at all foreign to me.

But I was convinced the Avalanche eventually would regret passing on Jones, and said so in the paper and on the air.

At the news conference in the Avalanche dressing room the day after the draft, Roy cheerily greeted me with: "Sorry to ruin your story." He was teasing.

The Avalanche official position was that the selection of MacKinnon was a group call. That might have been true by the time Joe Sakic stepped to the podium, but I'm convinced Roy's vote was cast early and decisively and swung the momentum in MacKinnon's direction. There was considerable sentiment in the Avalanche draft meetings that Aleksander Barkov Jr., the Finn playing in his homeland, would be the best choice. But Roy knew whom he wanted. He had unsuccessfully sought to land MacKinnon for the Mooseheads, he had seen him play numerous times, and he even had coached him.

The VP of hockey operations got his way.

SUMMER MOVES

A Colorado trade announced two days before the draft received surprisingly little attention. It was especially notable because it brought another familiar face back to Denver, with the Avalanche acquiring 33-year-old forward Alex Tanguay from the Calgary Flames.

Tanguay, who played his first six NHL seasons with Colorado, and defenseman Cory Sarich came to Colorado for veteran winger David Jones and defenseman Shane O'Brien. Now the Avalanche even had a former Patrick Roy teammate on the roster. In 2001, when he still was only 21, Tanguay scored two goals in Game 7 of the Stanley Cup finals against the Devils, guaranteeing his perpetual spot in Avalanche lore. Now he would have a chance to add to that.

In another departure from the Avalanche's previous standard operating procedure of relative secrecy, Roy at the draft proceedings also disclosed that he already had tentatively decided how his lines would look, at least going into training camp. From left to right, he said they would be: Ryan O'Reilly-Matt Duchene-P. A. Parenteau; Gabriel Landeskog-Paul Stastny-Tanguay; and Jamie McGinn-MacKinnon-Steve Downie. Lines are best written in pencil in the NHL. So the specific combinations didn't matter as much as the fact that Roy was signaling his willingness to play O'Reilly, a center by trade, at left wing; to try Tanguay, who almost exclusively had played center and left wing in his career, at right wing; and plug in MacKinnon as the center on the third line.

Next, the NHL's free agency period opened on July 5. Colorado's moves on the first day weren't monumental. On defense, the Avalanche signed Andre Benoit, 29, who had played only 41 games with Ottawa; and American Hockey League (AHL) journeymen Nate Guenin and Nick Holden, both thought as "organizational" guys who could add depth at Lake Erie and be call-ups in times of need.

With the early September opening of training camp approaching, the Avalanche signed Duchene and Landeskog to long-term contract extensions. Duchene had one year remaining on his $7-million, two-year deal; and the five-year, $30-million extension began with the 2014–15 season. Colorado locked him up through 2018–19. Landeskog had one year remaining on his three-year entry-level contract, and the extension was for seven years and a total of $39 million. So he was under contract through 2019–20. Yes, *2019–20!*

All of that was another collective counterstrike to ownership's image of making the Avalanche the second priority at the Pepsi Center; it also sent a message that following the "wait-your-turn" protocol would be a wise course of action for young Avalanche players. Landeskog, still only 20 years old, had been the Avalanche captain for nearly a year, and the popular Swede's beyond-his-years maturity and popularity were unquestioned. But after some bumps in the road in his first four seasons in the league, Duchene was developing into not just the Avalanche's best player but a leader.

The absence of moves on the goaltending meant Roy and Allaire were committed to going with their holdovers—Semyon Varlamov and Jean-Sebastien Giguere. For Colorado in 2013–14, the ideal scenario would be for Varlamov, 25, to get most of the starts, and for Giguere to play 25 to 30 games. The pressure was on Varlamov, who fulfilled one of his dreams when he met Roy: to win over his new coach and to live up to the faith the Avalanche organization had showed in him two years earlier.

NETMINDERS

NO. I, SEMYON VARLAMOV, 6'2", 209 LBS., BORN APRIL 27, 1988, SAMARA, RUSSIA

Varlamov moved to Yaroslavl, about 250 miles northwest of Moscow, when he was 13. There, he played in the Yaroslavl Lokomotiv programs beginning at age 16 and joined the local Russian League team at only 18.

Washington had two first-round draft choices in 2006 and took Varlamov with the second, at number 23 overall. Varlamov's regular-season work with the Capitals in 59 games over three seasons was decent to good; he was especially strong in the 2009 playoffs, and the Capitals had hoped they would serve as his breakout to star status. But he had been unavailable for extended stretches because of groin and knee injuries—nothing major, but enough to bring his durability and resilience into question. With his contract expiring after the 2010–11 season, Washington was wary of a long-term, high-priced commitment. In fact, young Czech goalie Michal Neuvirth played in all nine of Washington's 2011 playoff games, and the Caps believed farmhand Braden Holtby was ready to move up, so Capitals general manager George McPhee didn't offer Varlamov and his agent, Paul Theofanous, a contract worthy of an entrenched number one. They did make him a qualifying offer, enabling them to retain his rights as a restricted free agent. If he got an offer sheet from another team, the Capitals could retain him by matching it or would be entitled to draft choices as compensation. In this instance, it enabled them to trade him to Colorado.

When the 2011 free agency period opened, the Avalanche acquired Varlamov from the Capitals for two 2012 draft choices—a first- and second-rounder. He still was only 23, but the deal was risky for several reasons, mainly because the price the Avalanche paid implied they believed he could be the long-range answer in the net. To put it another way, they were hoping he could be the long-range occupant of the crease Colorado had been searching for since Roy's retirement. If he wasn't? The Avalanche would have wasted valuable draft choices, mocking their own "rebuilding" mantra.

The Avalanche also signed him to that new three-year, $8.5-million contract. Later that same day, they signed Jean-Sebastien Giguere as an unrestricted free agent, emphasizing that he would be Varlamov's backup. Greg Sherman essentially admitted what was at stake—among other things, his own credibility.

A week later, when Varlamov came to Denver, Sherman labeled him "someone we believe strongly is going to carry the load for us for many years to come." For his part, Varlamov spoke haltingly in English, and he said all the right things. He thanked both the Capitals for giving him his first shot in the league and the Avalanche for showing such stunning faith in him. "I look forward to helping the Avalanche get back in the playoffs and compete for and win the Stanley Cup," he said. "It may sound funny, but my NHL dream was to play for the Avalanche."

The reason for that?

"Because my favorite NHL player and NHL goalie was playing here, Patrick Roy," he said.

Varlamov said he had never met Roy, who then was coaching major junior hockey in Quebec. And what if joining the Avalanche opened the door for Varlamov to meet his hero?

"I will be a little bit nervous, for sure," Varlamov said with a laugh.

In 2011–12 with Colorado, Varlamov was up and down, mostly strong early and late in the season as the Avalanche posted 88 points and missed the playoffs. Most reasonable observers conceded that any conclusion about the wisdom of the Avalanche's commitment to him would have to be postponed.

During the NHL lockout in late 2012, Varlamov remained in Russia to play for Yaroslavl Lokomotiv. His lockout employment came with some angst, as he could look around the dressing room and think of the men who had been there. On September 7, 2011, the Lokomotiv team was heading for its season opener in Belarus when the plane crashed after takeoff, killing all 26 players on board—including two former Avalanche defensemen, Latvian Karlis Skrastins and Belarusan Ruslan Salei.

"I knew the whole team," Varlamov said after the lockout ended and he rejoined the Avalanche. "You always remember those guys. Going in the locker room could be tough. You can't forget. It was tough to see the city, how hard it hurt everyone."

In the Avalanche's horrible 2013 season, Varlamov struggled. His save percentage (.903) and his goals-against average (3.03) both were shaky, and his record was 11–21–3 for the Avalanche. Colorado averaged only 2.09 goals in the games he played, the second-lowest "support" figure for any goalie in the league. He also had stretches of excellent play, even if the record didn't reflect it. But he still had to be considered a disappointment in his second season with Colorado, and if he didn't deliver more, the trade for him would go down as a thunderous blunder.

Then Varlamov got the news that his new head coach was his childhood goaltending idol, and his new goaltending coach was Roy's own mentor. Over the summer, the young Russian worked with Francois Allaire in both Switzerland and Montreal. "I think Varly is looking for a fresh start," Allaire said. "I think he's open to trying something else. He didn't feel he was going in the right direction. He wants to flush everything out and start fresh."

The strategy was to tweak but not retool Varlamov's style. Although Allaire did the direct tutoring, Roy had input, too. The biggest change was that Varlamov was coached to keep his catching glove higher. "When he's going to face a shooter, the shooter is going to see less," Roy explained. "I think the connection right now with Francois is great, and I think he's going to have a huge impact on this organization."

On the eve of training camp, Roy again was asked about his goaltending situation.

"I'm very comfortable with our goalies," he said. "I never believe in number one, number two goalies. The number one goalie is the one who is playing, the number two is the one sitting on the bench."

That was almost funny, because it was hard to believe that Roy ever—even for an instant—thought of himself as a number two goalie on the nights he watched his backups play. But he was emphasizing that he considered Varlamov and Giguere a tandem.

"I want Jiggy to share his experience," Roy said. "Francois will do it, and I will do it as well. We're going to help Varly. I know there are a lot of question marks in Denver regarding Varly. But I can say one thing to you. I drove from Quebec to Montreal to see him practice with Francois. For fourteen days, he worked with Francois and Jiggy in Montreal. He was in Switzerland with Francois for about a week. He is putting in a commitment that makes me believe he deserves a chance to prove himself, and we will give him that chance."

By the time training camp opened, Varlamov seemed to have become accustomed to having Roy as his coach.

"Of course, he's a legend and he was my idol when I was growing up," Varlamov said. "But right now, he's my head coach. I think he's more worried about the team, not worried about me. He has twenty-five players on the team, and he has to take care of all of them. I have to worry more about my game and how I practice. Everybody knows I didn't play great last year. We finished twenty-ninth last year, so I don't think anybody was happy about last year. Same as me. We all want to play in playoffs."

NO. 35, JEAN-SEBASTIEN GIGUERE, 6'1", 202 LBS., BORN MAY 16, 1977, MONTREAL

In 1989, 11-year-old Jean-Sebastien Giguere's Pee Wee team from Blainville, Quebec, won the right to be on the ice with the Montreal Canadiens for a practice. After it was over, Montreal goalie Patrick Roy posed for a picture with Giguere, then signed a goalie stick and gave it to Giguere. That same year, Giguere attended Francois Allaire's goaltending school, and a long-term mentor/protégé relationship had begun.

Four years later, Roy led the Canadiens to the Stanley Cup for the second time in his career; Giguere, who had just turned 16 and was on the verge of joining Verdun of the QMJHL, was among those celebrating.

Giguere spent one season with Verdun, then most of the next three seasons with the Halifax Mooseheads, and was the Hartford Whalers' first-round pick in 1995. After playing eight games for Hartford, he was traded to Calgary in 1997 and was considered the Flames' goaltending hope of the future. He struggled in his trials with the Flames for two seasons, though, spending much of the time in the AHL. Anaheim picked him up in 2000 for a second-round draft choice, and he worked with Allaire to get his game back together.

By 2003, he was turning from disappointing prospect to the real deal, and in one of the best postseason goaltending performances ever, he led the Ducks all the way to the Stanley Cup finals against New Jersey. Early in the finals, he was asked about his longtime admiration of Roy, who was on the verge of announcing his retirement. "I don't read the paper right now," Giguere said. "I don't know what's going on with Patrick. Obviously, though, it makes me feel good to be compared to him. But at the same time, there is only one Patrick Roy. He was the best who ever played. I don't try to match him or anything like that. I try to be myself, as good as I can be. I don't know where that's going to bring me, but that's where I want to be."

After the Devils knocked off Anaheim in Game 7 in East Rutherford, some fans booed the announcement of the choice for the Conn Smythe Trophy as the NHL playoff MVP.

Some of the Devils, though, clapped.

Giguere was the fifth Smythe winner from the losing team in the finals, and he joined Detroit goalie Roger Crozier (1966), St. Louis goalie Glenn Hall ('68), Philadelphia winger Reggie Leach ('76), and Philadelphia goalie Ron Hextall ('87).

Giguere finished the postseason with a 15–6 record, a 1.62 goals-against average, a .945 saves percentage, and five shutouts.

Four years later, Giguere finally got to hoist the Cup when he and the Ducks beat Ottawa in the 2007 finals.

From there, though, injuries set in, including a sports hernia, and he had a lackluster stay at Toronto before signing with the Avalanche on the same day Colorado acquired Varlamov in 2011. His first two seasons with the Avalanche as Varlamov's backup were decent enough, and he made his mark more as a locker room leader, even grousing late in the 2013 season that some of his teammates were more concerned with their imminent postseason trips to Las Vegas than they were about being professional down the stretch. Giguere's "Quite frankly, I don't give a damn about your trip to Vegas" became the most memorable—and fitting—quote of the Avs' awful season.

After Roy took the Colorado coaching job, it meant he had two goaltenders who had looked up to him as kids. Giguere also was looking forward to working with Allaire again.

"I can pretty much say I would never have made it in the NHL without Francois's help," Giguere said after the Avalanche hired Allaire. "I had played some games, but I was never a regular . . . The day I got traded to Anaheim, he called me and said: 'Why don't you come over to my house? We'll watch some video.' We're from the same town [Blainville], so I could do that. The day I did that, everything changed. Everything started to become a little simpler. What a lucky break for me."

The issue with Giguere, at 36, was whether he could stay healthy and provide reliable backup goaltending—or maybe even more, if Varlamov faltered.

CAMP

Semyon Varlamov's off-season work regimen was one of the many illustrations of why NHL training camps have become jokes—at least if they're billed as a means of getting the players into shape for the season. Long gone are the days when players hunted, fished, played golf, sold insurance, painted the barn, and drank beer in the offseason, and rarely—if ever—put on skates between the final game the previous season and the opening of camp. In the old-world NHL, camp involved multiple on-ice sessions on most days, and it was the means to work the players into shape after a summer of relative sloth, to sweat out the beer, and to build back players' wind after an offseason of chain smoking. Now, there's too much money at stake, the players are in better condition than ever, and the true "time off" in the offseason involves days, not weeks. Many of the Avalanche players skated together in the offseason, often with other NHL players who live in the area. But even those who didn't hang out in Denver most of the summer generally worked out hard and skated hard, so when the Avalanche were set to open their first training camp under Patrick Roy on September 12, this wasn't going to be a bunch of out-of-shape players bending over garbage cans.

Roy was itchy. A three-day rookie camp whetted his appetite. Roy wasn't on the ice for that, with Craig Billington running the sessions most notable for the look they provided at Nathan MacKinnon and many of the Avalanche's other draft choices. Although MacKinnon still didn't need to shave very often, in the hockey sense he looked like a man among boys. "There was definitely some good pace out there," he said after the first workout. "I still need to get used to the altitude some, though. I'm used to playing at sea level, so it's definitely an adjustment."

Both the rookie and full-roster camps were on the same practice rink the Avalanche used when Roy played, Family Sports Center in suburban Centennial, just up the street from the Broncos' headquarters. Technically, the full camp would last only three days before the Avalanche held a Burgundy-White intra-squad game, cut down the roster considerably, and then embarked on a six-game exhibition schedule. The day before the full camp opened, Roy talked about what was ahead. He had a hard time containing his excitement—and, in fact, he failed to do so.

He told about sitting in a Starbucks alone, having coffee, when a fan came over and greeted him, "Hey, coach, how you doing today?" After eight years of coaching major junior, you'd think he was used to that, but in Denver, it was jarring, he said. "I thought, 'Oh, yeah, that's me!'"

This was ten years since his retirement and his departure from Denver. So much had changed. In his personal life, he and Michele were divorced in 2005. His sons, goaltender Jonathan and forward Frederick, had played for him with the Remparts and both had been involved in controversial incidents. Jonathan had beaten up an opposing goalie as part of an on-ice brawl and been suspended for seven games; his father—the coach—had been suspended for five games. But, by 2013, Jonathan had left hockey behind and was pursuing a music career. Frederick, who also had drawn a 15-game suspension for punching an opponent during a time-out, was with Rochester of the AHL. The boys had been very young during Roy's days as a player, and now their father was back in Denver, a bachelor without any of his children—neither the sons nor daughter, Jana—living with him.

"I've been walking the street, and there's a buzz for the Avalanche," Roy said. "The fans are excited about our team. And there's one thing a lot of fans have been saying to me: 'Make sure you're going to make them work.' I can promise them that I am going to make them work. But I will accept their mistakes. This is part of the game. And my objective is to make every one of them the best player possible. We're going to be extremely clear on the criteria that we're going to look for, for our team. If it's the sacrifice part, if it's the work habits part, if it's the discipline part, if it's the team concept, we're going to be crystal clear about that to our players. You don't have to play well every night to win games. You'll remember that in my years here, we were not perfect every night. We gave ourselves chances to win. When you pick that up as a player, you become a strong team. We want to have a Stanley Cup attitude, and we're going to work hard at it."

The "Stanley Cup attitude" sound bite would become a theme for his team.

"September is not the month you're going to win the Stanley Cup, but you're certainly going to prepare yourself," he said. "I've played with teams that have surprised the world of hockey. We'll see what we're going to do as a group." He said he had checked out the "expert" predictions, and noted: "Not too many experts put us in the playoffs. I would love to surprise them."

Although it had been outlined to the players, Roy and his staff would gradually install their "system" in the camp and the remainder of the preseason. It wasn't revolutionary, but it was a departure from what the Avalanche had done under Joe Sacco. To simplify it, under Sacco the system was more "hang back" whereas under Roy it would be "push up." Roy, with the help of Tourigny, implemented a new "triangle" defensive scheme. Although the system was not new to hockey, it was new to most Avalanche players.

Essentially, the system goes like this: Whichever forward was first to the opposing puck carrier was designated "F1" and would be assigned the responsibility of attacking that opposing skater. The other two forwards—"F2" and "F3"—were supposed to support F1 as quickly as possible, to surround the puck carrier and take away his time and space. F2's job would be to "lock the wall," or force the play as close to the boards as possible, while F3 would further serve as a buttress to any possible openings. The system could only work if the forwards had speed and a willingness to work hard, possibly sacrificing some offense in the process. It would also require the defensemen to move up higher in the three zones. If the defense sat back too far behind the forwards, big gaps would open up, allowing for too much time and space for the opposing puck carrier if one broke free from the attempted triangle forward scheme. Although Roy worried about the mobility of his defenseman corps to carry out the system effectively, he knew his speed up front might be able to compensate enough to make the whole thing work.

On the third day of the full workouts, a confrontation between Gabriel Landeskog and Steve Downie drew a lot of attention. Landeskog
took major exception to a hit from Downie during scrimmages and tried
to go after him along the bench. But Downie, whose helmet flew off on
his hit, was bending down to pick it up and couldn't engage much. So
later, Landeskog got Downie in the corner and pitchforked his feet
from under him with his stick, sending Downie down on the ice. When
Downie got up, he skated gingerly back to the bench. Downie had
suffered a season-ending knee injury in the second game of the lockout
season and was coming off reconstructive surgery, so his ire over Landeskog's move was understandable. He sat out a couple of shifts, but
when he returned for a face-off, with Landeskog lined up outside on
the circle, he skated hard to get next to the Swede in time for the drop
of the puck, and they pushed and shoved each other. The words flying
back and forth weren't for the meek or broadcast television, and proved
that Landeskog had picked up profanity in his second language. At one
point, Downie delivered what seemed to be a retaliatory hit on Landeskog. After practice, Landeskog shrugged it all off as just part of training
camp.

"All the guys at this camp want to show the management and this
coaching staff that they want to be here," Landeskog said. He noted
that once the season started, "We don't really get to [practice] as hard as
we do out here, so when you get a chance, you want to play hard and
make sure you don't give the guys anything to chirp about during the
season."

After the camp workouts, the Avalanche made the hour-long trek to
the Air Force Academy for the Sunday afternoon Burgundy-White
intra-squad game on the Cadet Field House's rink. What was most
interesting wasn't the outcome—Burgundy beat White 3–1 in front of a
sellout, standing-room-only crowd in a game that ended just as the
Broncos-Giants game was kicking off in New Jersey—but Roy's somber
initial reaction. He had watched from upstairs, and he wasn't happy. He
was as downcast as if the Avalanche had just lost 2–1 to the Red Wings
after Detroit scored with 2.8 seconds remaining. His message was calculated, and he was trying to make a point that sloppiness wouldn't be
tolerated. "I liked the effort, I liked the enthusiasm," he said, looking at
the final score sheet. "There's things I have a bit of concern about, how
we are going to manage our games. Sometimes decisions with and with-

out the puck, I think we're a little too high risk. I understand it was just a Burgundy and White game, but these are things we saw also last year in the games that I've been watching. We're going to have to start talking about those things."

It seemed strange to see Alex Tanguay, who had lived with Roy and his family as a rookie in 1999–2000, back in a Colorado jersey. He skated with the Burgundy squad, on the line with Paul Stastny and Landeskog. Roy was asked if he was going to apply anything he gleaned from that experience in dealing with the very young MacKinnon, who had just turned 18 on September 1. Responding, Roy disclosed that MacKinnon was moving in the next day with Jean-Sebastien Giguere's family, including Giguere's wife, Kristen; and children, Maxime-Olivier, six; Luka, four; and Felix, one.

"I think he's going to be in real good hands with Jiggy," Roy said. "Jiggy will do a super job with him. Nate's working so hard. Off the ice, he's such a class person. At the rink, I want him to be himself. I don't want him to try to feel that he has to impress the gallery every time he's on the ice."

In the dressing room, when his imminent living arrangement was brought up, MacKinnon asked: "Oh, is that out now?"

Well, yes, Nathan, it is.

"I'm excited," he said. "He played for Halifax, and I played for Halifax, so we have kind of a connection there. And his wife is actually from Nova Scotia as well. It's going to be fun. He's won a Cup and a Conn Smythe, so he's a very experienced player, and I'm looking forward to it. I've lived at home the past couple of years, so I didn't do much cooking or anything like that, so I think it's best that I live with somebody right now."

Said Giguere: "I think it's good for a young guy like that to be in a family environment. But sometimes, he will need to have some freedom as well. I'm not his dad. I'm going to give him some guidelines and I am going to share my experience with him, but at the end of the day, he's 18 years old. He's an adult. I've never done this before, so this will be a new experience for myself and my wife and my kids. We've made it so he has some privacy in the house, a nice little setup for him, and hopefully it's going to click for everybody. My kids are super-excited. They have a new buddy, a new kid to play with, right?"

This wasn't new for the Avalanche, given Tanguay's tenancy with the Roy family, plus other more recent examples. Duchene lived with Adam Foote's family for two seasons; O'Reilly lived as a rookie with veteran winger Darcy Tucker's family; and Landeskog lived in his first season with a Denver-area family he asked not to identify publicly.

"I tried to learn from Patrick," Tanguay said. "I saw how he prepared himself, and he gave me advice here and there that I'm still using to this day. One of the first things he told me is, 'Take care of your body, and your body will take care of you.' He said there were times you could have fun, but times when you need to be serious and prepare yourself. I learned that it's a long season, there are times to prepare and a way to prepare; you need to figure it out on your own."

❊ ❊ ❊

Roy was all about hockey in those first few weeks in Colorado. But it wasn't ALL just Avalanche hockey. He still watched a lot of Quebec Remparts hockey, having game tapes sent to him from staffers and poring over them, usually late at night at home.

Roy's ownership stake in the Remparts involved not only financial security, but that feeling of *Hey, if it doesn't work out here, I can always go back there*. But make no mistake: Roy wanted to make it work in Colorado. No way would he accept going back to Quebec with his tail between his legs, a loser in Colorado at his first NHL job.

So Roy came into training camp ready to work as hard as he ever had, which is saying something. And little of it was surprising to the veteran players, given the long phone conversations he had had with most of them, talking about his vision of what kind of team he wanted, and how that player could help accomplish it.

Roy also taught himself to be a better listener than he ever was as a player. If one thing could be said of Roy the player, it was that he was stubborn, set in his own ways, and had little time for anyone else's opinions about him or his game.

Roy the coach knew he had to open his ears fully, not necessarily to hear every gripe or throwaway muttering, but simply to let his players know he was there for them.

❊ ❊ ❊

The Avalanche surprisingly claimed center Marc-Andre Cliche on waivers from the Los Angeles Kings during the exhibition season. Cliche was envisioned as a penalty-killing specialist, and he had spent the previous six seasons with the Kings' AHL affiliate at Manchester.

As Roy's ways became more familiar, the Avalanche went 3–3 in the six-game exhibition schedule, finishing up with their annual trip to Las Vegas for the "Frozen Fury" meeting with the Los Angeles Kings. There were a couple of disquieting showings, starting when Dallas beat the Avalanche 2–1 in the first game on the schedule with most of the Stars' best players not making the trip and Colorado taking four penalties in the offensive zone. "This is what I mean by managing the game better," Roy explained. "We have to learn to win." Also, Semyon Varlamov allowed five goals in only 24 shots in a 5–1 road loss to Dallas.

Although the NHL insists on calling this part of the year the "preseason," it's a semantic sham perpetuated on hockey fandom, especially season-ticket holders. They're exhibitions. No more. They're significant only for those trying to make the NHL roster or to cement spots, and in this case, it involved the two Colorado defensemen signed for organizational depth—Nate Guenin and Nick Holden—stepping up, catching Roy's attention, and sticking on the season-opening roster. That was confirmation that Roy was open-minded about trying to improve the defense after it generally was terrible the previous season. Colorado also kept Cliche on the big club roster.

Watching Roy's practices was an illuminating experience, mainly because of what he was *not*. He barked, he whistled—his own shrill whistle through his teeth, with nothing hanging around his neck—and he skated hard on the ice as he supervised and even participated. This was far from unusual or unprecedented, but most striking was that he was a teacher. During breaks for talks, when the players gathered around him, they listened with rapt attention. When he spoke to an individual player, it was an audience. During one early practice, he skated into the corner and began a one-on-one rap session with veteran defenseman Matt Hunwick, but Roy's shoulder shrugs and palms-up demeanor seemed to suggest, "Why do you do it like this, when you should do it *like this*." (Hunwick wouldn't last long with the team, exiled early to Lake Erie.)

Many of the Avalanche hadn't really known Roy as a player, but they knew his cachet, his credibility, and, of course, they also knew he was their boss. Yet, it still could look more like a bunch of teenaged major junior players gathering around him, wide-eyed, than hardened pros paying attention—or pretending to pay attention—to the coach because that's what you're supposed to do. It was becoming more obvious every day that his eight years of coaching major junior had shaped his coaching philosophy as much as—and probably more than—his days as a player. At major junior, coaching also means commiserating about girlfriends who don't understand and homesickness, and cajoling about getting homework done and not being derailed by the temptations facing players with rock-star status in those markets.

Roy was far from the only major junior coach/former NHL player who made the leap to the NHL, because it's a rather common route. But he had that unusual credibility, and he was smart enough to come back as a teacher rather than as a superstar demanding to be heard.

"It's not been that tough so far," he said. "When I first coached in Quebec, I was thinking more as a player. Now, I'm more as a coach. Because if you're too emotional, you get your bench distracted, and it's tougher for your players. You don't need to scream at your players. It's more about being calm and trying to find solutions. I'm here because I'm passionate. I'm here because I love the game. I'm here because I love the fans here. I'm here because I have a chance to give back the great things I went through in Denver."

On Wednesday, October 2, the opening night opponent was the Anaheim Ducks.

Part II

Regular Season

GETTING STARTED

WEDNESDAY, OCTOBER 2, AT DENVER: AVALANCHE 6, DUCKS 1. RECORD: 1–0

Patrick Roy meant it. He really did. He was going to be calm, cool, collected, thoughtful, under control, restrained, reasoned . . . all of that. The player who initiated the two famous goalie fights against the Red Wings? The man who lost his cool after Mario Tremblay's "disrespect"? The goalie who didn't hide emotions and, in fact, was fueled by them? Even the fiery junior coach involved in several controversial incidents?

That was another Patrick Roy.

This Patrick Roy was a teacher, a coach, even a father figure speaking soothingly much of the time.

Oops.

That re-branding was forgotten in the final seconds of the Avalanche's rout of the Ducks. It was a dream night for the Avalanche. Roy got tumultuous cheers from the sold-out house in the pregame introductions and at other points when his picture was flashed on the new scoreboard screens, which were so huge and clear, the major temptation was to ignore what was going on below and watch the screens instead. The Avalanche dominated from beginning to end, getting two goals from Jamie McGinn and one apiece from Ryan O'Reilly, Steve Downie, John Mitchell, and Matt Duchene. Semyon Varlamov had 35 saves and was tremendous in the net, allowing only Jakob Silfverberg's goal with 6.4 seconds remaining.

That wasn't what the hockey world was talking about the next morning.

It was talking about Roy's actions as the game ended.

The Avalanche coach was irate about what he considered a dangerous knee-on-knee Ben Lovejoy hit on Nathan MacKinnon at the Colorado blue line with about 30 seconds left in the game, and there wasn't a stoppage until the lone Anaheim goal ruined Varlamov's shutout.

"I was not happy, first of all, seeing their defenseman kneeing our guy," Roy said later. "That was a knee-to-knee hit, and it should have been a penalty, in my opinion. I certainly didn't like that. When it's 6–0, I don't think this game needs this type of cheap shot."

After Silfverberg's goal, Roy indeed sent out his fourth line for the face-off, with enforcers Cody McLeod and Patrick Bordeleau flanking center John Mitchell. They weren't out there for a tea party, and McLeod and Bordeleau came off as guys looking to stir up trouble when the puck dropped. Then the clock ran down, with Bordeleau all but ignoring the puck and shoving the Ducks' Matt Beleskey. Forgotten was that Roy had the last change at home and could (and did) claim that he was just continuing to match lines, and Anaheim coach Bruce Boudreau had sent out *his* fourth line. The puck went over to the bench area, and amid the shoving and maneuvering, the final horn sounded.

But the skaters remained on the ice, compressed in that area; that's when it really got interesting. Several gloves came off and hit the ice in the rugby scrum. The Ducks' Corey Perry, a terrific player but also a noted yapper, was sitting on the dasher near the end of the bench, with his back to the ice and facing Roy. Pretty soon, words went back and forth between Perry and Roy, who came down to get closer, and that incensed Boudreau, who also moved toward the Colorado bench. A minor-league journeyman as a player who was an "opposing" player in *Slap Shot*, his vocabulary was well documented to be spiced with epithets after the airing of HBO's "24/7: Penguins-Capitals, Road to the NHL Winter Classic" in 2010—when he was Washington's coach. He was offended by Roy talking to his players, and said so, calling it "bush" . . . and a few other things. Roy pushed the glass between the benches, and the stanchion gave, bending toward the Ducks—and toward Boudreau, who reached up to stop it. Roy clearly was surprised that the wall had that much give in it.

Stationed between the benches for the Altitude television broadcast, freelance cameraman John Almering unflinchingly continued his work, filming away as Roy pushed it again, with even more vehemence, and this time he knew it would move as much as it did. It bent even further into the Ducks' bench as Perry and winger Patrick Maroon shoved it back. By then, more players were on the ice, theoretically for the symbolic skate to the goaltenders; surprisingly, nothing more broke out, especially because McLeod and Bordeleau still looked willing to stir it up. Finally, as things calmed down, the officials signaled that it was OK for the Colorado bench to empty, and the remaining players came out to congratulate Varlamov.

Afterward, Boudreau let Roy have it . . . verbally.

"I didn't expect that," he said. "It's not our job to go back and forth with their players. All of a sudden, I told him, 'That's bull, that's bush league,' and he did what he did. He's going to be in for a long year if he's going to yell at every player and yell at the refs at every stoppage of play. It's not the way the game is played."

He added, "At the end, obviously we're frustrated. But, I mean, he's got Bordeleau and McLeod on the ice. Even if they start something, a coach has no right to start yapping at players."

Footage from both team broadcasts was up on YouTube, seemingly before the teams left the ice, and was much commented on overnight . . . and beyond. The consensus: *Patrick Roy was being Patrick Roy*. It was easy to understand the reaction, but it also was a case of overreaction from those who hadn't been watching or listening to him on a regular basis since he had taken the Colorado job.

Roy was angry, but his outburst was more calculation than explosion.

He was standing up for his players.

It was opening night, and he was using the center-stage atmosphere to send a message—or two. Lovejoy's hit on MacKinnon was shaky and dangerous, and even more so, unnecessary in a 6–0 game. (That works both ways.) Roy would have had Bordeleau and McLeod out there for that face-off even if Boudreau had sent out his top line (which would have been stupid) or put out the trainer, the bus driver, the massage therapist, the video man, and the radio analyst. So there, Roy was probably being a bit disingenuous, but his message was clear and undoubtedly worth what it cost him.

It sure got folks talking.

Officially, Roy drew a game misconduct for the tirade; and the next day, one of the NHL's vice principals checked in. Colin Campbell, for one season a Colorado Rockies defenseman during his journeyman's career, announced that Roy was fined $10,000 and called his actions "irresponsible." In the statement issued by the league, Campbell also said: "One of the responsibilities of an NHL coach is to help diffuse volatile situations on the bench."

The next day, some of the media reaction in Denver came from personalities who hadn't been to a practice or an exhibition game and didn't seem to realize that Roy had been restrained until his explosion at the end of the game the night before. But the discerning caught on to the method in Roy's madness and even understood why he said he neither contested the fine nor apologized for his actions.

"This is the role of the coach at some point," he said. "I love my players, and I always will be behind my players."

By then, too, someone had told Roy that a similar Lovejoy hit on Calgary's Curtis Glencross had ended Glencross's season the year before, and he brought that up, too. "A 'D' that skates forward and gets his knee open is dangerous, and it's something that we do not accept," Roy said. "Then, at the end, Perry was talking to me, and I responded, and this is when Boudreau came in. I don't talk to players. I never talk to players. I respect all the players."

And Boudreau's comments?

"What Boudreau said was all lies," Roy said. "I'm certainly not going to get too involved in this one, but when you talk about classless, when you're lying, this is classless. This is the league policy, and I understand it now, but at the same time, I will always defend my players. Things happen. This is the way I dealt with this one. Would I deal with it differently next time? Maybe. Maybe not. I don't know."

The incident also drew attention around the league. St. Louis Blues' coach Ken Hitchcock, who also had coached in major junior with the Kamloops Blazers before moving up to the NHL as an assistant, was quoted in the *St. Louis Post Dispatch* as calling it "junior hockey. It's got no place in our game. You can't be pushing barriers down."

The Avalanche—still struggling to regain their popularity in the market and at the box office—couldn't have bought that kind of publicity. They not only had won their opener, but Roy also had a lot of folks talking—even in Denver, where many media types thought blanket sports coverage meant discussing how tight Peyton Manning's spiral had been in practice that day, and that Nuggets' exhibition games and preseason coverage were worthy of being played ahead of the Avalanche's real season. The Broncos were 4–0, but for one day, at least, they had to share the spotlight.

FRIDAY, OCTOBER 4, AT DENVER: AVALANCHE 3, PREDATORS 1. RECORD: 2–0

The scheduler had a sense of drama, bringing the Predators (with Seth Jones) into Denver twice in the first month of the season to face the Avalanche (and Nathan MacKinnon). Although they didn't play in the same league, the two teenagers ran across each other all the way through the draft process and played against each other in such events as the World Junior Championships—MacKinnon with Canada and Jones with the United States. They could say they were friends and not be stretching the point.

The Avalanche won the first meeting between the Central Division rivals with two goals from winger P. A. Parenteau and one from, yes, Patrick Bordeleau. Varlamov again was solid for Colorado, making 26 saves. He had allowed only two goals in two games.

The controversy in this one came when Steve Downie left his feet and nailed Nashville defenseman Roman Josi, making partial contact with his head and knocking him out of the game. Predators Shea Weber and Gabriel Bourque both tried to go after Downie. Nashville coach Barry Trotz later characterized it as the sort of hit the NHL was trying to legislate out of the game, or at least discourage, and he said he assumed the league would fine or suspend Downie, who drew a charging minor. Roy shrugged it off. "That was a great hit," he said. "I thought it was a fair check. What I like about Steve is that he is a great leader, and he plays hard. He doesn't go wild."

* * *

To the shock of many, NHL discipline czar Brendan Shanahan, the former Red Wing, the next day said the Downie hit wasn't deserving of extra discipline.

"I play on the edge," Downie said. "I'm going to make that hit. It was a borderline hit. I've just got to keep my feet on the ground and keep my elbows down and drive through with my shoulders. That's my focus. In no way am I going out there head-hunting."

He had noticed that Roy had defended him and praised his play, emphasizing that despite the controversial hit, he was playing under control.

"It's great to play for Patrick," Downie said. "He's a fighter, and he showed the boys on opening night that he's in our corner. And we've got to battle for him. If he's going to go out and put his neck on the line like that for us, then we've got to do it for him too."

Downie was playing right wing on the Matt Duchene-centered line, with Ryan O'Reilly on the left side. The skepticism about O'Reilly's suitability to play wing, rather than center where his hockey savvy and two-way strength were so valuable, was dissipating. "Right now, I love what I see so far," Roy said of having O'Reilly on the wing. "He has been clicking really well with Matt. He's very good along the wall, gets the puck out of the zone, smart with the puck. He makes good decisions, supports well, and is really reliable in our end. I think he makes Dutchy a better player."

YOUNG GUNS

NO. 9, MATT DUCHENE, 5'11", 200 LBS., BORN JANUARY 16, 1991, HALIBURTON, ONTARIO

When Patrick Roy shoved the glass that first night against Anaheim, one player on the Avalanche bench was chortling, feeling he was flashing back to watching as a kid as Roy challenged not one, but two, Detroit goaltenders during the heyday of the rivalry.

"You always have that kid part of you, and I'm still pretty young at heart," Duchene said. "I'm good at relating to young kids and keeping that fun childhood side. I just remember watching those battles and dreaming of being there one day. When you're young, you don't have any clue what it's about, but it looks like a lot of fun. You're playing for something so big. Especially being from Canada, where we eat, sleep, and breathe hockey, seeing those battles going on was pretty cool. Then, seeing Patrick getting fired up like that the first game I was playing for him, brought back some childhood memories, for sure. That's where I went to at that point. All that was going on, and I was trying not to laugh. Everybody was all mad and swearing and yelling, and trying to fight each other, and I was sitting there, trying not to laugh. I was in another place."

That "other place" was childhood.

In Haliburton, Ontario, officially a "village" about 135 miles northeast of Toronto, young Duchene at first wanted to play the same position Roy played.

"As a kid, I was obsessed with goalies," Duchene said. "I almost became a goalie. I would have been one if my dad had let me. I loved the gear. When I was starting hockey, if my dad had said, 'All right, I'll buy you all the gear, and you can play in net,' I would have. My dad was a goalie, so he knew what it was like. He knew the pressures. Parents know what's best, what their kids need, for the most part, and he saw that I had some talent as a forward. He said, 'You can play net in ball hockey at school and with me.' He got me new road hockey gear every Christmas, so that was the first thing. Then, when Patrick came over from Montreal to Colorado, I was just watching, and I loved the way he stood and played. He was the reason I became an Avs fan, which is pretty cool now that I'm playing for him."

Duchene had a framed and autographed Joe Sakic jersey hanging in the basement of his family's home, and, as the years passed, he switched his loyalty to the Avalanche almost exclusively. He followed all the Colorado moves—including the goalie fights—with rapt and wide-eyed interest. His father, Vince, and his mother, Chris, indulged him, never suggesting that he follow a team closer to home. When Alex Tanguay scored what turned out to be the game-winning goal in Game 7 of the Stanley Cup finals in 2001, young Duchene had a bucket of popcorn in his lap and jumped up, spilling the popcorn all over.

"The goalie side of me really loved to watch Patrick; and the player side of me, when I was playing, every game I pretended to be a player," Duchene said. "My mom would always say, 'Who are you going to be today, Matt?' I was five, six, seven years old, and I would be either Joe Sakic or Peter Forsberg. Those two guys, plus Patrick, were the guys I looked up to. They made me a diehard Avs fan, for sure. I used to take it personally when they lost. I took it harder back then when they lost than I do now. I know that sounds crazy. You're day by day now, and you're more mature, but when they lost in the playoffs, I bawled my eyes out a couple of times as a young kid."

Meanwhile, when it became apparent that the young Duchene might have a bright future in the game, his family went along with Matt playing his minor hockey in Lindsay, Ontario. Because it was a "zone" or hub-type program for the region, he wasn't the only player traveling significant distances, but he might have been the mileage champ. "I drove an hour and fifteen minutes to practice six times a week," he recalled—making it clear he wasn't the one doing the driving, and that it all represented family sacrifice. As he starred in the Lindsay program, he always sought to "play up" an age classification, but some resented that and tried to block it. "There were some tears shed over that, because it got so personal with me," Duchene said. "I fought that for eight years. My dad fought hard for me to get that. It was a key to development. I played up until my last two years of minor hockey, and they had found a way to keep me from playing up, but that was OK because by then it was time for me to play at my own age.

"Hockey parents are crazy, and we came across some that were crazy. We were just trying to mind our own business, and my dad, who's a very smart hockey guy, was trying to do whatever he could to help me develop into what I could be, and he knew what I needed, and we did whatever we had to do. He probably seemed like a crazy hockey parent, too, but he knew what he was doing."

Eventually, at age 15, Duchene left Haliburton to play major junior for the Ontario Hockey League's (OHL) Brampton Battalion. "I went from a town of 1,500 people to a [high] school of 2,500 kids," he said. "It was very different for me."

Eligible for the NHL draft after his second season with the Battalion, Duchene was considered a sure bet to go near the top of the first round. The Avalanche had the third choice, thanks to their Western Conference-worst 32–45–13 record and no reshuffling of the order in the draft lottery. The selection order ended up what most had considered likely going in—center John Tavares to the Islanders, Swedish defenseman Victor Hedman to the Tampa Bay Lightning, and then Duchene to Colorado. Greg Sherman announced the choice at Montreal's Bell Centre; Duchene, who quickly donned an '09 Avalanche jersey, couldn't contain his excitement.

"I keep looking down at the logo, going, 'Are you kidding me?,'" he said that day. "I used to draw their logo every day in school. I'm just so happy. Every kid dreams of playing for his boyhood team. It's crazy. They have not had a top pick in many years, and the one year I'm available and rated up there, they have it. It's kind of fate, I guess."

Two weeks after the draft, on July 9, 2009, Duchene and several top Avalanche prospects skated in a development camp workout at Family Sports Center. Then they went en masse to the Inverness Hotel, filed into a ballroom, sat in the back row of chairs, and watched and listened as Sakic officially announced his retirement. "Obviously, it would have been great to skate with him at least in camp, or whatever," Duchene said that day. He seemed embarrassed when he was asked if he had considered the irony of taking his first skate as a member of the Avalanche on the day Sakic retired. The question, of course, came with the assumption that the torch might eventually pass from Sakic to Duchene. "I don't know," he said. "I guess you guys can decide that. I don't really know what to say to that. I haven't been to a camp or been to a game yet."

Under Joe Sacco, Duchene got off to a slow start as a rookie. He was such a student of the game, though, that he could recite virtually game by game the progression of Tampa Bay wunderkind Steven Stamkos the previous season. His point was that Stamkos hadn't burst out of the gate, either, before finishing with 23 goals. Eventually Duchene got going, scored 24 goals, and was a Calder Trophy finalist in the season. He finished third, behind Buffalo defenseman Tyler Myers and Detroit goalie Jimmy Howard, but he was the top vote getter among the 2009 draft crop. Myers had gone to the Sabres in 2008 and Howard to the Red Wings in 2003.

In his first two seasons Duchene lived in the basement at the Adam Foote household, with the Avalanche defenseman; his wife, Jennifer; and sons, Callan and Nolan. Duchene at times seemed like a third Foote child, playing video games with the two boys. At the rink, his relationship with Sacco was strained, and even Duchene at the time acknowledged that he needed to be more attentive in the defensive end of the ice. He was named to the All-Star Game in his second season, and he wasn't out of place, but his relationship with Sacco was deteriorating.

In a November 4, 2010, game against Vancouver, Sacco humiliated and angered Duchene by keeping him on the bench for the final fourteen minutes of the second period in a 3–1 loss to the Canucks. Sacco was certainly within his rights to bench him, as Duchene in his first three years occasionally was plagued by too much dipsy doodle play with the puck, things that might look pretty on a YouTube video but drove the old-school Sacco crazy.

Duchene could accept being benched for stretches of a game. If he deserved it, he wouldn't whine about it. Well, maybe a little. The thing that seemed to really drive a wedge between Sacco and Duchene, among others, was Sacco's stubbornness in sticking with a system that they were convinced wouldn't work.

In the 2011–12 season, Duchene's third, he moved into his own Greenwood Village condominium and had a team-high 12 goals at the Christmas break. But he suffered a knee injury the next week and scored only two goals the rest of the season in limited work, playing in only 58 games. He signed a two-year, $7-million contract, seemingly accepting the challenge to prove himself worthy of a longer-term commitment.

By the time the truncated 2013 season opened, Duchene was in better condition than he had ever been, partially because of a gluten-free diet and a new trainer, Andy O'Brien. "I've changed everything—eating, stuff in the gym, stuff I do before games, everything," he said. "I eat fish almost every day, taking some different supplements and stuff. What I wanted to do this summer was learn more about my body and what made it tick. I was doing some stuff that worked for some guys, but it didn't work for me. I'm the type of guy who doesn't accept failure, and last year obviously didn't go the way I wanted in the second half, so it was time to make some adjustments."

In the Avalanche's otherwise horrible 2013 season, he was one of the bright lights, with 17 goals in 47 games.

Duchene was the most outgoing of the Avalanche's young stars, capable of talking as fast as he skated—well, almost—and willing to speak frankly, sometimes defying the conventions. Although his casual wardrobe—he could look like a guy headed off to do his chores on the family farm after practice—drew some teasing, he also had ranked near the top of his high school class and dabbled in art, guitar playing, and writing.

His summer 2013 contract extension was a reward, an expression of faith from the organization following Sakic's elevation and Roy's hiring. Early in the season, he finally spoke publicly about his dissatisfaction with Sacco.

"There were very few people in this room who were happy," Duchene said. "Our style of play—it wasn't right for this team. We knew it would fail. That was the hard part. We knew success was going to be short-lived. It was hard to really be excited about it. For myself, it was really hard to look at what we were doing and think it would keep on working.

"I think there's always been a plan [here]. People are professionals, and they always have a plan, but is it the right plan? We've had a young, fast, offensively gifted team for four years and haven't been able to show that every night. The only time we ever seemed to play that way was against a team that really opened it up and let us play that way."

Of the changes under Roy, Duchene said: "The one thing with Patrick is, there's no doghouse. If you're not doing what you're supposed to do, he's going to bring you in, he's going to sit you down, and you're going to correct it constructively, and then you're going to move on from there. You don't stay in that doghouse. It's the first time I can honestly say everyone in this room is excited."

The major issue, of course, was whether this was a honeymoon period—or whether it would last.

NO. 90, RYAN O'REILLY, 6'0", 200 LBS., BORN FEBRUARY 7, 1991, CLINTON, ONTARIO

The quiet, reflective O'Reilly—a yoga devotee often found stretching in corners of locker rooms or hallways—was one of the young stars, but he wasn't one of the boys. He wasn't a loner or outcast, he just wasn't in one of the packs very often. He lived in a downtown loft, drove a fire-engine red Audi sports car, played the ukulele and mandolin, and included Billie Holliday among his musical tastes. In short, O'Reilly was more of an eclectic personality than your usual hockey player.

His family lived in rural Ontario, outside the small town of Brucefield, about a two-hour drive west of Toronto. "The town had stop signs at each end and maybe fifty houses, something like that," Ryan recalled. "And a big barn at one end." There, his parents, Brian and Bonnie, were social workers for the province. About the time Ryan was born, juvenile home shutdowns in the area challenged the system, so Bonnie and Brian started to take in kids themselves. Payment came from the province, but the motivation wasn't financial. Somebody needed to do it, and Ryan was raised with other kids—troubled kids—passing through the O'Reilly home for stays of various periods. "We would have maybe four or five at a time," he said. The total would be about fifty by the time Ryan left home to play major junior with the Erie (Pennsylvania) Otters of the Ontario League. "I was living with all these different guys, all these kids who didn't have good childhoods, were abused and having problems getting along in school and with anyone," O'Reilly said. "It was grade eleven or twelve before I realized how lucky I was to be raised in that environment and learn how to be accepting and get along with everyone."

Part of the deal was that these houseguests were expected to at least try to take part in the family games, including hockey in the driveway, where Ryan and his brothers, plus his mother and father, all took part. "We always had friends from down the road who would come over, too," Ryan said. "We all got along that way, and hockey was how we got connected, things we did together."

Bonnie O'Reilly played an especially fierce game.

"She's probably the most competitive athlete in my family," Ryan said of his mother. "She plays broomball, still plays to this day. I bug her, I say the NBL, the National Broomball League, is calling her, and she takes it serious. She was an amazing basketball player, and she plays hockey."

Ryan laughed.

"She's a little more feisty than I am," Ryan said with a laugh. "She's not afraid to use her stick and won't back down from anything."

Because their hometown was rural, Ryan and his brother, Cal—who eventually would make the NHL ahead of Ryan with Nashville, but not be as successful—traveled long distances to play. "I don't think it ever hurt me," Ryan said. "I look back on it now—I think it was more beneficial, coming from a small-town area. We'd be driving an hour, an hour and a half to practice. My parents spent so much money so my brother and I could play, travel hockey at a high level. We'd have games in Windsor, three hours away; we'd go down and maybe play two games that day, and it just shows the sacrifice our family made to do that, drive that much. That helped so much, so when you go to junior, you're used to sitting around or driving three hours a day to play. Some of the kids came to Erie from Toronto, and everything had been in Toronto; they'd never had to travel. No matter what, we had to drive. My parents spent so much of their life helping me do what I want to do and what I love."

After sounding him out, the Otters took him first in the OHL draft.

"I was excited for it," O'Reilly said. "They had guys who I think would have been first overall picks who didn't want to go there. They asked me, and I said, of course, I'd like the chance to go first overall. I went down to the city, and I liked it. I still have close friends from Erie, and I go back there every summer."

After two seasons with the Otters, and playing against Matt Duchene and Brampton, O'Reilly expected to go in the first round of the 2009 draft—a few picks after Duchene, perhaps, but not long after him. Even then, he was highly regarded defensively, but it was unique for a center with only 16 goals in his major junior season to be ranked that high. Instead, he wasn't taken in the first round, and Colorado pounced on him with the third pick of the second round.

"I was disappointed not to go in the first round," O'Reilly said. "From halfway through the first round, my agent said there was a good chance I could go, so that kind of got my hopes up, which I shouldn't have done. I was seeing other players going and I was like, 'I'm better than him,' and stuff like that." He smiled. "You're a young kid; you can do that. But once the second day came, the draft started and, boom, I was gone. I wouldn't change anything now. I think being drafted at that pick was the best thing that could happen for me. I came in hungry, and I came in with no pressure on me, and I think that's what helped me make the team and get a spot."

Only the high first-round picks generally make NHL rosters right away, so the assumption was that after attending training camp, he would be returned to Erie for the 2009–10 season. Instead, he stuck with Colorado. The biggest surprise wasn't that O'Reilly quickly proved himself a legitimate NHL center; it was his considerable offensive skill, which had seemed latent in major junior. Suddenly, he seemed to be a primary example of a heady playmaker who made the players around him better as he quickly stamped himself as one of the better defensive centers in the league. In his first three seasons, he had 8, 13, and 18 goals, and seemed on an upward curve there. Then came his acrimonious contract battle, when he didn't reach an agreement before the lockout began in 2012 or after the teams went back to work.

His father's militancy and grousing (often on Twitter) that the Avalanche didn't appreciate Ryan's intangible contributions were understandable, if unfortunate. It all seemed to slightly contradict O'Reilly's image as the ultimate rink rat who stayed on the ice long after other teammates left and loved the game above all else. The Avalanche still were thinking at the time that in a perfect world, after rebuilding, O'Reilly would be the best third-line center in the league, a penalty killer and defensive stalwart—an honorable and valued status, but not a superstar in the making. The Flames forced Colorado's hand with the two-year, $10-million offer sheet, though, and the Avalanche matched it. O'Reilly had six goals in twenty-nine games down the stretch for a team that got worse, record-wise, after he signed. "When you're in that situation, yeah, it's a business," O'Reilly said. "You have to protect yourself and do what's necessary because you're only going to play the game so long."

When Roy announced after the draft that he was going to take a look at O'Reilly on wing, on a line with Duchene and P. A. Parenteau, it seemingly acknowledged that the new coach would have to be imaginative to get his top six forwards all on the top two lines. The issue was whether being on the wing would diminish O'Reilly's effectiveness if he couldn't take as much advantage of his savvy, both making plays and defensively, as if he were at center.

"When I knew we were going to take MacKinnon, I knew that someone was going to have to move," O'Reilly said. "I figured it would be me. I was excited for it. It was just another challenge. I had played on the wing over at the [2013] world championships, and I was kind of starting to get comfortable with it."

By early in the season, he was developing chemistry with Duchene, learning to live without being a primary face-off man. "I love taking face-offs, and that's one of the things I miss most about it," O'Reilly said. "Just starting a shift with that, it's a pressure situation, and it's getting the puck back to the boys. But Dutchy's been great on face-offs, and we usually have the puck. Sometimes I think of the game in a centerman's way and be more defensive. I'm still learning every game. It's going to be a while before I'm really comfortable. I've always been a natural centerman, but I like it.

"I think I got into the league because I was good in my own zone, and that's kind of been the staple in my game, playing in my own end first and being successful there. It requires me to be more physical and forecheck with my feet more and be more aggressive, whereas before as a center, I had to sit back a little more and try to read the play and support more. I like it. It helps generate a little more offense for me, and it's good."

NO. 92, GABRIEL LANDESKOG, 6'1", 204 LBS., BORN NOVEMBER 23, 1992, STOCKHOLM

It happened, over and over, in his first couple of years in the NHL. Landeskog, who served as captain of major junior's Kitchener Rangers in the Ontario Hockey League, an honor that usually goes to hard-nosed Canadian lads, would be talking on his cell phone to his parents or someone else back home. The teammate would hear him, sometimes stop and sometimes keep going, but often be blindsided by a sudden realization.

This teenager, who in the everyday business of the locker room and the Denver street sounds as if with a little coaching he could play Othello in Stratford-on-Avon, is speaking *Swedish*—which makes sense, after all, because he's from Stockholm. But part of the deal about Landeskog's single-minded approach to reaching the NHL was to immerse himself in English-language classes, even more so than the typical multilingual Swede in the NHL who at least retains a slight lilting intonation. "I knew if I learned English and understood it well, it would only help me with my dream," he said after the Avalanche drafted him in June 2011.

His father, Tony, played two seasons in the Swedish Elite League and several more years in the second division, but never had the chance to venture to North America and the NHL. His son wanted more. In Stockholm, where Tony was in the insurance business, and his wife, Cecilia, was a chef, young Gabriel also played soccer but played hockey with more passion and an eye on the future. At age eight, he put a poster of the Avalanche's 2001 Stanley Cup championship team on his bedroom wall. Although he said only a limited number of NHL games were available on television, he learned all he could about the Colorado team with so many stars—including the superstar Swede, Peter Forsberg, and the goalie named Roy.

Swedes are accepted only reluctantly in the three major junior leagues playing under the Canadian Hockey League umbrella—so reluctantly that each team is limited to two "imports." Not only does the player need to be extraordinarily talented, but be able to cope with the tribulations of being so far away from home. At 16, Landeskog was a natural to make that move because of his uncanny maturity and his English proficiency, which would help in the mandatory high school classroom work that is part of major junior's routine for the younger players. The option was to stay in the Swedish Elite League, which he got a brief taste of in the 2008–09 season, playing three games for Djurgarden.

"At that time, I had to make a decision to either stay in Sweden and play in the senior hockey there and get five or ten minutes a game, or go to major junior and hopefully get more ice time and develop and get used to the culture and systems," Landeskog said. "I think for me, that was the right decision. I wanted to come over here, I wanted to do this, and I wanted to get used to the hockey over here. One day, this is where I wanted to be, so looking back, I made the right decision."

The Plymouth Whalers took him in the OHL draft but traded his rights to Kitchener. Right away, Landeskog played with a sharp-edged playing style that in old-school thinking made him look more like a kid from Saskatoon than Stockholm. The soft Swede stereotype was long dead—or, at least, it should have been—but Landeskog's physical play nonetheless took some by surprise. He had 24 goals in 61 games in his first season with the Rangers. Was he challenged? "If it was anything," he said, shaking his head, "it was me challenging guys. I wanted to prove myself. I don't think there was any resentment towards me being European or anything like that. I came over here to play hockey just like everyone else in the OHL."

The Rangers named him their captain for his second season. "I was a little surprised," he said. "We had a couple of older guys that had been there a few years, and it was a tremendous honor to get that, to be the first 17-year-old captain there, especially as a European."

Holding the second pick in the draft, the Avalanche pounced on Landeskog after Edmonton took Ryan Nugent-Hopkins in 2011. Unsurprisingly, although his maturity never was questioned, he struggled at times as a rookie. Ultimately, he came on to score 22 goals and become the third Swede to win the Calder Trophy, following Peter Forsberg (1995) and Daniel Alfredsson ('96). As his honor came two years after Duchene finished third in the Calder voting, the Avalanche seemed to be at least assembling a precocious core.

Another shocker came in the summer of September 2012, when the Avalanche announced that Landeskog would succeed Milan Hejduk, entering his twilight and likely to play even fewer minutes in the upcoming season on the third or even fourth line, as captain. The NHL lockout was under way at the time; not only would the teams not go into training camp as scheduled, but the labor dispute lasted months. It was noted that when he was named, Landeskog had become the youngest captain in NHL history. He was 19 years, 297 days old when the announcement was made, or eleven days younger than Sidney Crosby had been when he was named captain of the Penguins.

It was a major endorsement of Landeskog's maturity and likely status as a long-term Colorado cornerstone. He was the fourth Colorado captain, succeeding Joe Sakic (1995–2009), Adam Foote (2009–11), and Hejduk (2011–12), but the emphasis on the youngest-in-history angle— by eleven days!—seemed almost contrived and theatrical. It was reasonable to infer that the Avalanche even was delivering a not-so-subtle message: to Duchene, then 21, that he still had some maturing to do before being considered captain material; that Paul Stastny wasn't forceful enough (although Hejduk certainly never was, either); and that Colorado still didn't have complete faith that Erik Johnson was going to live up to what was foreseen for him when the St. Louis Blues took him with the top overall choice in 2006.

Landeskog didn't do anything "wrong" as the captain in the abbreviated 2013 season, but he missed twelve games with a concussion and had only nine goals. The team's struggles couldn't be laid at the captain's doorstep, either, but it was at least fair to say that the experiment had mixed results. It wouldn't have been a shock if Roy had announced he wanted a fresh start, including a switch of the "C." He could have couched it that he was trying to take some pressure off Landeskog, too.

Roy decided to stick with the status quo—and with a 20-year-old as his captain. In chats with Landeskog, he emphasized that he wanted his captain to come see the coach if there was anything that needed to be discussed, and that Sakic led more by example than through rhetoric. When questions came up about the appropriateness of Landeskog serving as the captain, Roy said there were veterans on the team who could help out on the leadership front, and that even a goaltender named Roy didn't need a "C" on his jersey to speak up.

NO. 26, PAUL STASTNY, 6'0", 205 LBS., BORN DECEMBER 27, 1985, QUEBEC CITY

John le Carré could have written this Cold War thriller. Except it was real. After playing for Czechoslovakia in a tournament in Innsbruck, Austria, young Peter Stastny was with his brother, Anton, in a car speeding the wrong way down a one-way street, and Peter caught himself thinking that if they just made it through this ride, that might be the easy part. They were trying to defect from the clutches of the authoritarian Czechoslovakian Soviet-dominated regime and from the compliant men who ran the nation's hockey program.

This was 1980, six months after the brothers played for Czechoslovakia in the Olympics at Lake Placid, losing 7–3 to the Americans' "Miracle on Ice" team in group play and finishing fifth overall. As proud minority Slovakians in the nation patched together after World War I, the Stastnys—Peter, Anton, and a third brother, Marian—never had been comfortable representing Czechoslovakia, and the Soviet dominance of the nation added to the enmity.

As they were being raised in Bratislava, their father was a clerk for a power company. Rink time was sparse, and the brothers and their friends played hockey on the street, or, when it got cold enough, on makeshift outdoor rinks. Eventually, they were the core of the Czechoslovakia national team, and the three brothers had a combined 16 goals in six games at Lake Placid. Peter was the second-leading scorer in the Olympic tournament.

After Peter (along with his wife, Darina) and Anton defected and joined the Quebec Nordiques, brother Marian was able to join them a year later. Peter became the biggest star of the three, scoring 450 goals and getting 1,239 points in 15 seasons with the Nordiques, Devils, and Blues. While Peter was with the Nordiques, Darina Stastny gave birth to Paul in December 1985. Predictably, young Paul was on skates soon. "A quarter mile from our house, there was an outdoor rink under the train tracks, and that's where I did my first real skating," Paul recalled. Peter played nearly two full seasons with a young Joe Sakic before the rebuilding and struggling Nordiques mercifully sent him to the Devils in 1990. One of Sakic's most vivid memories of his early seasons was Peter Stastny tracking him down in a hotel coffee shop, informing Sakic that Stastny had just been traded, and telling Sakic that he had enjoyed

playing with him and that he would be one of the game's stars soon—
and for a long time.

In New Jersey, Paul often went to the rink with his father. "I was the
little kid on the ice at the Christmas parties, trying to skate with the
pros," Paul said.

Next came the move to St. Louis, when Paul was seven. A year later,
Peter was the flag bearer for Slovakia at the 1994 Winter Olympics in
Lillehammer, Norway, where he played for the reborn nation's hockey
team. "I was eight years old, and I didn't realize how big of an honor it
was," Paul said.

Darina and Peter stayed in St. Louis after his 1995 retirement,
meaning that Paul thought of himself as an All-American boy—albeit
one born in Canada with Slovakian roots. The family, Paul included,
still spoke Slovak in their home. "As I got older, I tried to speak it more
because it's one of those things that if you don't practice it, you lose it,"
Paul said.

After Peter retired, he worked for the Blues as a scout and skated
with the team's alumni squad when he could. Sometimes, he brought
along Paul. When Joel Quenneville was coaching the Blues, he went on
the ice with the alumni and a little kid who didn't respect his elders. "I
wondered, 'Who is this little guy who keeps taking the puck away from
me?' I couldn't get it back," Quenneville recalled.

Paul played one season with the Omaha-based River City Lancers of
the United States Hockey League, and then enrolled as an eighteen-
year-old freshman at the University of Denver. He had committed to
the Pioneers when they were struggling, but by the time he came to
DU, they had won the NCAA title in 2004. In Stastny's freshman season, the Pioneers repeated as national champions, and the Avalanche
took him in the second round of the 2005 draft. After his sophomore
season, he signed with the Avalanche, and the consensus at the time
was that he should have remained at DU at least one more season. "I
think I had to leave after two years," he said. He noted that star teammates Gabe Gauthier and Matt Carle had departed. "So guys a step
ahead of me were gone, and when you play with better players, you get
better. When you're one of the better players in the league, there's not
that much to improve on. I needed the next step. We thought the next
step, whether it was the NHL or the AHL, there would be faster and

stronger guys. I knew it wasn't a foregone conclusion I was going to make the NHL."

But he did, in part because veteran center Steve Konowalchuk had to retire when a heart defect showed up in his physical exam at the start of training camp. Stastny had an astounding rookie season, finishing second in the Calder Trophy voting to the Penguins' Evgeni Malkin. It was clear that he was the sort of player who thrived in better competition, with wingers who could take advantage of his playmaking instincts and at a level where savvy two-way play was even more valuable and prized. The kicker that season? He encountered older teammates, including Sakic, and even older opponents who knew of his father's incredible story and asked him about it. Paul was embarrassed to realize that some of them knew more than he did.

"They would bring up different things, and then I would ask my dad," Paul said. "He wouldn't say anything about it unless you asked him. Then, when I was with him at things like Christmas parties, engagement parties, and weddings, and people would ask him about it, I'd perk my ears. It's one of those stories that no matter how many times you hear it, it's always fascinating. It's one of those surreal things you can't imagine anyone going through these days."

While Paul was settling into the NHL, Peter was shuttling back and forth between St. Louis and Europe, where he had a home in Bratislava and served as a representative for Slovakia in the European Parliament. He also served as the head of Slovakia's national teams in World Cup and Olympic competitions.

The two major reasons Paul's career became such a flashpoint for criticism was that his rookie season's goal total—28—still was his career high as he began his eighth season in the league, his first under Patrick Roy. He drove some Avalanche followers nuts because he was playing under a five-year, $33-million contract he had signed under Francois Giguere's watch as GM; and he was more of a playmaker and two-way player than a scorer, meaning his contributions didn't always show up on the score sheet to "justify" anything close to that salary. Still, it was obvious early in his deal that he would be overpaid barring a breakout. Whether the conclusion was that he had hit a plateau as a player at a young age, or that he could only end up with eye-popping numbers with stars on his wings, he was a solid, smart, two-way player whose contributions couldn't be fairly measured in conventional scoring stats.

"I know I've got some genes for things that can't be taught," he said. "I get that from my dad and my uncles, the vision for things you see in your head. But I always loved the game growing up; I've always been a student of it."

His dual citizenship gave him some flexibility in international hockey, and it wasn't surprising that his first opportunity came to play for the United States, beginning with the 2007 World Championships, when he played on the American squad with his older brother, Yan. "And being in the States since I was so young, it's basically what I remember, and the way I was brought up was All-American," he said.

Paul was on the silver-medal Olympic team at Vancouver and had a goal and two assists in six games. Incredibly, 30 years after the Miracle on Ice, NBC didn't make much of the connection that this was an All-American story—a son playing for the United States as his father, who played for Czechoslovakia *against* the Americans in 1980 and then defected, watched. Stastny also had some Avalanche fans shaking their heads when he did well in the 2012 and 2013 World Championships. In the latter, he had seven goals in ten games for the Americans. On the bigger international rink, he was more effective.

Roy already was frequently challenging Stastny in practice, trying to prod him to be better, even if that meant occasionally ignoring his instincts to be unselfish.

"When you're not playing well, you'll have a talk," Stastny said, shrugging. "He can get a feel for what I'm seeing, and I can get a feel for what he's seeing. It's nice, because he's one of those coaches that doesn't just tell you, 'Hey, you have to be better.' He'll tell you, 'Hey, you have to be better, and here's what I think you should be doing,' or, 'Here's what you're doing right, and here's what you're doing wrong, and let's fix this.' I think that's what he's been doing with every individual, and I think that's why a lot of guys really like him and really respect him. He understands if you're playing good hockey and it's not going in, it's going to come. If you're playing bad hockey, that's when he puts you in your place and tells you to get out of that comfort zone and get back to the way you were playing."

As time went on, Stastny would be on the bubble for possible selection to the 2014 Olympic team, and the subject of trade rumors because that five-year deal was expiring and the Avalanche were overstocked with natural centers.

"I'm 28, I don't feel old, but we have a young team," Stastny said. "Every year, I've kind of grown. As a player, from my first year to now, I feel I've gotten stronger, smarter, become a better skater, better defensively and a better two-way player. You learn that when you're on a winning team, good things happen. When you're on a losing team, it's frustrating, but you also learn a lot about yourself. Sometimes you have to take a look at yourself in a mirror, and learn from what happened in the past and move on. In my head, I have certain numbers I think I should be getting, but at the same time, I know that for us to do well, I have to be playing good two-way hockey. I know we have guys drafted first, second, third overall who are more gifted than me offensively, and I know when I play better defensively, it opens up opportunities for them. We have a good mix of players here, and Patty's done a good job of bringing everything together. Sometimes guys worry about their stats, but when you win, everything takes care of itself, everyone's playing with more confidence.

"The rest, you can't really worry about. Last summer, I wanted to see what would happen, going into it with a new coach and management. The way things are going now, it's going well, and I want to stay here, and I want to play well. We have to keep winning and keep progressing, and I want to be part of that. Being overloaded at center is a good problem to have. Having six, seven centers on the top three lines is interesting, but you're a center, you understand the game, and you can play both positions. I try not to, but I tend to think about all that, and people bring it up. I try to forget it as soon as I can and take it for the short-term."

"WHY NOT US?"

As the Avalanche prepared to leave on their first road trip, Patrick Roy understood that he would be the center of attention as the team arrived in Toronto and played in the arena located a short walk from the Hockey Hall of Fame. "Maybe I will, but I would prefer our players to be," he said. "The reason we're 2–0 is that the players are playing really well. The coaches are there to help them and communicate with them and stuff like that, but the players are responsible for the start we have and certainly deserve all the credit."

In Toronto, Roy was greeted with—among other things—a ridiculous story in the *Toronto Star* for which the newsroom writer, after citing the opening-night incident in Denver, consulted "anger management experts" and passed along tips from them to Roy for help in controlling his temper. The online version of the story came with video of the Roy tantrum available at the top. It was so bizarre, even the most intelligent readers of the usually credible paper probably initially wondered if it was an *Onion* satire on what used to be called the "Experts Rolodex" phenomenon in journalism. (Call an expert!) It opened with: "Relax, Patrick Roy. It's just a game." After that, readers heard from a University of Toronto associate professor and a psychological counselor, and the message to Roy throughout was the same: Chill. Most likely, the column was supposed to be taken seriously, but the net result was unintended satire.

After the morning skate in the Air Canada Centre, Roy's media availability in the ice-level corridor drew a throng. In Toronto, even the most low profile of opposing coaches can find themselves speaking to a large group after a morning skate, but this was extraordinary—truly a throng. And, of course, one of the first things Roy was asked about was the opening night fireworks in Denver.

"Things like this happen sometimes," Roy said. "The objective was to protect our players. But I'd rather talk about this game, if you don't mind." But he was asked about maintaining that kind of fire over an 82-game schedule. (Yes, even in hockey-crazy Toronto, the questions sounded the same.) "I'm passionate about what I'm doing," he said. "I love to win, and that always comes first. I learned a lot during my junior days, that you have to control those emotions, and it's been easy, and it will be very easy, because I am here to win. I always have to be really calm when the game is on the line. Everything has to be calculated. If it can turn the game around, then turn it around. If it's at the end of the game and I think it's time, then it's time."

Roy also sat down with Paul Hendrick of Leafs TV for a five-minute interview, and it wasn't hard to infer later that he had at least hinted that he didn't need to talk about the Anaheim game again. Hendrick's interview for the Leafs' own network was a quick run through aspects of his gravitating to goaltending as a young boy, his coaches, his early days with the Canadiens, even his nicknames and superstitions as a player. Periodically through the interview as aired, footage of Roy running the morning skate was shown as he talked to Hendrick.

Near the end, Hendrick remarked that he'd heard Roy say he approached every game as a goaltender as if it were his first in the NHL, and asked if he had approached it the same way as a coach. "Yes, I do," he said. "I have a lot of respect for the game. I have a lot of respect for our fans. I think the fans are coming to watch us, and they deserve us to be on the top of our game. I think the same thing as a coach. You always have to come up with solutions, you always have to come up with options for your players, and I think it is important. I am passionate about the game, but at the same time, I have a lot of respect for the game, and especially our fans."

TUESDAY, OCTOBER 8, AT TORONTO: AVALANCHE 2, MAPLE LEAFS 1. RECORD: 3–0

The Avalanche passed perhaps their first test of legitimacy, beating the previously unbeaten Maple Leafs on goals by P. A. Parenteau and Cory Sarich. Nathan MacKinnon had an assist on Parenteau's goal, giving him four assists in his first three NHL games.

"I'm trying to be patient. I have two great linemates, and I think we're working hard together," MacKinnon said. "This was my first road game, and it was pretty good it was at [Air Canada Centre] against the Leafs."

Semyon Varlamov allowed only one goal for the third consecutive game, making 27 saves as he equaled his road win total for the entire previous season. This was almost hard to believe, but it was the Avalanche's first 3–0 start since the move to Denver. This was easier to believe: the Avalanche never had won three in a row in the previous season, albeit a shortened one.

Some of the game stories out of Toronto portrayed it as quite an upset that Roy hadn't exploded on the bench during the game. The headline on the Canadian Press story on Canada's MetroNews site:

**Patrick Roy stays calm as
Colorado Avalanche out-work
Toronto Maple Leafs**

From Toronto, the Avalanche headed off to Boston—and a dinner date.

✺ ✺ ✺

"Why not us?" was the playoff motto of the 2004 Boston Red Sox, the formerly cursed-by-the-Bambino franchise that became the first team in Major League Baseball history to win a playoff series after being down three games to none—against the hated New York Yankees, no less. Pitcher Curt Schilling came up with the motto, and it hadn't been dusted off again until the Avalanche convened for a team dinner at Tresca, a restaurant in Boston's famed Italian North End.

The Avalanche's host was the restaurant's co-owner, Ray Bourque, who would pick up the tab for the entire dinner.

Bourque and Roy were acquaintances in their many years of playing against each other when Bourque was a Boston Bruin and Roy a member of the Canadiens and Avalanche. To call them friends would be a stretch. The Bruins and Habs were Original Six blood rivals, and no love was lost between the teams. But when Bourque, who was seeking a chance to be on a Stanley Cup winner before his retirement, was traded to Colorado in the spring of 2000, he and Roy hit it off instantly. Roy compared it to having a "big bear" in front of him.

In Bourque, Roy had someone who shared his intensity for the game, but also someone he could relax and talk with about life over a glass of fine wine and top-end steak. Not many teammates ever got too close to Roy, partially because his accomplishments in the game were just too intimidating for anyone to relate. Roy had few peers in the game, but Bourque was someone he could respect—despite the fact that Bourque had never hoisted the Stanley Cup in the first 20 years of his career when he landed in Denver in early 2000. That spring, for the second season in a row, the Avalanche lost to the Dallas Stars in seven games in the Western Conference finals, but Bourque soon announced he would return to Colorado, presumably for one last shot at the Cup.

Despite having three Stanley Cup rings by 2001 and a roomful of other awards, it was Roy who was more nervous when the playoffs began than Bourque, who by then had let Roy know this would be his final season, win or lose. It was Bourque who would have to sit with Roy to calm him down and get his confidence back up after a shaky start to the Western Conference semifinals against Los Angeles. The Avalanche lost Game 1, 4–3 in overtime, to the Kings and were in danger of losing Game 2 as well when a Glen Murray shot was headed toward the net late in the second period of a scoreless game. But Bourque came to the rescue, knocking the puck out of midair just as it was about to cross the goal line. The Avalanche went on to win 2–0, but the rest of the series was a dogfight. There were moments when Roy began to doubt himself, and the stress caused by his wanting so badly to send Bourque into retirement with a first Stanley Cup compounded the situation. Bourque told Roy, "Quit worrying about me and my story. This is about all of us, not me."

The irony was that Bourque was more secure about himself than was Roy, despite Roy's more championship pedigree. Roy would later admit he was scared before every game, scared that he would suddenly lose all his ability and be a laughingstock. In Bourque, Roy would come to find a wise, mature older friend he could lean on for advice.

From there, Roy was more relaxed, and the Avalanche beat the Kings, then the Joel Quenneville-coached Blues in the Western Conference finals, moving on to the Stanley Cup finals against the New Jersey Devils—yes, the former Colorado Rockies.

By Game 7 against the Devils, after Roy had just shut out New Jersey in Game 6 at the Meadowlands, Roy knew he would be invincible—and he was in the Cup-clinching 3–1 win. If you ask Roy about that game today, however, he'll still shake his head a little. After hearing from his coach, the crafty Bob Hartley, that he'd overheard some trash-talking from the then wife of Devils goalie Martin Brodeur—that it was going to be "fun when we get it again," meaning a second straight championship—Roy told Hartley the Devils would not score a goal the rest of the series. That one goal, scored by Petr Sykora in Game 7, still makes him mad. But with Alex Tanguay scoring twice, the Avalanche won that game, too; the photos of Bourque holding what for him had been the especially elusive Stanley Cup overhead immediately were iconic. In a move Joe Sakic perhaps was remembered for as much as anything else in his career, the Avalanche captain accepted the Cup from NHL commissioner Gary Bettman but made what amounted to a quick touch pass to Bourque.

On this night a dozen years later in Boston, in Bourque's restaurant, the Avalanche players included Tanguay, but no others who had been teammates of either Bourque or Roy. Bourque looked out at the young faces, even spotting Nathan MacKinnon, who had yet to celebrate his sixth birthday when Bourque, Roy, and their teammates won the franchise's most recent championship.

Bourque asked Roy if he could say a few words to the team.

Sure, said Roy.

Bourque then stood up and told the young Avalanche players how good a new coach they had in his friend, how things would turn around finally under his watch, and he then suggested a motto with which to go forward: "Why not us?"

"It worked for the Red Sox, when nobody believed they could do something, and it can work for you guys, too," Bourque said.

It sounded good to Roy and the boys. Why not go with "Why Not Us?"?

THURSDAY, OCTOBER 10, AT BOSTON: AVALANCHE 2, BRUINS 0. RECORD: 4–0

In the TD Garden the next night, the Avalanche stayed unbeaten, largely thanks to Jean-Sebastien Giguere, who had 39 saves in the shut-out. Ryan O'Reilly scored in the first period, on a redirection of an Andre Benoit shot, and Matt Duchene added an empty-netter. With the Avalanche nursing the one-goal lead most of the game, Roy didn't use MacKinnon as much as in previous games, and the defensive tandem of Erik Johnson and Jan Hejda logged marathon minutes.

Also memorable was a typical pushing-and-shoving post-whistle scrum with 51 seconds left in the second period when Milan Lucic, with words and shoves, tried to goad Gabriel Landeskog into a fight after Landeskog grabbed him from behind and pulled him away from P. A. Parenteau in the scrum. Landeskog barked back but declined the invitation, something that offended those in the macho wing who believe that one of the obligations of a physical power forward—and a captain, no less—is to answer the bell. Boston coach Claude Julien, in fact, later labeled Landeskog "soft." For shoving Landeskog in the face, Lucic drew a ten-minute misconduct to go with one of the roughing calls doled out to Lucic, Jarome Iginla, Landeskog, and Parenteau.

"He grabbed P. A. from behind, and I had to do something, so I tried to get him off P. A. He wasn't too happy with that. He wanted to fight, and I think I did a pretty wise choice not fighting him," Landeskog said. "That's one of the best fighters in the league. It's one thing to stand up for your teammates, but you can't be dumb doing it. For me, just coming off a concussion last year, you've got to be smart. I respect him as a player, and he's one of the toughest in the league, and I don't want to fight him. A guy who's had only one fight in the league, I think guys around the league would agree that's a bad trade-off . . . On top of that, we were up 1–0 in Boston, and we have to be smart and think about the team first. I wasn't going to do that for my personal pride. I have to be smart."

Roy wasn't singing "Peace Train," but he at least endorsed Landeskog's decision. "We don't have anything to prove, fighting with him," Roy said. "There's no need for Gabe to go in the box for ten minutes. We need him on the ice. I thought it was smart for him." Also, the man infamous for a pair of goalie fights added: "I don't think that fighting is that important in our game."

SATURDAY, OCTOBER 12, AT WASHINGTON: AVALANCHE 5, CAPITALS 1. RECORD: 5–0

It was an emotional night for Semyon Varlamov. Since he came to Colorado, the Avalanche and Capitals had only met once—in Denver in December 2011—and Giguere had played that night and come away a 2–1 winner. In the 2013 season, the Avalanche schedule was against only Western Conference opponents, so this not only was his first game in the net against the Capitals, it was his first trip to Washington with the Avalanche.

He made 40 saves overall, 19 in the second period alone, as the Avalanche won easily to get to 5–0 for the season. Yes, the team that had finished 29th out of 30 teams in the overall NHL standings the season before had a perfect record after five games under Roy.

"I got too excited to play against my old team," Varlamov said. "That's why I think I am too nervous. In the warm-ups, my legs were shaking. The whole first period, my legs were shaking. But after the first period, I feel so much better."

It wasn't just Varlamov, as MacKinnon also broke through for his first NHL goal, on a power play late in the second period. He one-timed a Paul Stastny pass from behind the net to give the Avalanche a 3–0 lead and then did a Lambeau Leap into the glass. "I can't do a nice ice sweep like Dutch," he said of Matt Duchene, "so I have to jump into the glass." Earlier, Duchene had scored his third goal of the season.

The Avalanche had won three straight on the eastern trip, and although other teams were off to fast starts as the Western Conference dominated inter-conference play, Roy's presence behind the bench added to the intrigue as scribes and other media members along the Atlantic seaboard were asking where this had come from.

"I think we have come a long way and really jelled as a group," Landeskog said. "We've definitely gotten a lot more confident, and Patrick brings a lot of confidence to our hockey club. He's calm, cool, and collected, and he brings that confidence to our team."

Roy brought up Bourque's message without mentioning his name, and it would become a common postgame narrative.

"Right now we're saying, 'Why not? Why not us?,'" he said. "We've been working hard every day, we've been remaining humble and know we're playing against very good teams. It was a tough trip, but we're very happy with how it went."

As a Denver franchise, the Avalanche never had opened 5–0 before, though the 2000–01 Stanley Cup team had tied its first two games—back when ties were possible—and then run off nine consecutive victories. And the slightly sobering note for those with long memories was that the 2011–12 team, under Joe Sacco and with Varlamov and Giguere as the goalies, had lost its opener to Detroit at home, then won all five on a long road trip and raised hopes. And that team had finished 41–35–6 and missed the playoffs.

TUESDAY, OCTOBER 15, AT DENVER: AVALANCHE 3, STARS 2. RECORD: 6–0

After five games—all wins—the major aspect of the Avalanche winning streak that involved red-flag raising was that they were allowing 34 shots a game, the fifth-highest total in the league. One reason for that was they had been ahead much of the time, but it also was true that they were getting superlative, difference-making goaltending from Semyon Varlamov and Jean-Sebastien Giguere.

It happened again in Game 6, with Varlamov stopping 37 of 39 shots and Duchene scoring twice as the Avalanche remained perfect with the win over the Stars. "I guess goaltending is crucial in this league," Roy said mischievously. The man who had stolen a few games for his own teams over the years said of Varlamov's work: "That was a steal."

A couple of intriguing twists were involved. One was that the Broncos, who had beaten lowly Jacksonville two days earlier, and the Avalanche both were 6–0. The other was that the victory had enabled Roy to equal what seemed to be more of an "achievement" than a "record"—the most consecutive victories out of the chute for a first-time NHL head coach. The other man to win his first six games was Mario Tremblay at Montreal, who accomplished that with Roy as his goaltender after taking over from Jacques Demers after the Canadiens opened the 1995–96 season with five consecutive losses. Also later over-looked was the fact that the Canadiens did go 12–1–1 in the first four-teen games under Tremblay before the wheels came off. In other words, bringing up Tremblay's quick start as an NHL head coach prob-ably reminded Roy of how quickly and drastically fortunes could change.

Whether or not it was a "record," Roy now had a chance to outdo Tremblay.

"I don't care about the 7–0," he said. "That's what I said to the guys before the game. We have to take care of the things we can control. What we control is how well we play the game."

BLOOD FEUD, REDUX

The Red Wings' move to the Eastern Conference meant that Colorado and Detroit would meet only twice a season—once in each building—for the foreseeable future. Both on the day before the game and on the morning of the first meeting of the season with the Red Wings, and the only one in Denver, Patrick Roy was peppered with questions about the Detroit-Colorado rivalry and his re-involvement in it. He called the rivalry the "best of my career, no doubt about it. We were into it. There are a lot of good memories. Every time we played them, we knew the winner had a good chance to go far in the playoffs, if not win the Stanley Cup."

He complimented both Red Wings' general manager Ken Holland and coach Mike Babcock, and noted how well Detroit had drafted. Then he downplayed the current and likely future state of the rivalry and again brought the conversation around to trying to win back the Colorado fans.

"Right now, to me, until we're making the playoffs and we establish ourselves among the top teams, we need to be patient, and a rivalry will come back," he said. "It's going to be created by playoffs, by which team we're playing a lot. Obviously, I think the one with Detroit has disappeared a bit, especially now with them changing conferences. I think we're living a lot in the past right now, and I'm trying to move on and look at what's next for us. Let's make the playoffs a couple years in a row, and I'm sure we'll find someone. Right now, Chicago is in a class by itself. It's funny how things have changed since my last game. You could play in Chicago, and there was like ten thousand people in the building, and everybody came here in Denver. There was a full house every night. Now it's the opposite. But we're confident we're going to bring back our fans."

After the game-morning skate, Roy went to the Pepsi Center's Blue Sky Grill, where he sat down to be interviewed by a member of the Red Wings' Fox Sports Detroit broadcast crew for fourteen minutes. The edited footage was played on the air that night. Roy's interviewer was Chris Osgood, his opponent on April 1, 1998, in the second of the Avalanche coach's two goalie fights in the notorious games with the Red Wings.

Osgood broke the ice by saying how much he had admired Roy over the years, and Roy said he had caught Osgood on a broadcast earlier and pronounced his work "perfect." Osgood, clearly nervous, thanked him and then prompted Roy to talk about the transition from player to coach; about trying to teach young players to win; and about whether he was tempted to coach the goalies himself rather than entrust those duties entirely to Francois Allaire.

When talking about nurturing Varlamov and conceding he had given the Russian goalie a pep talk or two, mainly emphasizing the need to have fun, and then starting to talk about Giguere, Roy caught himself. He stopped and asked Osgood: "Do you have another question? Just kidding. I've been going on!" He added, "Our goaltenders have been the big reason we are 6–0 as we talk."

Osgood noted that he had been on the Detroit bench, watching Mike Vernon play in that fateful December 2, 1995, game at Montreal, and said he believed Mario Tremblay had "left you out to dry." He asked Roy how he would handle a similar situation as a coach. "Because I am a partner with them, I will always protect my players," Roy said. He added, "I'm not going to judge what Mario did. We all have our opinions." He went on to explain that he was there to support his players after inevitable bad nights and to emphasize to them that, hey, it happens and to move on. He didn't specifically answer the question, but the inferences were easy to draw.

When Osgood asked him about playing in Detroit, Roy referred to the infamous March 1997 game when the avenging Darren McCarty jumped Claude Lemieux, leading to all hell breaking loose and to Roy's fight with Vernon. Roy said the game knocked the Avalanche off their focus, that they were too concerned with revenge after that rather than winning, and it was instrumental in the Red Wings beating Colorado in the '97 Western Conference finals and even took "a couple of years" to recover from.

Eventually, Osgood confessed he had idolized both Grant Fuhr[1] and Roy growing up, and then asked the Avalanche coach: "What were you thinking when you came after me at center ice? What were you thinking exactly?"

Smiling, Roy asked: "Other than kick the shit out of you?"

Osgood responded in kind, saying: "I was thinking holy shit, what is going to happen?"

Roy turned serious. "It didn't matter who it was on the other side," he said. "You could get rattled in those games, and I think after our fight, this is where I realized it was overboard. This is not what we were there to do—fighting. It was to win hockey games. I think we had a lot of frustration with Claude and that game, and we simply lost our focus. The problem is when you lose your focus, and it's the leaders of the team that lose the focus, it's hard to get back. And I think that that night was probably the night that a lot of things clicked in my head and probably the night I said, 'Hey, we're not heading in the right direction here.' And I think in some ways that was a good turnaround for us."

Maybe it was a start, but there were more trials. The Avalanche lost to Edmonton in the first round of the 1998 playoffs, then fell to Dallas in the Western Conference finals in both 1999 and 2000 before winning the Cup again in 2001.

The interview underscored that Roy could and would use even that sort of environment—a virtual fireside chat—to hear what he wanted to hear in the questions, to steer conversations and news conference answers to what he wanted to say, to points he wanted to make. That was a knack a lot of coaches never developed. If you're going to be dealing with the press, you might as well use it to get your message out there.

---

1. The standout goalie best known for his days with the Edmonton Oilers as a Wayne Gretzky teammate.

THURSDAY, OCTOBER 17, AT DENVER: RED WINGS 4, AVALANCHE 2. RECORD: 6–1

That night, because Kroenke Sports officials had come up with a more efficient way to keep track of standing-room-only tickets sold, the official crowd of 18,101 for the Red Wings' only appearance of the season in Denver was the largest in franchise—and state hockey—history. Perhaps one-third of the seats were filled by Red Wings fans, a familiar phenomenon since the Avalanche's arrival in Denver, but one increasingly prominent in recent years, after the huge slip in season-ticket sales. Once the schedules came out and then single-game seats went on sale, Detroit fans successfully scrambled and—to their credit—bought up enough tickets to make the Pepsi Center seem like Joe Louis Arena West on the game nights.

Varlamov had his first less-than-sterling game. The Avalanche were in a hole early after Cody McLeod drew a major for boarding and a game misconduct after blasting defenseman Niklas Kronwall into the end boards only 2:13 into the game. Kronwall later said he shouldn't have turned his back at the last second, and he absolved McLeod of some of the blame; nonetheless, it was an inexcusable and dangerous hit. The veteran Swede stayed down and was hauled off on a gurney. Word soon came that he had suffered a concussion and cuts to his right ear, meaning he wasn't hurt as seriously as he appeared to be at first. McLeod later said he had visited Kronwall after the first period and apologized, noting that although he played a physical brand of hockey, he didn't want to hurt anyone.

On the long power play, the Red Wings took a 1–0 lead on the first of Johan Franzen's two goals of the game, and the score was 2–0 after the first period, so Roy delivered his first pep talk of the season after a terrible start.

"Hey, guys, we're fine," he said. "Let's go out and have fun. You win the next two periods, and you're going to win the hockey game."

Nothing was thrown. No walls were punched. It was Roy, the coach, as he had come to be as he reached the NHL.

"I think if you look at us in years past, we'd kind of deflate and lay down," said Erik Johnson.

The Avalanche did come back to pull into a 2–2 tie early in the second, but Franzen and Pavel Datsyuk scored in the third, and the

Red Wings sent their fans into the Colorado night in a celebratory mood. The Avalanche goals came from Johnson, on a virtual end-to-end rush with the puck on a power play, and Gabriel Landeskog. Johnson's came after Todd Bertuzzi, playing his 480th regular season game after his attack on Avalanche forward Steve Moore on March 8, 2004, drew his second minor of the night. And, yes, many of the Colorado fans continued to boo Bertuzzi every time he touched the puck.[2]

Roy found himself left "tied" with Mario Tremblay, an annoyance he didn't bring up. Asked how his first loss felt, he surprised the media with his answer. The most naive in his audience were expecting him to snap off a terse answer and perhaps add to his reputation as a hothead, but he was calm and philosophical. Yes, again, his attitude was the result of calculation.

"It felt good," he said. "I thought our guys played hard. I loved the energy we had for the entire game. No one gave up."

He only quarreled mildly with the major called on McLeod. "I didn't look at it [on video] because I didn't *want* to look at it," he said, triggering laughter. "I didn't want to make a comment on it. But from the bench, I thought that Kronwall turned his back at the last minute. Does that make it a dirty hit or not? I guess [Brendan Shanahan] is going to have to make that decision, but from the bench, I just saw a defenseman turning his back at the last second. For everyone that knows the game, I mean, it's hard for a player to stop."

      ❋ ❋ ❋

After the Avalanche's chartered flight landed in Buffalo, Roy rented a car and drove ninety miles to see his youngest son, Frederick, play for the Sabres' AHL affiliate, the Rochester Americans, in a 4–1 win over the Toronto Marlies. Frederick, a 22-year-old left wing making the transition from major junior scorer to pro agitator as a third- and fourth-liner, didn't figure in the scoring but got in a fight with 5:44 left in the third period. Frederick was memorialized in Avalanche lore as the ten-year-old shown in a championship T-shirt and hat, with his father on the ice in Denver after the Game 7 victory over the Devils in 2001. Now in his second season with the Americans after playing major junior for his

---

2. A full narrative of the Moore-Bertuzzi "incident" is in *Playing Piano in a Brothel* or at www.terryfrei.com/stevemoore.html.

father at Quebec, Frederick likely faced long odds against making it to and especially sticking in the NHL, but given the genes, it wouldn't be wise to count him out.

Meanwhile, Patrick Roy got word that McLeod was suspended indefinitely, pending a Monday hearing in New York.

SATURDAY, OCTOBER 19, AT BUFFALO: AVALANCHE 4, SABRES 2. RECORD: 7–1

When the Avalanche arrived in Buffalo, the Sabres were 1–8 and Joe Sacco—the former Avalanche head coach—was going through the misery after catching on as an assistant to head coach Ron Rolston.

It got worse.

The Avalanche were up 4–1 by the middle of the second period and coasted home, and the goals came from Ryan O'Reilly, Gabriel Landeskog, Matt Duchene, and Paul Stastny—in other words, from the young guns Sacco had attempted to ride to long-term security in his four-season tenure behind the Colorado bench as Roy's predecessor. Buffalo didn't get its first shot on Jean-Sebastien Giguere until the 13:30 mark of the first period, and that drew a Bronx cheer from the disgruntled crowd.

"Our saying in here is: 'We don't lose two in a row,'" said Duchene, who did not meet Sacco for buffalo wings at the Anchor Bar after the morning skate. "We wanted to bounce back from that first loss, and we came out with the kind of start we wanted. We kind of smothered them early, took the life out of them."

✿ ✿ ✿

Hey, did you know that Sidney Crosby and Nathan MacKinnon both (kind of, if you don't get too technical) are from Cole Harbour, Nova Scotia?

Oh. You already do. Well, bear with us, anyway. The NBC Sports Network knew it had an easily hyped angle and jumped all over it for the nationally televised Tuesday night Avalanche-Penguins game in Pittsburgh. Crosby, the league's top player, and still only 26 years old after seemingly outgrowing the "Sid the Kid" nickname, was going against the 18-year-old Colorado rookie who revered him. It wouldn't be right to give in to temptation and say *"once* revered him," as if signing a professional contract and becoming a professional contemporary were enough to erase that awe. The only "problem" with identifying such an angle in advance was that it led to underplaying the more significant long-term story line—that this was another test as we assessed the early-season work of this first-time NHL head coach with such a famous name.

Heading into the first Crosby-MacKinnon meeting in the NHL, Crosby said, "I've known of him before and then trained with him a little the last couple years. He's obviously got a lot of talent, being a number one pick, and he's already doing well, so that's good to see. He's got a real good shot and good speed, and he isn't afraid to go into the hard areas to get the puck."

Asked what he thought of MacKinnon saying that Crosby was his idol growing up, the Penguins' captain responded, "It definitely means I'm getting a little older."

✿ ✿ ✿

With NBC Sports carrying the game, that meant Pierre McGuire, the love-him-or-hate-him-but-you-never-ignore-him hockey analyst for NBC and TSN, was at the rink early. He makes a habit of that on games he covers, and on this day in Pittsburgh, he was curious about how early Roy might arrive at the rink himself.

"I had a test for him," McGuire said, his big, expressive eyes moving downward in his way of showing seriousness. "I got here at 7:30 like I always do, which is usually before all the coaches get here. I wanted to see if Patrick Roy would be here that early, too. I get here, and the first person I see is Patrick Roy. That said something to me right there."

McGuire was an assistant to both Scotty Bowman and "Badger Bob" Johnson in Pittsburgh, and he called them "two of the hardest workers the game will ever see. I lived with Scotty right here in Pittsburgh. It was all hockey all the time. I can see some of those same things in Patrick just the little bit I've been around him so far as a head coach in the National Hockey League. Guys like Mike Babcock, they're always the first ones at the rink every morning, and they don't leave till one o'clock after a game. You've just got to put in the time, do the work."

In the wake of McLeod's hearing in New York in front of Brendan Shanahan and others, the Avalanche heard that the winger's suspension would last five games, leaving him unavailable through the November 1 game at Dallas.

MONDAY, OCTOBER 21, AT PITTSBURGH: AVALANCHE 1, PENGUINS 0. RECORD: 8–1

In most ways, the Penguins dominated, and that led to a 34–14 advantage in shots on goal. Giguere was in the Colorado net for the second straight game, and seven of his saves in the shutout came on Crosby shots. Amazingly, the Penguins were 0-for-7 on the power play. Roy said, "I have to give Francois Allaire credit for this one, because he thought Jiggy would still be sharp and that Varly would benefit from more rest for games at home this week. Jiggy was outstanding, but I like the way our guys helped him out with blocked shots and clearing rebounds."

The Avalanche goal came in the second period, when Landeskog exited the penalty box, took a lead pass from defenseman Ryan Wilson, and beat Marc-Andre Fleury with a shot from about 30 feet out. With the Penguins desperate to get something past Giguere, Crosby played 26 minutes, 40 seconds, while Roy used MacKinnon relatively sparingly, barely more than ten minutes. With Colorado spending much of the night killing penalties, his limited ice time was understandable.

Still, MacKinnon was making a concerted effort to be "responsible" defensively. He was mindful of what Sakic had told him in a heart-to-heart. Sakic mentioned that he had to change to become an all-around player, emphasizing defense, and added that he wished he had done it sooner. He told MacKinnon the best way to earn his coach's trust was to stick to the staff's systems and play well in the Colorado end. He also told MacKinnon to relax, not put too much pressure on himself, and not get caught up with what was being said about him.

FRIDAY, OCTOBER 25, AT DENVER: AVALANCHE 4, HURRICANES 2. RECORD: 9–1

In a workmanlike performance, Colorado got two goals from Duchene and one apiece from Johnson and Alex Tanguay in matching the Quebec-Colorado franchise's best start ever. The '95 Nordiques also opened 9–1 in their final season in Quebec, and the 2000–01 Avalanche started out 8–0–2, also for 18 points.

The Colorado victory meant that the Hurricanes still had never won a game in Denver as a Carolina-based team. The only previous win in Denver came in 1996, when they still were the Hartford Whalers. (This was just a cheap way to make you unable to get the Whalers' catchy theme song, "Brass Bonanza," out of your head.)

SUNDAY, OCTOBER 27, AT DENVER: AVALANCHE 3, JETS 2. RECORD: 10–1

This was the Avalanche's first true come-from-behind win, and they were down 2–1 after two periods. During the second intermission, Roy was calm, showing a couple of video clips that backed up his message to open up their game and move the puck more.

Jan Hejda got the tying goal with 12:47 left, and then Stastny converted a pass through traffic from Tanguay to put Colorado ahead with 5:28 remaining.

"I think we wanted to show ourselves and the fans and everyone that we could win games like this, too," Landeskog said.

The Avalanche had allowed only 16 goals in 11 games. A considerable portion of the credit, of course, deservedly was going to Varlamov and Giguere, who were doing tremendous work in the Colorado net. Varlamov had 23 saves against the Jets and had a 7–1 record at the end of the night. Watching again, Giguere remained at 3–0, and he still had allowed only two goals.

Duchene, among others, continued to take every opportunity to praise his new coach, and he did it again after the comeback victory.

"I've enjoyed every second of playing for him," Duchene said. "He's not a yeller and a screamer. He's not negative. When we need a kick in the ass, we get it, but that hasn't been very often. He's not getting panicked, worried about us slipping. We're never playing not to lose. We're playing to win. We're playing loose, and different guys step up every night, and it's exciting."

This time, the 2012–13 Avalanche didn't have to share any distinctions with previous Quebec/Colorado teams. The 10–1 start was the best in franchise history.

Because the Avalanche weren't playing again until the next Friday, November 1—getting an unusual break of four days without games— Roy announced that the boys wouldn't have practice the next two days. He assumed, of course, that the break would do them good.

GLASS HOUSES

After the Glass House, a two-tower upscale condominium/apartment project in what older Denver natives knew as "The Bottoms" area near both downtown and the Pepsi Center, opened in 2007, many Avalanche players—usually young and single—lived there during the season. Semyon Varlamov and his Russian girlfriend, Evgeniya Vavrinyuk, were among those quartered there in the fall of 2013. She subsequently said they had known each other for about four years and been "a couple" for about a year, spending part of the NHL lockout period in Yaroslavl when the goalie was playing for Lokomotiv.

On Wednesday, October 30, the Avalanche reconvened for practice, and nothing seemed amiss with Varlamov, either on the ice or in the dressing room. In fact, afterwards, Associated Press writer Pat Graham interviewed Varlamov for an off-day feature, and all seemed routine as the Russian spoke about his play and the team's surprising start.

Yet at roughly the same time, Denver Police Detective Darlene Vita was preparing an affidavit and arrest warrant for Varlamov, and Denver County Court Judge James Brees signed it at 1:43 p.m.

Based on Vavrinyuk's accusations of domestic violence, Varlamov faced possible second-degree kidnapping and third-degree assault charges. (Kidnapping could mean forcing someone to go somewhere against his or her will, even if it was just another room.) The lid stayed on for several hours. After the Avalanche organization was notified of the charges, Joe Sakic and Patrick Roy met with Varlamov at the team offices. They grilled the goalie as extensively as they could, given the language issues. Right away, they were convinced Varlamov was telling the truth when he told them the charges were unfounded. Their moves over the next few days and beyond would reflect that belief.

Varlamov turned himself in early Wednesday evening, and he was taken to a Denver Downtown Detention Center cell, where he would spend the night while waiting to go before a judge on Thursday morning.

As initial and sketchy reports hit the media that night, the Avalanche issued a statement, saying the team was aware of the allegations but would have no additional comment.

By Thursday morning, or Halloween, as Varlamov waited, the frenzy intensified. The police report (officially the affidavit and arrest warrant) was an open record, so media outlets obtained it. In the version released, Vavrinyuk's name was "redacted," or blacked out. While Varlamov heard the charges and was freed on a $5,000 bond at around noon, his Avalanche teammates were on the ice at Family Sports Center. They were scheduled to take a chartered flight to Dallas later Thursday afternoon and play the Dallas Stars Friday night. Many members of the Denver media flocked to the practice rink to seek comment from the Avalanche players and Roy; it probably was the highest media attendance at practice since the glory years.

If accepted at face value, the allegations in the police report were ugly. Detective Vita wrote that Vavrinyuk told her the attack at their Glass House apartment occurred on October 28. The day of the week wasn't mentioned, but the 28th was a Monday. The time of day wasn't specified, either.

The report also stated that on Wednesday another detective had interviewed the woman who had come to the apartment on Monday to "do [Vavrinyuk's] makeup." The woman, whose name also was redacted in the report, soon was revealed to be a Lithuanian professional makeup artist with her own business in Denver. She also just happened to be the fiancée of the attorney representing Vavrinyuk.[1]

The report said that Vavrinyuk told the makeup artist "that due to Mr. Varlamov drinking she was having concerns about him assaulting her." The makeup artist told the detective that she could see Vavrinyuk's "upper chest area and did not see any bruises or marks."

---

1. For several reasons, we've decided to leave out the names of the attorney and his fiancée.

The makeup artist said that the next morning—Tuesday, the 29th—Vavrinyuk called her, said Varlamov had attacked her, and asked for help. The makeup artist said she picked up Vavrinyuk at the Glass House and put her up for the night. She said that as Vavrinyuk was getting dressed Wednesday morning, she noticed bruises on her "left arm and upper chest area." Police were contacted. The arrest warrant was issued that afternoon.

Varlamov's agent, the New York-based Paul Theofanous, who speaks Russian and specializes in Russian clients, quickly issued a statement saying the goaltender was innocent and the charges were baseless.

The Avalanche remained tight-lipped, and when the players came off the ice at practice Thursday, it was obvious they had been told not to comment on Varlamov's situation. They actually knew far less at that point than the reporters, who had read quickly posted stories from the courtroom and the just-available police report online and in e-mail attachments. In addition to setting the bail at only $5,000, the judge cleared Varlamov—who entered the court wearing a yellow prison jumpsuit—to travel, and he was released on bond. So, in theory, he could make the trip to Dallas.

The media pack first approached captain Gabriel Landeskog.

"Right now, I'm more than willing to talk hockey, but anything other than that, I can't comment," Landeskog said.

His teammates took that stance, too, as reporters circled the room.

Matt Duchene would go so far as to say, "We all love Varly in here. I can't say enough great things about him. I think we're all pretty confident this is going to get resolved pretty quickly."

By then, as careful as the players were being, the whispering was starting around the practice rink. The most common speculation was that regardless of what else did or didn't happen, perhaps Varlamov had made it clear to Vavrinyuk that the relationship was over, and a pending case against Varlamov would enhance her chances of remaining in the United States beyond her planned three-month visit. (The speculation didn't necessarily make sense, but it was the speculation.)

It got even more bizarre. When Roy went to the podium in the upper-level practice rink media room, maneuvering around the numerous cameras there to capture his reaction to the Varlamov news, he opened with something that was unprecedented in Avalanche history.

The coach announced a trade. Or maybe it should be: The vice president of hockey operations announced a trade.

"Before we start, we made a trade this morning," he said. "We have acquired Maxime Talbot from Philadelphia. The reasons are Talbot has won a Stanley Cup with Pittsburgh, he's a great penalty killer, and we feel he's going to bring a lot of depth to our team. He's a guy that has performed so really well in the playoffs, and we think he will be a great addition to this team. Obviously, in return we had to give Steve Downie. Philly wanted Steve Downie back, and we thought it was the price to pay to get Talbot."

Maxime Talbot for Steve Downie?

The quick speculation was that perhaps Downie's training camp hassle with Landeskog and his sometimes undisciplined play in the early part of the season wore out Roy's patience. He loved grit, and his comments about admiring Downie's fire were genuine, but Downie had also taken some suspect penalties. Colorado also seemed to realize it wouldn't try to re-sign Downie in the off-season, when his contract expired, so getting something for him wasn't all that bad.

But the media corps wanted to talk about the guy in the police report, not a newly acquired veteran forward.

Asked whether Varlamov would be making the trip to Dallas, Roy said he didn't know the details of what had happened in court that morning. He was told that the court had permitted Varlamov to travel, but Roy remained reticent to comment on the next moves. "I'd rather wait until it is confirmed by his lawyer than start projecting things, and then at the last minute we have to turn back and say he can't play."

The word came about 90 minutes later: the Avalanche were not recalling a goalie from Lake Erie. Varlamov was making the trip to Dallas.

That afternoon, Vavrinyuk appeared at what amounted to a news conference at the office of her Denver attorney. Reporters seemed to have no qualms about allowing the attorney's Lithuanian fiancée to interpret Vavrinyuk's remarks. She also had been a figure in the drama, with her observations included in the police report.

The next day, the *Denver Post* recovered, enlisted visiting Russian journalist Vsevolod Pulya, managing editor for the Moscow-based *Russia Beyond the Headlines*, to view video of Vavrinyuk's remarks and provide a fresh interpretation. The differences from the original translation mostly were minor, but the major one was that the original stories about her news conference reported she said the beating happened on Monday, which was what the police report said. Pulya's translated version said she said the beating happened at 6 a.m. Tuesday (which was the 29th), and from here on, that will be the version relied upon here.

Vavrinyuk said (in Pulya's translation) that Varlamov attacked her after he returned home; she also said he had been drinking since the previous afternoon. Curiously, at that news conference, she didn't mention some of the allegations she had made in the police report. Then she said that this was the fifth time Varlamov had beaten her—and that the previous times were in Russia, including when Varlamov was playing for Yaroslavl Lokomotiv during the lockout, and in Male, the capital of the Republic of the Maldives in the Indian Ocean. "Currently, I am in the U.S., the country which stands for human rights," she said. "I know I will be protected here. I want everyone, all of the fans who love him and chant 'Varly, Varly' all the time to know that he's a violent man, that he acts like this with his beloved girlfriend."

Asked why she hadn't left him after the alleged earlier beatings, she said: "There's a limit to everything. I used to love this man. I wanted to have family with him. I was thinking that he would change over time. But people don't change. And this event was my limit, my last drop. I didn't want to go to the police this time either. But when I got back home, I saw my stuff by the door. I was thrown out like a dog. And that was the reason I decided to go to the police." She said that when she texted Varlamov and told him of her plans, he "just replied wishing me good luck. He thought that this time he would also remain unpunished." She added that she was getting threats from Russia via social media and acknowledged she was being accused of wanting to get money from Varlamov. "I want to tell everybody that I came to the police not to get any money from him," she said. "I don't need his money at all. I went to the police for him to be punished."

She said she had been living in Hong Kong and broke a modeling contract to join Varlamov. She also said she had several "marks" on her body and pointed to the areas, but she didn't show them.

As the two versions of the interview reached the public, the most common reaction was to assume that the truth probably was somewhere in the middle—that something had happened, but that Varlamov wasn't the monster his girlfriend had portrayed him to be. Her admission that she had decided to go to the police only when he essentially tossed her out of the apartment by leaving her belongings outside the door also seemed curious, given her insistence that the fifth beating had been the final straw. The time frame of that wasn't specified, either. Plus, of course, even those most prone to be sympathetic to victims of domestic violence—and that includes almost everyone—were incredulous that she claimed to have come to the United States with Varlamov after he beat her abroad four times previously.

When it became apparent that whatever happened, whether only an argument or a beating, almost certainly had happened on Tuesday morning, not on Monday as originally reported and stated in the police report, suddenly, stories simply started mentioning Tuesday without pointing out the apparent original error. For the sake of argument, assume for a second that Varlamov indeed had begun drinking at 2 p.m. the day before the incident and kept it up overnight before coming home at 6 a.m. So if the confrontation had happened Monday, that would have meant he was drunk when he was in the net for the Avalanche's win over Winnipeg Sunday night. It was obvious that it mostly likely was just a mix-up, but nobody pointed out the sudden correction in the date and day of the alleged incident. It could have been left up to the judgment of individual readers whether the confusion over the date and day of the week in the police report and early coverage, plus the direct involvement of her lawyer's fiancée, diluted her credibility.

Of course, it hadn't taken long for cynics and Roy detractors to start making snide remarks about the Avalanche coach also having experience in facing domestic violence allegations. The fact that most of them displayed either faulty memories or utter disregard for the truth didn't seem to matter in the world of Twitter and largely unmoderated, anonymous comment on the bottom of online stories.

What they referred to happened early in the morning hours of October 22, 2000. It followed a night of celebration for the Roy family and friends—including Ray Bourque and his wife—in the wake of Roy breaking Terry Sawchuk's long-standing record with his 448th career victory, making him the winningest goaltender in NHL history.

◊ ◊ ◊

Wine flowed freely and spirits were high during dinner at Del Frisco's in suburban Greenwood Village. The night before, Michele Roy was on the ice with Patrick and their children as the team honored him for attaining the milestone before a game against the Florida Panthers. On the way home from the restaurant, an argument started between Patrick and Michele that would continue behind closed doors at their home. Michele later would say they were arguing about her "in-laws." Patrick's parents were divorced; although his mother, Barbara, was in Denver for the celebration, only his father, Michel, was staying at the Roy home.

In Michel Roy's book about his son, *Patrick Roy: Winning. Nothing Else*, he recounted: "I was awakened by the sound of people shouting. According to my watch, it was 2:20 a.m. Michele and Patrick were screaming at each other at the top of their lungs. Suddenly I heard a sharp cracking sound. I few moments later, Michele burst into my bedroom and flipped on the ceiling light. I sat up in my bed. 'Mr. Roy,' she said angrily, "you've won! . . . You can keep your son.'"

The goaltender's father wrote that he walked downstairs to see Patrick stretched out in a chair looking shell-shocked, with a police officer standing by him and another interviewing Michele in another room. Michele had dialed 911 and hung up the phone before talking to police, but the call was traced back to their home. Roy told police that the most-discussed part of the incident—he tore two lightweight doors, more partitions than real doors, off their hinges—happened only after Michele had made the hang-up call. When officers arrived on the scene, they discovered the disturbance and, under the terms of Colorado's 1994 domestic violence law, were required to make an arrest in a domestic violence incident—essentially, at the very least, to separate the parties and prevent something else from happening after police left.

They arrested Patrick Roy at 2:55 a.m. He spent several hours in jail, was charged in Arapahoe County Court with misdemeanor criminal mischief in an act of domestic violence, and was released on $750 bond. That was Sunday; he appeared in court the next morning to hear the charges, with his parents, brother, and sister all there to support him. He went to practice and read a statement afterward: "Obviously, this is creating a distraction, and my wish is that this distraction will soon be over," he said. "I am thankful for the support I am getting from my family and every one of my teammates."

Roy wasn't prevented from returning to his home and his family, and the court essentially seemed to recognize it was about an argument—a heated one, but not one involving physical contact—rather than violence; and about the inflexibility involved with enforcing the progressive and much-praised Colorado law. In most ways, his family life returned to normal, and he and Michele would remain married for five more years, including through the first years of his retirement. The charges later were dismissed, but they caused damage to Roy's reputation and caused him considerable stress. He had trouble eating and sleeping for a while and lost about ten pounds.

Without passing judgment on the validity of the charges made by Varlamov's girlfriend, what he was alleged to have done was exponentially worse and more troubling than what Roy had done in a high-decibel argument with his wife. But that point seemed to escape many who insisted on bringing up the 2000 incident again in the wake of Varlamov's arrest. It also was fair to say, as Roy himself openly conceded, that his own experience was a factor in his decision to give Varlamov the benefit of the doubt and to not assume the worst.

FROM THE NOTEBOOK OF ADRIAN DATER

This was one of the many instances where my coauthor and I publicly disagreed.

Terry wrote that the Avalanche should at least give Varlamov the weekend off and recall one of the Lake Erie goalies to back up Giguere. His point was that Varlamov would be distracted and that playing him would at least appear insensitive and cavalier about the seriousness of the charges and the domestic violence issue.

He was wrong, of course.

I felt strongly, and wrote a column saying it, that Varlamov should remain on the active roster and keep playing. Hadn't the judge freed Varlamov on minimal bail and not banned him from working? If it was good enough for the judge, it should have been good enough for the Avalanche. Wasn't the American way still innocent until proven guilty? Of course it was. Even for Russian hockey players. I was adamant that unsubstantiated allegations alone shouldn't prevent him from doing his job.

So I had no problem with the Avalanche allowing Varlamov to continue to play.

Plus, I was absolutely convinced that Roy and Sakic had questioned him intensely and believed his version of what happened. Say what you will, but they knew if they publicly backed him and it turned out to be false faith, they would look foolish. That was another reason I believed the Avalanche did the right thing when they took him on the trip. Guys like Roy and Sakic aren't played for the fool too often.

STAYING ON TRACK

FRIDAY, NOVEMBER 1, AT DALLAS: AVALANCHE 3, STARS 2 (OT). RECORD: 11–1

Semyon Varlamov didn't just make the trip; he played against the Stars. The reasoning was that the game was on the road and out of the Colorado spotlight, and that Giguere could play the next night, back in Denver against the Canadiens.

Paul Stastny, who also had scored in regulation, ended the game with the goal at 3:36 of overtime, firing the puck through traffic off a rush. Varlamov had a shutout going into the third period but allowed two goals in the final two minutes as the Avalanche fell victim to what so often happens in those situations, trying to sit on the lead. He had 26 saves and, on the whole, played well—especially under the circumstances.

"Honestly, I had no doubt," Patrick Roy said. "Coaching sometimes, you have to make decisions, and we took one. We were comfortable to make that decision."

Varlamov, as he knew he would be, was asked about his situation, and it couldn't have been a coincidence that his first public comment sounded much like Roy's first public response in October 2000. "I don't want to comment about anything regarding the process," Varlamov said. "At the same time, I want to thank the Colorado Avalanche, the whole team, for their support. I ask that everybody reserve their judgments and not rush to conclusions." To another wave, he said, "I think I am the luckiest guy in the world because I play in the NHL and I play for this team. I've got such good teammates, so I don't think about what's happening."

That night, the Avalanche traveled back to Denver, where they were facing the Canadiens less than 24 hours later.

❖ ❖ ❖

At some point on Saturday, Varlamov—who knew he wasn't playing against the Canadiens—consented to a Russian-language video interview with Kirill Kissilev of NHL.com. It was a strange mix of hard-core hockey and a discussion of his situation. He said he considered playing against Dallas merely a confirmation of a previously planned-out schedule. He was asked about the support he was receiving, including from Russia. "Of course, it helps me," he said. "But again, believe me. Your personal life stays your personal life, and sport is sport. And personal life shouldn't interfere with sport. That's why all my focus is currently on hockey, on the game, on communicating with the team."

SATURDAY, NOVEMBER 2, AT DENVER: AVALANCHE 4, CANADIENS 1. RECORD: 12–1

A Saturday night game involving a Canadian team made this a natural: The *Hockey Night in Canada* crew was in town, and the game was shown across much of the nation. The CBC folks had much to cover, including again touching on Roy's surprising start as an NHL head coach, and the pregame ceremony honoring Adam Foote and raising his number 52 banner to the rafters, where his retired number joined those of Joe Sakic, Ray Bourque, Roy, and Peter Forsberg.

The ceremony for Foote went well, which wasn't surprising given that the Avalanche had a lot of practice at it. He was emotional and graceful, and thanked his former teammates, especially his former defensive partners, including Randy Velischek, Alexei Gusarov, and Bourque—all present at the ceremony. He added: "I'd like to thank you fans for the energy you gave us, especially when we kicked Detroit's ass."

Of course, that drew thunderous cheers.

As Foote met the media after the first period, he naturally was asked if he had considered his road roommate—Roy—to be possible coaching material. "I knew that five years before I retired, I really did," Foote said. "I had a feeling that he was going to go to junior for a few years and then get back to the NHL. I wasn't sure whether it was going to be as a coach or a GM, but I knew he knew the game inside out. He has a passion for it. He's a hard worker, and that's what he does, that's what gets him going and gets him up in the morning. He loves to teach and loves to figure it out, and he's good at it."

The Avalanche won again, breaking out of a 1–1 tie in the third period on goals by Nathan MacKinnon and Ryan O'Reilly, then getting an empty-netter from P. A. Parenteau. The attendance of 18,152— again boosted by counting the standing-room sales—was another franchise record, and the up-and-down nature of the box office in the first month illustrated that the fan pool still was huge, but fans had realized they could pick their spots after the deterioration in the season-ticket base. The negative was that Alex Tanguay suffered a knee injury in the second period and didn't return. The Avalanche players gathered up the puck at the end of the game and presented it to Roy as a keepsake from his first coaching victory over his former team.

Giguere had 29 saves, and the Montreal native had allowed only three goals in his four games played. "Honestly, he looks like a 25-year-old," Roy said.

Karen Crouse of the *New York Times* was in town to do a column on the Avalanche and Varlamov's situation. In the postgame session, she asked Roy if his own 2000 incident factored into his handling of Varlamov.

"I was hoping to never have to answer that question again," Roy said dryly. "The answer is, yes. I guess Varly is like me, appreciating that nobody is making a judgment. The best article, I think, was written by Terry Frei, and he said let's not make a judgment before the process is done. I thought that was something I appreciated at the time, and I'm sure Varly appreciates seeing that support from our fans and a lot of people around him."

FROM THE NOTEBOOK OF TERRY FREI

Yes, Roy saw me among the reporters in the news conference and knew I was there when he made reference to the column I wrote that ran in the Denver Post *on the morning of October 23, 2000, or the day after his arrest and the day he was scheduled to appear in court. As the news conference ended, and I went to the podium to retrieve my recorder, Roy asked me: "Remember that one?" I said yes, but my recollection was only vague. I looked it up shortly after I got home. Here it is, slightly condensed:*

Last week, as Patrick Roy was about to break a record he so obsessively sought, and the telecast of the Avalanche-Washington game was shown across the United States and Canada, shots of Michele Roy's reactions followed every replay of game action. When the Avalanche won the game in overtime, making her husband the winningest goaltender in National Hockey League history, Michele's undiluted joy at her seat was on international display.

Friday night, Michele was introduced to the Pepsi Center crowd and walked across the red carpet placed over the ice, joining her husband—and their children—for the celebration and commemoration of his accomplishment.

About 30 hours after that emotional ceremony in Denver, after Roy accepted all the gifts in the convivial company of his parents, siblings, wife and children; after he heard the warming ovation from the crowd and then stepped into his crease to help beat the Florida Panthers, passions were reconfigured into anger in the Roys' Greenwood Village home.

Roy was taken into custody for investigation of domestic violence, criminal mischief, and destruction of property and released on $750 bond. He will appear in Arapahoe County Court this morning.

If it turns out that Roy's conduct merits him being lumped in with the other athletes who have tarnished their profession with disgracefully violent treatment of women, then I'll be back at the laptop, adding to the deserved derision.

But I don't think that's going to be the case, either.

Roy's temper is part of the record—meaning both his past, and also the record he was celebrating only a few days ago . . . So if it turns out that Roy argued with his wife, loudly and emotionally; then smacked and kicked a door, doing demonstrable damage for the po-

lice to see; sufficiently alarmed Michele to cause her to dial 911 and
then hang up; and was taken into custody because of the understand-
ably and necessarily inflexible standards of police response to domes-
tic disturbances, that is not a completely stunning development.

It also is not a heinous offense . . .

As instances of athletes' domestic abuse are exposed with disquiet-
ing regularity, it can be so tempting to react to each case—and to this
one—with just-another-jock disgust. That probably will be the ap-
proach taken by journalists who tend to pontificate about the evils of
stereotyping, then see nothing wrong with stereotyping athletes. It
isn't that simple.

Each instance deserves to be considered with case-by-case fair-
ness. Broncos wide receiver Rod Smith, for example, never deserved
to be lumped in with the thugs who cavalierly and violently maltreat
women—whether the thugs are athletes, journalists, plumbers, attor-
neys, professors, police officers, or cocaine dealers.

Because of the proliferation of that violence, and because of the
inexplicable pattern of the abused often staying with violent spouses,
the standard for responding officers is both justifiable and necessary.
If the police are called to a home, which was technically the case
because of the 911 hang-up call in the Roy incident, and there is
evidence of violence, they must take someone into custody.

Even if the evidence of violence is on a door.

Before that standard was enforced, there were too many instances
of spouses saying the dispute was over, whether honestly or under
duress; then of something tragic happening after the officers left. So
Roy was taken into custody early Sunday morning.

I'm uncomfortable, and I bet you are, too, with knowing that
Roy's private life has become such a public issue. There will come a
point today, and probably in any discussion over the next few days,
that Roy will have every right to say: "That's none of your business."
I admit I'm hoping he doesn't have to say it very many times, or for
very long, because that will mean that the details that do come out
won't create a firestorm.

⁂

At practice three days later, Varlamov faced a group of Denver reporters. By then, it seemed the Avalanche had decided that trying to qua-
rantine him or rule him off-limits to the media would be counterpro-

ductive. All knew that he would have to say he couldn't talk about specifics of the case, anyway. But in this era when media members can advance their careers by grandstanding and calling attention to themselves, it wouldn't have been a shock if someone—with cameras and recorders rolling—tried to demand that he address the specifics of the police report or Vavrinyuk's statement at her news conference. That didn't happen, but reporters understandably at least alluded to his situation. "The life of a professional athlete is public," he said. "Truth is truth. Lying is lying. Sometimes life puts you in a good situation. Sometimes life puts you in a bad situation. You can't listen to everybody."

Roy dropped this hint for the record: "As we speak, we have different info that makes us believe we should trust him."

That day, *Sports Illustrated* reporter Sarah Kwak called Vavrinyuk's attorney and asked if she could interview her. In a subsequent story, Kwak said the attorney asked, "What kind of fee are you offering?" Kwak said she told him her magazine doesn't pay for interviews, and that he responded: "Oh, OK. She's a little tired from giving interviews. I'm sure you can understand. Thanks so much for the call."

WEDNESDAY, NOVEMBER 6, AT DENVER: PREDATORS 6, AVALANCHE 4. RECORD: 12–2

With his team still having only one loss at that point, Roy was hearing questions about whether the Avalanche were getting the respect they deserved or whether he thought they were winning over the hockey world. At the morning skate before the Nashville game, Roy enunciated what repeatedly had been—and would remain—his stand.

"I don't think about those things," he said. "I'm not saying I don't care what people think about our team. Every comment I've been reading so far since the start of the year has been outstanding, the reporters have been great to us. I always go back to one day at a time. We cannot control what people think. We cannot control where we're going to be three months from now or four months from now. What we can control is what we do tonight."

"Tonight" turned out to be the Avalanche's first stinker of the season, and Varlamov struggled, contributing to the problems through mishandling the puck and allowing soft goals. "Tonight, I gave up five goals, and it was not my greatest game this year," he said simply. (The Predators' sixth goal was an empty-netter.) "It's a long season, and it's very important for the goalie to forget about this game and look forward to working hard."

Roy said he hadn't considered yanking Varlamov, who finished with 22 saves. "No, because he was fighting out there," Roy said, adding that the Avalanche hadn't played well in front of him. "It's a team loss. It's as simple as that."

FRIDAY, NOVEMBER 8, AT DENVER: AVALANCHE 4, FLAMES 2. RECORD: 13–2

Bob Hartley was back in town, and that meant reunions. The second-season Flames coach, who had coached the Avalanche from 1998 to 2002 and hoisted the Stanley Cup with them in 2001, was popular with the Denver media. After his father's death in Hawkesbury, Ontario, the hockey goalie abandoned plans to attend college and became a young breadwinner for his family. He worked, first, in a paper mill and then a windshield factory in his hometown. Soon, as a young married man and father, he also began serving as a volunteer goaltending coach for the local Junior A team, became the head coach, and moved to Laval in major junior, then to the Avalanche's AHL affiliates at Cornwall and Hershey. When Marc Crawford departed in 1998, Hartley moved up to be the head coach of the Avalanche.

Roy and Hartley, fellow French-Canadians, had their moments of disagreement when one was the goalie and one was the coach. The most notorious was when Roy smashed some video equipment in Anaheim, angered that a coaching stratagem, briefly replacing Roy with Craig Billington to buy some rest for his power-play unit, cost Roy credit for the win as he so zealously chased Terry Sawchuk's record. But their relationship survived that, and they became friends after Roy's retirement, as Hartley, who coached at the major junior level before climbing the ladder, acted as an unofficial adviser and confidant as Roy began coaching.

"I have a lot of respect for Bob," Roy said on game morning. "Over the past years, he always said, 'Hey, call me if you need something; I'll be there for you.' He's been there for me in my junior years and even since I've been in the NHL. He called me when I got the job, he called me in the summer, and he called me before the start of training camp. We're talking a lot. I have a really close relationship with him."

Would he be able to forget that friendship that night?

"When the puck drops, I'm going to be focusing on our team." Roy smiled and added, "I can't look at him too long because he'd take advantage of it."

Hartley's banged-up team put up a fight, but John Mitchell's goal broke the 2–2 tie in the second period, and Duchene's empty-netter with three seconds left made the final gap two goals.

Down the hall, Hartley was in surprisingly decent spirits, despite the loss.

"We talk every week," he said of Roy. "We talked before the game, and I just went to say bye to him. It was fun to see him across the bench. Sometime you coach those great players and you never think that one day you're going to be coaching against them. It's just a sign that hockey's a big cycle. And everything keeps going."

DIVISIONAL BATTLES

A month into the season, it was clear that Patrick Roy was not going to be a social butterfly his first year back in Denver. In the fall and beyond, he would mostly limit himself to two frequent haunts: Elway's, the restaurant near his home in the Cherry Creek area; and the home of Avalanche PR guy Jean Martineau.

Before moving back to Denver, Roy split with his longtime Quebec girlfriend. Roy is not much of a cook, so as a bachelor again, and with his three grown children living elsewhere, he either ate his meals out or eagerly ate the home cooking of Martineau's wife, Brigitte. The three had known each other since grade school. Roy joked that he only passed English language classes at age 13 in Quebec because he worked out a code with Brigitte to pass along the correct answers via foot signals. "I should not have done that," he said. "I might have been better today."

Mostly, though, Roy's personal life in his first season back in Denver was going to be virtually indistinguishable from his work life. It was mostly all hockey all the time. Roy subscribed to the CenterIce package and clicked around the dial of games most nights.

When the weather and other circumstances allowed, he also played some golf. Roy carries a two handicap and doesn't look out of place playing with current and former PGA pros he has met over the years; Fred Couples is one of his buddies.

SUNDAY, NOVEMBER 10, AT DENVER: AVALANCHE 4, CAPITALS 1. RECORD: 14–2

Late in the second period, the Pepsi Center went pin-drop silent. Washington's Alex Ovechkin had just slid headfirst into the end boards, and he stayed down, motionless, as the Capitals' trainer rushed out. The best player in the world—or maybe the second best, if you were a Sidney Crosby advocate—appeared to be seriously injured. Colorado defenseman Jan Hejda was involved in the contact that sent Ovechkin into the boards, but it wasn't a dirty hit from behind. "My stick was on the ice, but he stepped on it, so it was very bad luck," Hejda would say later. "I wasn't going to hit him hard or something, I was kind of poke checking on the puck."

Semyon Varlamov, Ovechkin's fellow Russian, was in his crease, bent over and watching, concerned. After a minute or two, Ovechkin stirred, then got up and headed to the visiting bench. Varlamov joined in the stick taps from the players on the ice, and the applause from the crowd was polite but sincere.

The new scoreboard screens came into play. Much, much larger than life, Ovechkin's reaction when he reached the bench was shown, and it didn't require major lip-reading expertise to know what he was saying in reaction to nothing being called on Hejda, the Czech veteran. It wasn't in Russian, and it was quite graphic. It would have fit right in with Patrick Roy's opening night exchange with Bruce Boudreau.

Ovechkin didn't miss a shift. It looked ridiculous, as if a soccer game had broken out. Ovechkin should have drawn a red card for bad acting.

For the rest of the Avalanche's victory, the crowd gave him the Bertuzzi treatment, booing every time he touched the puck.

All of that spiced up an entertaining game, and the crowd again showed it wasn't going to be reluctant to chant "Varly" at appropriate moments. One was when he made several tough saves when the Capitals had a two-man advantage for 56 seconds early in the third period, with the Avalanche clinging to a one-goal lead. By the end of the game, he had 33 saves and had allowed only two goals by his former team in the two Avalanche-Capitals meetings.

"The guys did an unbelievable job for me, blocking shots," Varlamov said. "This team is playing unbelievable right now, on the PK especially. I can tell the boys I appreciate what they are doing for me right now."

What was he thinking when Ovechkin was down?

"That was a scary moment, I think," Varlamov said. "For him, for Russian national team, when you see a leader like Ovechkin lay down on the ice, it's a pretty scary moment, but I think he's good, he's fine, he still was playing in the game. So I hope he's feeling good."

Mostly, Ovechkin was mad.

"I thought it was a trip," he said. "Hit my head on the boards." He went on to label it a "dangerous play."

Nick Holden had one of the goals, his first in the NHL, and Patrick Bordeleau also scored before P. A. Parenteau and Gabe Landeskog opened up breathing room in the third period.

The full house and loud atmosphere were another reminder of the glory days, when the Avalanche had the hottest ticket in town. "Best player tonight for us was our fans," Roy said. "Simple as that. They were loud. It was awesome."

The 14–2 start again was the best mark for the franchise at a certain point, with the previous best after sixteen games being the Nordiques' 13–3 break from the gate in 1995—the lockout-shortened last season in Quebec.

TUESDAY, NOVEMBER 12, AT RALEIGH: HURRICANES 2, AVALANCHE 1. RECORD: 14–3

Roy was calm and philosophical after the Avalanche's first road loss of the season. He knew Colorado had played significantly worse games than this one, but sometimes—especially on the road—you just lose and have to move on. Folks in and around the NHL were still expecting him to detonate after every loss. They were wrong.

"I have to give it to them," he said of the Hurricanes. "They played well at the start of the game. I thought maybe we tried to be a little bit too perfect. But I would say the second half of the game was ours."

Paul Stastny's second-period goal got the Avalanche within one goal, but that was all the scoring.

The second and final stop on the road trip was going to be at St. Louis. Although Blues-Avalanche wasn't one of the league's more notorious rivalries, it was one of the more intriguing matchups, especially in 2013. When Blues coach Ken Hitchcock reacted from afar in the wake of Roy's opening-night fireworks, pronouncing them "junior hockey," the Avalanche coach filed away all of that. One of the many things Roy had shown, both as a player and now as a coach: he didn't forget.

THURSDAY, NOVEMBER 14, AT ST. LOUIS: BLUES 7, AVALANCHE 3. RECORD: 14–4

Chris Stewart drove the Avalanche organization crazy—when he was with the Avalanche. Colorado's first-round draft choice in 2006, he alternately was embraced as a budding superstar and written off as a washout, sometimes even within the same week. All the while, he was an intriguing story.

His father, Norman, emigrated from Jamaica to Montreal at age 23. Soon, he was married, and he and his wife, Sue, settled in Toronto, where he worked as a swimming pool installer and played cricket. Yes, cricket. The Stewarts' two young sons, Anthony and Chris, went to games and were mystified what their father saw in this glacially paced game. Chris gravitated to soccer, football, and hockey. He and Anthony had five younger sisters. In hockey, Anthony was the star; Chris, the little brother. "Anthony got the new equipment, and the new stuff for me was his old stuff," Chris said.

Chris enjoyed playing tight end in football, but he decided to try to join his older brother with major junior's Kingston Frontenacs. At age 16, Chris set out to make the roster as a fourth-line "energy guy," meaning he fought his way through training camp and had a black eye swollen shut when he was told he would be joining his brother on the roster. He made such quick progress with Kingston that the Avalanche took him in the first round. They left him in major junior for more seasoning, and as that season was winding down, he got the horrible news that his mother, Sue, had suffered a fatal heart attack while watching television with Norman. She was 52.

It took a long time for Chris to get over it.

He went up and down between the Avalanche and the AHL several times, but eventually led Colorado in goal scoring in 2009–10 with 28. But he remained inconsistent, and he continued at times to act like the kid trying to make the Kingston roster by fighting everyone who would drop the gloves. At one point, he suffered a broken hand and missed significant time. Joe Sacco, who also had coached him in the AHL, didn't want to take the passion out of his game and didn't try forcefully enough to drive home the point that he had become too valuable to be fighting so often. Stewart had 13 goals in 36 games for the Avalanche in 2010–11 when he was part of the major trade that brought Erik Johnson to Colorado. In the ensuing two years, Stewart's play for the Blues was familiar, meaning he was in and out of the doghouse. When the Avalanche came to town for the first of the four games of the season between the two teams, Stewart had only two goals in 16 games. And although he still had a lot of friends in the Colorado dressing room, he was in a foul mood.

Stewart had a power-play goal during the Blues' four-goal second period, when they pulled away from a 1–1 tie to a 5–1 lead and guaranteed that Jean-Sebastien Giguere would suffer his first loss of the season in the Colorado net. It was 4–1 when Patrick Bordeleau delivered a big hit on St. Louis defenseman Ian Cole, and the ripple effect was that Stewart went at it with Avalanche defenseman Cory Sarich. Given the conventional standards of the sport, that wasn't anything untoward, but when Stewart showboated after winning the fight, with bush-league raising of his arms that looked more fitting for pay-per-view wrestling, it crossed the line. Later, Bordeleau drew a ten-minute misconduct for lining up next to Stewart, with officials clearly trying to head off additional trouble.

Roy seemed to issue a challenge about the teams' later meetings. "We're going to see them again, and let's make sure we're ready when we do," Roy said. "There's no reason for us to get down on ourselves. We're 14–4, and we played a really good game at Carolina. The puck didn't bounce our way tonight, but I think we learned a lot from this."

Johnson logged 22 minutes of ice time; although he didn't collect a point, he was plus one and had three blocked shots. The former Blues defenseman wasn't Colorado's problem in this one.

SATURDAY, NOVEMBER 16, AT DENVER: PANTHERS 4, AVALANCHE 1. RECORD: 14–5

Goalie Tim Thomas, who had sat out the previous season while holed up at his home in the Woodland Park area near Colorado Springs, returned to the state and had 32 saves to help the lowly Panthers deal the Avalanche their third consecutive loss. Again, as the game wound down, and the Avalanche seemed listless and out of sorts, the story was going to be how Roy would react.

He was calm—so calm, he seemed to be almost overacting.

Worse than the loss, Matt Duchene suffered an oblique injury during the game and likely would be out of the lineup for at least a week.

"We have to stay positive, there's no doubt about it," Roy said. "But I hate to lose a game like this in front of our fans. They deserve better."

❄ ❄ ❄

The Chicago Blackhawks had won the Stanley Cup twice in their four seasons under former Avalanche coach Joel Quenneville. By early in the 2013–14 season, it was arguable that although the Avalanche management had been unrealistic about the quality and depth of talent in the organization in 2008, when Quenneville left, the rebuilding approach at least had been semi-validated.

The Blackhawks, who had taken advantage of high draft choices to acquire the core stars—most notably, center Jonathan Toews (third overall pick in 2006) and Patrick Kane (first overall in '07)—were the model the Avalanche were trying to follow. Part of that was unspoken, too, because the Blackhawks had been widely derided as parsimonious and behind the times in the final years of patriarch owner Bill Wirtz's control, even in such things as not televising home games. Crowds in the Chicago Stadium were sparse during the down years. Yes, even in an Original Six market. But once Wirtz's son, Rocky, took control, the organization turned calendar pages to the present, and the marketing moves in conjunction with landing the young stars through the draft led to a Blackhawks' renaissance on the ice and at the box office. Quenneville was in the right place at the right time, but he also was the right coach. He even kept the ship afloat after the first Cup title, when salary cap issues forced the Blackhawks to unload several major contributors and essentially do a quick depth rebuild on the fly.

Quenneville and Roy were together with the Avalanche for about thirteen months, starting with the goaltender's arrival from Montreal and ending with Quenneville's departure to become the coach of the Blues in January 1997. "I played for Joel in '95–96, and that was the first time I met him," Roy said the day before the teams' first meeting of the season. "Ever since that day, I have a lot of respect for him, and I learned a lot from him. He was an assistant coach then, and I had no doubt in my mind that he would turn [out] to be a great NHL head coach, and that has been the case. He's won two Stanley Cups for Chicago, and that speaks for itself."

From his viewpoint as the vice president of hockey operations, Roy admired the Blackhawks' approach. "It's a mix of a lot of things," he said. "They built on draft picks. When you get Toews and Kane and [defenseman Brent] Seabrook and Duncan Keith, it helps to start with a pretty solid foundation. They've been drafting well, especially in the late rounds, and they have a lot of depth. But the core of their teams have remained the same. There's a team that a lot of teams, and especially us, look up to."

After the Blackhawks' game-morning skate, Quenneville returned the compliments to Roy. "He's the one player as a coach you always knew that he had a different level of how he saw the game and viewed the game," Quenneville said. "Putting it all together as a coach, he brings a lot of different elements to what coaching is all about. He's a competitive guy. He understands the game, understands people, and understands what it takes to win."

He also seemed to be more impressed with the direction of the Avalanche organization than when he walked out the door five years earlier. "Things change quickly," he said. "You get some young kids in your system, and all of a sudden these kids are top players in the league, and you have a different type of team." He noted that in the Nordiques' final season in Quebec City, "we had about seven, eight, nine, ten guys that were young and ready to take off in their careers, and it all came together nicely."

TUESDAY, NOVEMBER 19, AT DENVER: AVALANCHE 5, BLACKHAWKS 1. RECORD: 15–5

Minus Matt Duchene, the Avalanche romped. Roy's players acted as if his attitude—along the lines of, "Oh, we've lost three straight? I didn't know that"—rubbed off. There hasn't been an NHL coach who didn't accept the inevitability of losing streaks and slides, however brief, but this again was a test of a first-time NHL head coach who was expected to react emotionally to every twist in the season. In this case, his even keel was both noticeable and underplayed.

The victory also marked the first time an Avalanche team had reached 15 wins in the first 20 games. The two Stanley Cup teams came up short of that through 20 games, winning 13 in the 1995–96 season and 14 in 2000–01.

The Avalanche got the first five goals of the game—from Paul Stastny, Gabriel Landeskog, John Mitchell, P. A. Parenteau, and Cody McLeod—and Semyon Varlamov stopped 36 shots.

Remembering that he had been asked the day before about how the Avalanche could emulate the Blackhawks, Roy came up with an addendum. "There's a lot of things we can learn from Chicago, but one is they put a lot of shots on net," he said. "They shoot from everywhere and drive the net hard."

This was the coach who, early in training camp, had dryly reminded the Paul Stastny-centered line that someone generally needed to take a shot for a line to score. For the first time, too, Roy brought up what likely would become a season-long issue: with the Western Conference dominating inter-conference games in the realigned league, it was becoming obvious that a pretty good team or two—with decent or better point totals—wouldn't even make the playoffs in the West.

The top three teams in the Central and Pacific Divisions would get the conference's first six playoff spots, with two wild-card berths going to the next two teams regardless of division. It was beginning to look as if nine or ten teams would be fighting for the eight spots. The one season when the Avalanche notched 95 points under Quenneville but didn't make the playoffs was the ominous reminder that a decent season—and in this case, tremendous improvement—might not be enough to make the postseason.

This time, Roy used an innocuous first question about the significance of beating the defending Stanley Cup champions to emphasize that winger Brad Malone and defenseman Tyson Barrie, the undersized "scooter" defenseman counted on to add offensive punch from the blue line, had been able to step into the lineup seamlessly after being recalled from Lake Erie the day before. It was a bit of praise he knew would trickle down to Monsters coach Dean Chynoweth. "We had a meeting before the season started to make sure we played the same way [in Cleveland], and I thought the guys were not lost," Roy said. "They knew what was going on."

Roy was hoping that Barrie came back from Lake Erie a changed man—one who understood his need to jump into the play but also be just responsible enough defensively. If he did, that would help give the defensive corps more balance.

BLUELINERS

NO. 6, ERIK JOHNSON, 6'4", 232 LBS., BORN MARCH 21, 1988, BLOOMINGTON, MINNESOTA

In Minneapolis, Bruce Johnson took his young son, Erik, to a nearby apartment complex with a small oval rink. Together, father and son set a modest goal: for Erik to make it a full lap without falling down. At first, that seemed impossible. Erik fell and fell again. Soon, though, very soon, making it through that lap was easy.

Yup, Bruce Johnson thought, *the kid had potential.*

It wasn't long before Erik was trying hockey. "I just loved playing," Erik said. "It wasn't anything that my dad had to push me into. I loved watching the Gophers on TV right away. We didn't have a net at the time at our house, so I just shot at my sister's old baby cradle. She was two years younger, so she was about four, and it was discarded there in the garage. I had a stick and a ball. Then we moved into the suburbs, and I got a net for my birthday."

Also, the Johnsons' Bloomington neighbors had had a makeshift backyard rink, and as Erik practiced there and participated in youth programs in one of the sport's longtime U.S. hotbeds, his dad decided it was time to try the same thing. So Erik spent much time after dinner and even before going to school skating in his own backyard. He also played baseball, but it was a sidelight. Hockey was serious stuff as he played for the Jefferson Jaguars in public-school leagues, then switched to the Academy of Holy Angels in time for his freshman year. That was a compromise in the family because Erik had wanted to go to Shattuck-St. Mary's in Faribault, where he would have been a year behind a kid named Sidney Crosby.

"They recruited me, and my parents and I went down to Faribault and took the tour there," Johnson said. "I had some friends who had already gone there, so I really wanted to go there. But my mom said, 'No, that's too far away from home.'"

He played for state tournament teams at Holy Angels as a freshman and a sophomore.

Johnson was smiling at this point as he told of the National Team Development Program (NTDP), based in Ann Arbor, Michigan, approaching him.

"I said, 'Mom, you wouldn't let me go to Shattuck; I'm going to Ann Arbor,'" Johnson said. "She thought Faribault was far away, but it was only an hour from our house. This was 13 hours away, so in hindsight, she probably wishes I had gone to Shattuck."

He played two seasons for the NTDP, for under-17 and under-18 teams, and was impressive in an appearance with the U.S. team in the World Junior championships. Although he loved his time in Ann Arbor, he added that he wasn't certain how crucial it was in his own development.

"It's hard to think how it would have turned out if I didn't go," he said. "I think the good players are the good players, no matter where they go, but I think it helped me realize what it took to be a pro. And just the way you train there helps. You go to school from 8 to 1 and you're at the rink from 1:30 to 6. You're doing weight training and all the nutritional stuff. To be prepared at 16 and 17 like that is a pretty cool opportunity."

Johnson made the most of it. When the Blues made him the number one overall choice in the 2006 NHL draft, it was notable: not only had an American-born player gone at the top of the draft; an American-born *defenseman* had gone at the top of the draft. (This was seven years before the Avalanche pondered whether to take American-born defenseman Seth Jones at number one.) "It was pretty cool being the highest-drafted Minnesotan ever, with all the great players that have come out of Minnesota," Johnson said.

The Blues were fine with Johnson going to college for a year to play for his beloved Minnesota Golden Gophers. "They knew that was my dream, so they let me do that," he said. "We were one of the best teams in the country, and that definitely was a thrill to be able to live in my hometown after being away for two years. It was good to live in the dorms and be able to drive home for dinner at night if I wanted to."

During that freshman season, he had four goals in seven games for the United States in the World Juniors, and that might have ended any chance that St. Louis would either tolerate or recommend that he stay in college one more season. The Gophers lost in overtime in a 2007 regional final to North Dakota—at the Pepsi Center, no less—and Johnson signed with the Blues.

He had a decent rookie season in 2007–08, when he still was a teenager, until the final two weeks of the regular season. "It's really hard for a defenseman to go in that position," he said of the status of being a top overall choice. "Probably people expect, 'Hey this guy is first overall; he's probably going to be Bobby Orr every night.' Those expectations are unrealistic. Any person coming into the league as a high pick is going to face high expectations, so I think I was kind of lumped in with a lot of guys that way. I don't feel that pressure anymore, but I definitely felt it for a couple of years."

He sustained a serious knee injury in a golf-cart accident on a team outing, underwent ACL surgery, and missed the entire 2008–09 season. "I don't like to make a lot of excuses," he said. "I think a lot of people go through injuries like that at one point or another in their careers. That was a pretty serious injury for me when I had just turned 20. It was hard. I think the biggest thing was that I learned a lot about myself in that time. It really required me to do a lot of rehab and hard work and even rehab mentally. I read Drew Brees's book, and when he went through his shoulder injury, he thought his career might be ending, and then he came back and rehabbed hard and thought he came back stronger. With me, and a knee injury like that, you don't know how it's going to affect you, but I think it made me tougher mentally. I came back the next year, and had my best year and made the Olympic team after missing an entire year. I was pretty proud of the way I responded. I could have felt sorry for myself, but I kept working hard and got my career on track."

After returning, he had 10 goals and 29 assists and averaged nearly 22 minutes in 2009–10. He also was one of the standouts on the U.S. team that won a silver medal at Vancouver.

The stunning trade that brought Johnson to Colorado came on February 8, 2011.

"It was hard to leave St. Louis," Johnson said. "I really liked living and playing there. The trade wasn't a surprise because I didn't think I was playing that well and I thought a change probably was going to happen at some point or other with a new GM there and everything. But I had thought I was going to spend my whole career there potentially."

The Avalanche were betting that Johnson, at 22, still had tons of potential to go with his obvious talent, and that he would become the superstar hybrid-type defenseman so coveted in the game, capable of being a major physical force in the defensive end of the ice and a major offensive threat at the other end. The example repeatedly cited was Chris Pronger. He was similarly doubted early in his career, before Hartford gave up on him and shipped him to St. Louis, where he was named both the NHL's most valuable player and top defenseman in 2000, earning him the Hart and Norris Trophies, respectively. He was 25.

Johnson was heartened that he came to Denver, a city he liked, and to a team with many players he already knew—including Paul Stastny, his roommate at the 2007 world championship in Moscow and at the 2010 Olympics. But that's what made one post-trade incident so notable. Paul's father, Peter, the Hall of Fame winger who lived part-time in St. Louis, blasted the deal, portraying it as a disaster for the Avalanche because of the departure of Stewart.

"Everyone has an opinion," Johnson said at the time. "He chose to voice that. It's not going to change what I feel about Paul or his family at all. We're still going to be friends, and I'm still going to have respect for the Stastnys."

Colorado signed Johnson to a relatively modest four-year, $15-million contract extension in the summer of 2011, showing more faith. Near the end of the 2013 season, Johnson turned 25. He was coming to the end of that period when "potential" and "upside" explained away deficiencies.

In his initial round of phone calls to holdover players, Patrick Roy told him: "Don't live in the past. Don't worry where people say 'first overall.' It's over! Be who you are."

In the early stages of the season, Johnson wasn't lighting it up offensively, and the Avalanche clearly needed more out of him there. Yet, he was playing major minutes in the top pair with Jan Hejda and doing strong work in front of the Colorado goaltenders as the tandem almost always was out against the opposition's top line.

"Defense is a tough position to learn," Johnson said. "Everyone always told me that when I was 19, 20. I was like, 'Oh, yeah, I guess I'll believe it when I see it or experience it.' But sometimes it takes a little longer. Some guys, it happens for right away. It's taken a little bit longer for me. Sometimes that's just how it goes. This year, I understand the game, and I think my maturity on the ice is really helping me out a lot. I go into every game so confident that I'm going to play well. I don't know if I had that in years past. That has a lot to do with Patrick and how he's instilled the belief that I'm a guy who can go out there and play big minutes and be a big contributor on this team. I don't want to say that I couldn't do it without Patrick giving me that confidence, but it's definitely helped a lot to have a guy who's so positive and has such a belief in me as a player. I think that's how a lot of guys in here feel that way, that he has faith in their abilities. It feels good to finally assert yourself and know that you're going to go out and be a good player in this league every night, as opposed to you're going to play a couple of good games, and you don't know what's going to happen the next couple of games. The consistency level that I never found my first couple of years, I think I've finally got."

Some of it was stylistic, with Johnson the defenseman equivalent of Matt Duchene feeling unleashed.

"You know, I'm a player that can make plays," Johnson said. "You go out there and make a mistake and go back to the bench, and [Roy's] like, 'Don't worry about it. That's a great try. Go out and do it again next shift.' In the past, we played a lot of D-to-D, chip-it-up-the-wall type of hockey. Now, there's a lot of flow to our game, where we come out of the zone with speed. We're really utilizing our best asset, which is our speed. The biggest thing we've learned from Patrick so far this year is 'short memory.' You have a win, you forget about it, the next day you're on to the next game. You lose, you learn from it, and you're on to the next game. As a player, you have a good game, you forget about it, and you're on to the next game. You have a bad game, you forget about it, and you're on to the next game. I think when you have that short-term memory, it serves you well, both through the good and the bad. For us, it's been really good to have that mentality."

The expectation, at least in Denver, was that Johnson was a lock to be chosen for the U.S. Olympic team in Sochi. "I played in the last one, definitely want to play in this one," he said of the Olympics. "Anytime you get a chance to represent your country, it's a pretty special deal. I'd love to be there and hope to be there."

Did coming so close to winning the gold in Vancouver—Canada won the gold-medal game in overtime—whet his appetite for a return? "It was a little bit of a bitter taste," he said. "But at the same time, I have an Olympic silver medal, and that's going to be a pretty cool thing down the road when you have kids and grandkids, to show them. It's definitely a pretty special moment that we got to medal and everything. Yeah, it's a little bitter taste when you're one goal away from the gold."

NO. 8, JAN HEJDA, 6'4", 237 LBS., BORN JUNE 18, 1978, PRAGUE

The veteran defenseman was one of the first Avalanche off the ice after a morning skate, then went to the dry erase board at the end of the dressing room to go over some strategy with assistant coach Andre Tourigny. It was pure NHL: Tourigny's first language is French; Hejda's is Czech, and he speaks Russian. But they communicated in English, the Esperanto of the Avalanche and the NHL.

Hejda still was picking up the language, but he was quite skilled at speaking and comprehending it, given that he hadn't come to North America to play until he was in his late 20s.

When he was young and his country still was Czechoslovakia, Hejda followed his father and grandfather into the sport in Prague. "It was just something that was natural for me," Jan recalled after returning to his stall. "It was, 'These are skates and this is a hockey stick . . . and go.' Especially my father was all about hockey." Smiling, he added, "I was in bigger trouble if I didn't go to practice than if I didn't go to school. Hockey was first."

In the aftermath of the breakup of Czechoslovakia into two separate nations, the hockey system sometimes could be chaotic, and Hejda said that as he approached NHL draft age, he signed on with a Czech agent who turned out to be incompetent. "Back then the agent had to sign a player up for the draft, and when I thought I was supposed to be drafted and I wasn't, it was a surprise because I had a pretty good rating in Europe," Hejda said. "I asked what happened, why I wasn't drafted. The agent said, 'Oh, I thought you were one year younger than you are.' He had messed it up. Obviously, I fired him. I just played in the Czech League and kind of waited for later."

He settled into a solid career in the Czech league, and NHL teams weren't impressed enough to offer a one-way contract that would be more attractive than a comfortable living in Europe. He played six seasons for his hometown Slavia Praha in the Czech League and for the national team in the world championships in 2004, when he was 25. "We had a good team, we were in the playoffs every year, and one year in the Czech Republic, we won the championship," Hejda said.

Finally, after his sixth season, the Buffalo Sabres took him in the fourth round of the 2003 draft. "That was the year they went to the Stanley Cup final," Hejda said. "They offered me [a] two-way contract and said, 'This is what we have, where we are, we just went to the Stanley Cup final, and obviously we're not going to change our team too much, so you most likely are going to spend all the season in the minors.'"

Instead, he took an offer from CSKA in Moscow and played two seasons there before joining another Russian team for one. In retrospect, he considers the limited schedules in Europe a blessing and believes they enabled him to have less mileage on his odometer in his mid-30s than he would if he had come to the NHL sooner.

After he played for the Czech Republic for a fourth time in the 2006 world championships, he took a call from Edmonton Oilers scout Frank Musil, who asked him if he was ready to give the NHL a shot. Hejda said yes, if the offer came with assurances that he wasn't coming over to play in the AHL. The Oilers stuck to an offer of a two-way contract, but assured him he would have little trouble sticking with them. "I was kind of tired of the Russian league, and I was also thinking this was an opportunity to play in the NHL," Hejda said. "Edmonton gave me that option, and I was thinking, 'If I never try, I'm never going to have that experience.' I really just wanted to try."

The Oilers sent Buffalo a late-round draft choice for his rights and signed him. He indeed stuck with Edmonton for the start of the

2006–07 season . . . for six games before the Oilers sent him down to Hamilton of the AHL. "They treated me as a rookie anyway, even though I was 28 with a first place in the world championship and first place in the Czech League in my pocket," he said. "I knew that I had an option to go back to Russia and finish my career there."

So he considered heading back to Europe. He consulted with his wife and family, and they decided Hejda would stick it out for a bit before making a decision. "Finally, after six games in Hamilton, things turned in a good way, and I was lucky that some guys got hurt and I jumped on a plane," Hejda said. "Basically, from my first game I played with Jason Smith, and he was a great player, defenseman, and captain; and it's kind of weird, but from my seventh game in the NHL, I played against top lines."

He had only a one-year deal, though, and signed with Columbus as an unrestricted free agent after the season. With the Blue Jackets, he developed as a player and developed a grudging respect for coach Ken Hitchcock. "He knew what kind of defenseman I was, and he knew my style, and he taught me a lot," Hejda said. "He was a good coach. He wasn't a very good psychologist, I would say that, but he was a good coach."

After four seasons at Columbus—and a 2010 Olympics appearance with the Czech Republic—he signed a four-year, $13-million deal as an unrestricted free agent with the Avalanche in 2011. That was a major expression of faith in a player who hadn't come to the NHL until his late 20s and would be on the verge of turning 36 at the end of the contract.

In his first two seasons with Colorado, he was solid, but he took his lumps along with the rest of the defensemen during the awful 2013 season. But Roy showed faith, essentially installing Hejda in the top pairing with Johnson and leaving him there.

"Obviously, we had tough seasons, but finally things are turning up; and right now, I'm probably having the best time I've ever had in the NHL," Hejda said. "I'm pretty happy that Erik Johnson and I have figured out how to play together, because, if you remember, we played together when I signed the contract here for some games and that wasn't working. I think I know why. I was trying to be too much offensive and he is offensive. We both played offense, and we didn't play too much defense; and I figured out, right now, he's offensive, and I have no problem staying back and being backup for him. I knew points are coming anyway, and I'm happy that he's playing well, and I'm also happy that we are playing together."

And playing for Roy, Tourigny, and the Avalanche staff?

"It's awesome," Hejda said. "It's not just these two guys, but the whole coaching staff are super smart guys. They all coached junior as head coaches, so they know what they are doing, and they are also like friends, like teammates. This is not like sometimes the coach thinks he's the coach and the players are players. These coaches are just part of the team."

In the Pepsi Center dressing room, Hejda and Cory Sarich were side by side, and Hejda enjoyed pointing out that although he was two months older than Sarich, he had played far fewer games because of the shorter European schedules and his long wait to come to North America. But Sarich had something Hejda didn't have—a Stanley Cup ring.

NO. 16, CORY SARICH, 6'4", 207 LBS., BORN AUGUST 16, 1978, SASKATOON, SASKATCHEWAN

Early in the season, one of the questions most often asked was whether the Avalanche had expected to get the sort of solid play from the veteran Sarich they were getting after essentially accepting him as the throw-in in the deal for Alex Tanguay.

The answer, if folks were honest, was: probably not. By then, Sarich was considered over the hill, perhaps even destined to be out of the league after his five-year contract expired following the 2013–14 season.

"It's nice to be here and get a fresh chance," Sarich said.

Although he played most of his major junior career with his hometown Saskatoon Blades, he was Buffalo's second-round pick in 1996 and divided time in his first two pro seasons between AHL Rochester and the Sabres before going to Tampa Bay in a trading deadline deal in 2000. In six seasons with the Lightning, he was steady and reliable, and the highlight of his stay was the 2004 Stanley Cup championship that preceded the yearlong NHL shutdown and lost season. He didn't miss a game from 2003 to 2007 and once had the longest consecutive game streak in the league, a run that ended at 149 games. He signed a five-year deal in 2007 as an unrestricted free agent with the Flames and had a decent run there, at least until Bob Hartley became disenchanted enough with him to keep him in street clothes often as a scratch in 2012–13.

"It was just the opinion of a coach. Or coaches," said Sarich. "The last two years, they didn't play me for a bit, and then I come back and I was—not to toot my own horn or anything—but I was a really solid defenseman for our team. It just seems that the start of every season, it gets overlooked a little bit. So it's nice to have some people putting some faith in me again."

With Colorado, he was playing well.

"I've never thought that 35 was old," he said. "Maybe other people were convinced it is, but I still feel good and still feel like I can contribute. I feel like I can help us be solid in our end and get us out of our end."

Sarich was adjusting to Roy and Tourigny's defensive scheme.

"It was different for me, more of a man-to-man coverage versus more traditional kind of zone coverage that I'd experienced before," he said. "But I like the way our team is responding, and it keeps our team on our toes. It's a fun way to play."

NO. 4, TYSON BARRIE, 5'10", 190 LBS., BORN JULY 26, 1991, VICTORIA

Tyson's father, Len Barrie, was a major junior superstar, scoring 85 goals in 70 games in his "over-age" year for the Western League's Kamloops Blazers in 1989–90. Len's head coach there was a portly fellow named Ken Hitchcock, who was about to move to the NHL as a Philadelphia Flyers' assistant coach. Len played 184 games for four NHL teams, but he spent the majority of his career in the AHL or International Hockey League (IHL) and Europe. Tyson was born early in his dad's pro career and, as a hockey kid, spent much time hanging around the various pro locker rooms and rinks.

After retirement, Len went into the real-estate and resort development business, and initially did so well, he became a part owner of the Tampa Bay Lightning before business reverses—mainly a resort project bankruptcy—led to him unloading his interest in the team and seeing homes and property go into foreclosure. Barrie had recruited several players, including former goalie Sean Burke, to invest with him in the resort project named Bear Mountain, and they lost their collective shirts.

Tyson was able to pursue his own hockey career, first playing for the WHL's Kelowna Rockets at age 15. Ultimately, he played four full seasons for the Rockets, and their best season was 2008–09, when Barrie had four goals in a 22-game playoff run that ended with a loss to the Windsor Spitfires in the Memorial Cup championship game. Shortly thereafter, the Avalanche took him in the third round of the same draft in which they claimed Matt Duchene and Ryan O'Reilly but watched as he remained in the WHL two more seasons.

All along, the asterisk was Barrie's size. He never was going to be able to dislodge power forwards from in front of the net. But he was a terrific skater and puck handler, and for Colorado fans especially keeping track of such things, the issue was whether he could ever be on the team at the same time as a physical and stylistic duplicate, defenseman John-Michael Liles. But in June 2011, the Avalanche shipped Liles to Toronto, which brightened the organizational outlook for Barrie. He spent most of the next two seasons with Lake Erie but came back up after the lockout was settled and played 32 games for the Avalanche in 2013. But that breakthrough, that flash, didn't come, and he had only two goals in that season. The reality: if he didn't provide offensive punch from the blue line, it did no good to have a 5-10, 190-pound defenseman around.

Among other things, that's what Roy recognized. Barrie was tentative and turnover-prone at the outset of the season, and his demotion to Lake Erie came with a challenge: Get your confidence back, find a balance in your game, and maybe you'll be back. "At the beginning of the year, I thought I was going to be a top four defenseman," Barrie said. "I had all the expectations. I don't know if I was totally sure what they wanted as far as my game offensively and defensively. I was being a little too cautious, trying to prove to them that I could play defense. Then to struggle early and to be sent down was a bit disappointing. There was a reason for it. I had to go down and work on my game."

In part because of injuries, he was summoned back to Denver in mid-November. Tourigny delivered a challenge. "He explained to me that they really wanted me to move my feet more, jump into the play a lot more," Barrie said. "Instead of going 'D to D' with the puck all the time, just go. Go, and put the other team on their heels."

After he returned, he was destined to be an integral part of the defensive rotation, playing on the point on the power play. Before long, it would be clear that four-on-four overtime, with its more open ice, was made for him. The trick still was to mitigate the disadvantages of his small stature, especially for the position. "Skating is one of my bigger assets," he said. "So if I can stop [an opposing forward] from getting to the front of the net earlier or impede them or get in their way to make it longer for them to get there, so Varly can see the shot or whatever, that's big. If he does happen to get to the net, I think instead of trying to push him out, a big guy I'm not able to move, I have to try and get in front of him, maybe front the shot."

It wouldn't be long, either, before Roy mused that Barrie reminded him of Sandis Ozolinsh, the wandering Latvian defenseman whose of-fensive contributions were so important in the Avalanche's 1996 Stanley Cup run.

"TELL PATRICK TO . . ."

THURSDAY, NOVEMBER 21, AT GLENDALE: AVALANCHE 4, COYOTES 3 (OT). RECORD: 16–5
SATURDAY, NOVEMBER 23, AT LOS ANGELES: AVALANCHE 1, KINGS 0 (OT). RECORD: 17–5

Matt Duchene remained in Denver and skated, but the Avalanche managed to get four points in the two games without him. Ryan O'Reilly had the overtime goal at Phoenix, and Jamie McGinn had the goal 2:32 in overtime at Los Angeles.

On the day between games, word came from Denver that the Denver District Attorney's office had moved forward, filing a third-degree misdemeanor assault charge against Semyon Varlamov. The good news for the Avalanche goalie was that there was no kidnapping charge.

The next night, he collected his twelfth career shutout against the Kings. "Varly's been like this since the start of the year, and he's been very focused," Roy said. Of the charges from the D.A.'s office, Roy added: "I thought it was positive for him, but in the end I'm not a lawyer and I'm not a D.A. I think he needs to remain focused, and we'll see what transpires. The most important thing was the support he got from our fans."

Varlamov's response was familiar, too. "It's a long process, and I can't say anything right now," he said. "We'll see what's going to happen."

❊ ❊ ❊

Ah, the rematch of the embarrassing game at St. Louis was coming up—a chance for the Avalanche at home to avenge the embarrassing loss of a few weeks earlier! Chris Stewart better watch out as the Avalanche make him accountable, not so much the fight with Cory Sarich, but for his bush-league showboating after!

Going in, Roy refused to play along with that story line, and the reaction was mixed. Those who hadn't been around the team much tended to chuckle and assume it was just gamesmanship, that surely the former goalie who so notoriously fought would endorse retribution. To others, it was part of a consistent message—each game was an individual entity (yes, the dreaded "one game at a time"), and he wasn't going to allow anything to distract his team from the mission at hand. Again, he was thinking back to the height of the Avalanche-Red Wings rivalry and his conclusion that Detroit had outsmarted his team.

"I don't live in the past, unfortunately," he said. "You know what? The Blues did what they had to do. They were ready for us, they played a hard game, they played a strong game, and they played really well. I'm sure their coach was very happy with their performance against us. Now they have to come into Denver, and we're going to have to be ready and play a good game. But it's not about a rematch: it's about playing a good hockey game."

He was asked directly if he was summoning those lessons learned in the Red Wings rivalry—the lessons he alluded to in his sit-down session with Chris Osgood. "It's what I said to them after the second period [in St. Louis]," he said. "We're not going to play that game. We're going to play hockey. Our team is about speed; our team is about playing hockey. Are we capable of playing physical? Yes, we are. But we're not going to fight, and we're not going to be part of that game. We're going to make sure we play our way. That's how we're going to win our games, and that's what we've been doing since the start of the year. Why lose our focus? I thought it was important to address that after the second period and make sure in the third we were back in our game. That's what we did."

But Roy wasn't playing. As a coach, he noted every slight. He didn't forget. At some point, he would need to develop the short memory he preached about to his players, but for now, this could make things more interesting.

WEDNESDAY, NOVEMBER 27, AT DENVER: BLUES 4, AVALANCHE 1. RECORD: 17–6

The Blues had the Avalanche's number.

The word came shortly before the pregame warm-up that Paul Stastny wouldn't be able to go because of back spasms, and that led Duchene to decide to play. Rather than sitting out one more game with his oblique issue, he would go, even if that meant he was considerably less than 100 percent.

It went downhill from there.

The Blues roared off to a 3–1 lead after one period, and that was all the scoring until Stewart scored an empty-netter with 1:44 left. Stewart behaved, skipping the showboating this time.

Surprisingly, there were no fights at all, but there was some skirmishing near the benches at the final buzzer, some of it involving Patrick Bordeleau, who clearly had wanted to go with Stewart in the game at St. Louis—but was thwarted by the officials. In this one, Bordeleau had Colorado's only goal. In those final seconds, with the milling around and shoving along the boards near the benches, Blues coach Ken Hitchcock appeared to toss out a few words in Bordeleau's direction. But it wasn't an extended conversation or particularly striking.

In the Avalanche dressing room, Bordeleau was unapologetic for playing physical in the final minute of a blowout loss, and he was asked if he was conscious of trying to get *some* retribution. "Yeah," he said, then caught himself. "I mean no. It's been a while; and as a team and as a coaching staff and all the guys, we talked about that, how we're not going to revenge anything. But, like I said, whatever the score is of any game, regular season or playoffs, I'm still going to play the same way. It has nothing to do with the last game. If there's a guy I can hit, I'm going to hit him. 5–0, 10–1, 20–0, I'm going to be the same style. Thirty seconds, last 20 minutes: I'm going to keep playing the same game."

This was another time Roy had something to get off his chest, and he detoured to do it when asked whether Duchene was in the lineup only because Stastny couldn't go. Roy said yes and added that Duchene had played well under the circumstances, then noted that Bordeleau had been Colorado's best forward, at least offensively. "He was skating well," Roy said. Then he took off on Hitchcock, referring back to the veteran coach's reaction from afar to Roy's actions at the end of the opening night game against Anaheim.

"You know what?" Roy said. "I was very mad at the end because I've been jabbed by different coaches around the league, especially when Hitchcock, when he said that was junior stuff, talking to players and talking to the referee. But I saw a guy on the other side that was talking to players and then was also talking to the referee, even got the referee pissed off. It seems to me there are different rules for everybody in this league. I guess the old guys are allowed to do whatever they want; and I guess us, because we're younger, we cannot say anything. I'm a little pissed off about that."

Did he say anything back directly to Hitchcock?

"I can't [say] that here, I'm sorry," Roy said with a tight smile.

With that, he told the reporters—who were a bit taken aback because this seemed to have come out of nowhere—to have a good night and left the room. That prevented more follow-up questions about specifics.

FROM THE NOTEBOOK OF TERRY FREI

I was covering the game that night for the Denver Post *because Adrian was ill and Mike Chambers was off. Frankly, given the rush to file the "quick" game story to be posted as soon after the end of the game as possible and then get downstairs for the postgame interviews, I watched the end-of-the-game scrum and theatrics only out of the corner of my eye and didn't consider them at all significant.*

Sorry, folks, that's the reality of the business today. The next visionary editor is going to be the one who tells scribes covering games to stop worrying about all the in-game sideshows—tweeting and chat, among other things, and writing an "early" story that will be sent the second the game ends—and actually watch the game they're covering. Play-by-play type tweeting especially delivers minutiae to a secondary audience that in most cases, in my opinion, rarely or never actually ventures to a newspaper's site. So we're fouling up our newspaper and our later on-

line coverage to deliver small details to folks who aren't even among the
constituency we should care most about—our readers.

So when Roy finished off his rant about Hitchcock, I turned to others
in the interview room and mused that everything had been going so
swimmingly . . . and then this happened.

I knew I needed to try to find Hitchcock for his reaction. Later, I
fielded some criticisms of that, and I understand it. But Roy's comments
were on both the Avalanche radio and television broadcasts as part of
the postgame shows. So I wasn't "tattling" or going back and forth to
incite. If Hitchcock wasn't going to be asked to respond at the moment,
he would be the next day, anyway, after the comments were in the
paper. And, then, it would have to be only St. Louis writers doing the
asking.

I had covered Hitchcock as far back as the 1980s, when he was the
highly successful coach of major junior's Kamloops Blazers, I was the
columnist at the Oregonian, and his team came through to play the
Winterhawks. He had worked his way up through the ranks, coaching
minor hockey in the Edmonton area while working as a salesman, and
then catching on with Kamloops. At one point, he had ballooned to 470
pounds. To me, he was another example of hockey's unique open-
minded attitude about coaching backgrounds; in a sense, he was another Bob Hartley or former policeman Pat Burns. That's another reason Hitchcock's remarks belittling Roy's first-game antics as "junior
hockey" resonated with me. I had seen Hitchcock coach major junior
hockey. Also, of course, I had spoken with him many times when he
coached the Dallas Stars, including twice against the Avalanche in the
Western Conference final; and then at his subsequent NHL coaching
stops.

I walked back down the hall, where Hitchcock was standing outside
the visiting dressing room. I reintroduced myself to Hitchcock—that
never hurts—and then told him Roy had mentioned he had been talking
to players. Before I could even phrase it in the form of a question to suit
Alex Trebek, Hitchcock responded: "Aw, give me a break. Tell Patrick to
shut the fuck up. Give me a break. I'm talking to the players. Give me a
break."

He started to walk away, and then stopped. "Did he actually say
that?"

Yes, I said.

"When did I talk to the players?"

I said it was in the digital recorder and . . .

"Well," Hitchcock said, "tell Patrick to shut the fuck up."

With that, he went into the dressing room. I hustled back upstairs and updated the game story with the quotes inserted from both Roy and Hitchcock. Hitchcock's, of course, were censored. They also were in the morning paper—at least the later editions.

In hindsight, there was a better way to handle it. I should have asked Hitchcock if he would listen to Roy's comments on the recording—they would have been easy to find at the end of the session—and then react or give his side of the story. Again, those comments already were out there, on the air and in cyberspace. Or I should have waited for a minute or two after Hitchcock's volatile comments—remember, they were offered in a one-on-one conversation—and followed him into the dressing room, then essentially ask if that's really what he wanted his on-the-record response to be. Sure, that would have been "bad" reporting, but the right thing to do. In a sense, the fact that he knew me, or at least recognized me, probably caused him to, in effect, lower his guard.

✿ ✿ ✿

At practice the next morning, Roy closed the formal part of the team workout with a shootout competition. He said he would spice it up by making the top three in the competition his selections for the next time the Avalanche had a shootout.

The Avalanche hadn't been in a shootout in their first 23 games.

FRIDAY, NOVEMBER 29, AT ST. PAUL: AVALANCHE 3, WILD 1. RECORD: 18–6
SATURDAY, NOVEMBER 30, AT DENVER: AVALANCHE 3, WILD 2 (SO). RECORD: 19–6

The four points in the home-and-home set were potentially crucial, given that these two teams were major possibilities to be fighting for third place and the final guaranteed playoff spot out of the Central Division. "If someone would have said that we would pick up three points on them in the weekend in those two games, I would have been very happy and taken it in a heartbeat," Roy said after the second game.

At St. Paul, Jean-Sebastien Giguere had 27 saves in the win. Jan Hejda, MacKinnon, and Gabe Landeskog (empty net) had the goals.

At Denver, Roy carried through in his promise when the Avalanche went into their first shootout of the season. The Avalanche blew a 2–0 lead late, including allowing the tying goal with only four seconds left, but pulled out the two points in the shootout, when the coach's exclusion of Matt Duchene from the three-man original selections had folks scratching their heads. But it worked out, with P. A. Parenteau and Nathan MacKinnon failing to score before Ryan O'Reilly beat Josh Harding. Colorado won when Semyon Varlamov stopped all three Wild attempts.

"I had been told that Varly was pretty solid in shootouts," Roy said. "I guess I was pretty confident that we could win that game. Ryan scored a super nice goal, and Varly was outstanding from the beginning of the game until the end."

Roy confirmed that Duchene would have been next if the shootout had continued, but said he was committed to honoring the result of the practice competition when selecting his three shooters in the original rotation. He said "the three guys that scored" were his choices.

This was the first of several junctures in the season when well-meaning, but not particularly hockey-savvy, members of the Denver media would ask Roy about shootouts and shootout strategy, implying he had been a part of it as a goaltender. Roy would politely preface his answer that the shootout wasn't used in the NHL during his career, and then go from there.

Actually, Roy was involved in one famous shootout—at the 1998 Olympics in Nagano, Japan. In the semifinals on February 20, Roy was in the net for Canada, Dominik Hasek for the Czech Republic. With the score still tied 1–1, it went to a shootout, which under international hockey rules was to include five shooters per side in the original pool. (The NHL should go to that system and drop the point for the losing team, either in overtime or in the shootout.) Canada went first in the alternating shots, and in the first round, Hasek made a save on Theo Fleury, and Robert Reichel beat Roy.

Then, still alternating, Hasek made saves on Ray Bourque and Joe Nieuwendyk before Eric Lindros's shot went off Hasek's stick and then off the post. Meanwhile, Roy recovered to make saves on Martin Rucin-sky and Pavel Patera before Jaromir Jagr's shot went off the post. So, going into the fifth round, Canada's Brendan Shanahan needed to score to keep the shootout going, but Hasek made the save, and the 1–0 win in the shootout was good enough to give the Czech Republic, the even-tual gold medalists, the 2–1 victory.

The most curious aspect of Marc Crawford's shootout choices for Canada was his omission of Wayne Gretzky and his inclusion of Ray Bourque (two years before he would join the Avalanche). But many knowledgeable hockey folks—then and later—argued that Gretzky wasn't good on breakaways; and Bourque, despite being a defenseman, was renowned for his skill at penalty shots in practice.

Although Duchene was only seven years old at the time of the '98 Olympics, as a student of the game, he probably would have gotten the reference if someone had asked him if he felt a bit like Gretzky while watching the shootout that night.

UNRELIABLE SOURCES

On Monday, December 2, Semyon Varlamov appeared at an uneventful advisement hearing in Denver District Court. His bond was continued, and he assured the judge that he had read and understood Evgeniya Vavrinyuk's restraining order against him. His next appearance was scheduled for January 22, when he would enter a plea.

The same week, back in Russia, the news site Lifenews—that country's equivalent of TMZ, or TMZ squared—was running several recordings that purported to be of Vavrinyuk speaking with a friend. If taken at face value, they portrayed Vavrinyuk as calculating her trip to the United States as a means of setting up the Avalanche goaltender in this kind of scenario, and as a karate expert who wasn't reluctant to hit Varlamov as well in a combative relationship.

Varlamov still seemed a likely choice for the host nation's roster at the Olympics in Sochi in February. "He's probably going to be the number one goalie for them, and he'll be ready for it, no doubt in my mind," Roy said.

THURSDAY, DECEMBER 5, AT EDMONTON: OILERS 8, AVALANCHE 2. RECORD: 19–7
FRIDAY, DECEMBER 6, AT CALGARY: AVALANCHE 3, FLAMES 2. RECORD: 20–7
SUNDAY, DECEMBER 8, AT VANCOUVER: CANUCKS 3, AVALANCHE 1. RECORD: 20–8

The victory over Bob Hartley's Flames at Calgary—coming the night after the embarrassing blowout at Edmonton in which Varlamov and his teammates all had terrible games—salvaged the trip. "I was hoping we could put [Edmonton] behind us and come back here tonight with a big effort, and that's what we did," Roy said in Calgary.

Nathan MacKinnon, playing wing on Duchene's line, had his sixth goal of the season in Calgary, and Maxime Talbot scored for the first time in his sixteen games with Colorado. "It's about time," Talbot said. "I waited a lot of games for this. After this goal, you have 50 pounds off your shoulders." In net, Jean-Sebastien Giguere ran his record to 7–0 for the season.

Roy stuck with Giguere again in Vancouver, and the perfect season for him came to an end. Jamie McGinn had the only Colorado goal on Roberto Luongo, with 7.1 seconds left. Roy had pulled Giguere for a sixth attacker with five minutes left, and if Luongo had finished with a shutout, it would have been the 65th of his career, and he would have closed to within one of Roy, who was 14th on the NHL career list. Obviously kidding, Luongo said Roy pulled his goalie so soon because he "didn't want me to catch up to him on the shutout record." Roy conceded it was inevitable that Luongo would pass him in shutouts, but said, "He has some work to do on wins though."

Roy had finished with 551 career regular-season wins. At that point, Luongo had 361.

TUESDAY, DECEMBER 10, AT DENVER: COYOTES 3, AVALANCHE 1. RECORD: 20–9

Patrick Bordeleau had Colorado's only goal, and the Avalanche were reminded how frustrating it could be to try to come from behind against a Dave Tippett-coached team.

Duchene was looking like a center rushed back into the lineup, and he had gone seven games without scoring a goal since his return following the oblique injury. He also had played through a mild case of the flu. "Just snakebit right now," he said. "It happens."

THURSDAY, DECEMBER 12, AT WINNIPEG: AVALANCHE 4, JETS 3 (SO). RECORD: 21–9

Six minutes into the first period, Roy gave the referees a piece of his mind—and got a two-minute unsportsmanlike conduct penalty. It didn't seem particularly smart, with the Avalanche already trailing the Jets 2–0 and now facing their third shorthanded situation of the game.

But when the Avalanche managed to kill the penalty, Roy's barking served its purpose, providing a spark and awakening his team. He even acknowledged later, "I had to stop bitching, and I did not. That call was the correct call."

On a night that he snapped out of his slump, Duchene noted, "It's nice to see emotion from your coach. Obviously, we wanted to kill that for him. During one of the TV time-outs, Patty said to us, 'Just stick to our game plan.'"

Duchene had two goals and an assist during the Avalanche comeback and one of Colorado's successes in the shootout.

SATURDAY, DECEMBER 14, AT DENVER: WILD 2, AVALANCHE 1 (SO). RECORD: 21–9–1

Finally, the Avalanche had a one-point loss, falling in the shootout to the Wild. Most troubling was the lost opportunity to win in regulation, which would have been a big boost to Colorado in the race for a playoff spot with, among others, the Wild. Ryan Suter's goal for the Wild with 3:53 remaining tied it 1–1, and it came after the Wild pounced on a soft clearing pass by Nate Guenin.

Roy came away from this one bemoaning Colorado's struggles with a man advantage. The Avalanche had gone ten games without a power-play goal and were 0–26 with the advantage during that stretch.

MONDAY, DECEMBER 16, AT DENVER: AVALANCHE 6, STARS 2. RECORD: 22–9–1

It was Paul Stastny's turn to end a slump. His pointless streak ended at nine games, and he did it in style, getting two goals and two assists in the rout of Dallas. "I always put pressure on myself," he said. He said he had been frustrated, but noted: "You guys won't see it, no one will see it . . . It's a long season, an 82-game season, and you have to battle through it."

Both teams raced to the airport for their chartered flights to Dallas.

FROM THE NOTEBOOK OF ADRIAN DATER

Before the game the next night at American Airlines Arena, I spoke with Joe Sakic about trade rumors. I wasn't necessarily trying to pin him down about some of the rumors flying around about the Avalanche—at least not in that setting—and this was more of a social talk about the hockey grapevine.

Sakic gave a hearty chuckle.

"How many of them come true?" Sakic wondered out loud, meaning the trade rumors.

Before I could get my guess out, he quickly answered his own question.

"Gotta be less than 1 percent," he said. "They're always wrong."

As a restricted free agent, Sakic had signed an offer sheet with the New York Rangers in 1997, but the Avalanche matched it. (The Avalanche and Nuggets' CEO at the time, Charlie Lyons, a former assistant in the office of New York Governor Nelson Rockefeller, sent a framed photo of Rockefeller's famous giving-the-finger to 1968 Democratic National Convention protestors in Chicago as a gift to Rangers GM Neil Smith.) Otherwise, Sakic was the rare NHL player whose own name rarely came up in trade rumors. But it still happened. Occasionally over the years, a reporter from the Vancouver papers would openly speculate that the British Columbian native was about to "come home" to finish his career as a Canuck. Never mind that, for the past ten years or so of his career, Sakic had a no-trade clause and had no intention of even thinking of waiving it.

That still wouldn't stop the NHL rumor mill, which was more like the turbines of a working jet engine. For some reason, rumors in hockey reliably create frenzies among the fans, no matter how trivial or far-fetched. Websites that deal in rumor often outpace those of serious-minded newspapers in traffic. One of them, "Hockeybuzz," has accuracy statistics that the National Enquirer *would belittle and laugh at, but that doesn't prevent it from getting millions of monthly hits and considerable, um, buzz.*

The theory of why goes something like this: Because there is so much less media coverage of hockey in the United States, especially among talking-head TV pundits on "Shout as Loud as You Can" panel "debate" programs, hockey fans salivate over any scrap of information that dribbles their way. When a rumor is tossed out there, no matter how silly, hockey fans can't help but go, "Hey, did you hear what Crazyrumors.com just said? Think there's anything to it?" And other reporters and I have to decide whether acknowledging or debunking the rumors only contributes to a ridiculous process.

Case in point: In early December, Hockeybuzz.com reported "something major" was likely to go down between the Avalanche and Montreal Canadiens. What could it be? Was P. K. Subban coming to the Avs for Paul Stastny? Was Nathan MacKinnon on the block?

Turned out, nothing was going down, just as nothing ever did 99.99 percent of the time after titillating hockey rumors surfaced.

Another mid-December website story had Sakic feverishly "scouring the league" for a defenseman, with "all options on the table" to get what he wanted.

"You just roll your eyes after a while," Sakic said. "I mean, you're always wanting to get better if you can, and, yeah, trades happen sometimes. But almost everything you read is garbage when it comes to rumors. I guess you just throw enough spaghetti at the ceiling and hope something sticks."

TUESDAY, DECEMBER 17, AT DALLAS: STARS 3, AVALANCHE 2. RECORD: 22–10–1

Here's how rumors get started . . . or pick up steam.

The loss to the Stars seemed to illustrate why Sakic might need to do *something* about his defense. Whereas Jan Hejda and Erik Johnson formed a reliable 1-2 pairing, numbers 3 through 6 were often shaky. One of the team's more pleasant surprises early on, Guenin, found himself in street clothes for the second game of the Stars-Avalanche back-to-back, a victim of the dreaded "healthy scratch" decision by coach Roy.

Sakic and Roy had a dilemma: Should they try to make a big deal or two for needed help on defense, maybe shipping out Stastny and his expiring contract? Or, should they just look at the season as playing with house money, keep things as they were and hope to get lucky in the playoffs—and get some reinforcements the following season through their own system (e.g., prospects Chris Bigras and Duncan Siemens) and perhaps a free-agent signing or two?

It figured to be a damned-if-they-did, damned-if-they-didn't proposition for Sakic and Roy. If it really was a "Let's shock the world" and "Why not us?" motto for their team in 2013–14, why not roll the dice on a potentially game-changing trade and a long playoff run? Recent NHL history was full of lower-seeded, supposed Cinderella teams making long runs and even winning a Cup or two, such as eighth-seeded Los Angeles in 2012.

On the other hand, history was also full of teams that foolishly gambled their long-term future to make an unsuccessful run at the Cup. The Avs had suffered through too many recent poor seasons and accumulated too many good young assets through the draft to start giving any of it away now on a likely pipe dream of a Cup in 2014.

But Stastny's contract status created a difficult decision for Sakic and Roy. Either he had to be signed to an extension by the following season, or he had to be traded by March 5 to get some value in return.

In Dallas, Stastny and linemates P. A. Parenteau and Gabriel Landeskog were blanked, and that helped rule out any chance of the Avalanche sweeping the two-night series. Colorado at least did get its first power play goal in four weeks, when Matt Duchene scored the game's first goal. Eventually, the Stars got the game-winning, tie-breaking goal on Jean-Sebastien Giguere with 2:52 left in regulation.

Stastny's personal situation in a way mirrored the choice facing Sakic and Roy as the season wore on. Was this team really legit and worth being patient with, or did some big changes still need to be made?

As Sakic rode the elevator back down to the American Airlines Arena floor and quietly walked to the Avs' dressing room alone following the tough loss to Dallas, that very question seemed to be looming in a thought bubble over his head.

FROM THE NOTEBOOK OF TERRY FREI

Patrick Roy had been a Steve Moore teammate for eight games in 2001–02 and four more in 2002–03, when Moore was called up from Hershey. Roy was in his first season of retirement when Moore seemed to have secured a roster spot in the league during 2003–04 . . . before he suffered fractured neck vertebrae, a concussion, and cuts in the notorious attack by the Canucks' Todd Bertuzzi on March 8, 2004. I had visited Moore in the Toronto area in March 2005, a year after the incident, and even at that point, he was under orders from his attorney, Tim Danson, not to talk about the specifics of the Bertuzzi attack because of pending legal action in Ontario.

In late 2013, Moore still was living in the Toronto area, where he was raised before graduating from Harvard with a degree in environmental sciences and public policy. His much-delayed lawsuit against Bertuzzi still was pending, at that point scheduled to go to trial in September 2014.

Moore on December 18 broke his lawyer-mandated silence to speak with me and a couple of other reporters—Bob Duff of the Windsor Star *(where Steve was born) and Mark Spector of Sportsnet.ca—and unveiled the Steve Moore Foundation to be a clearinghouse and source of information about athletes' head injuries.*

He told us that after the Bertuzzi incident, "I spent the following five years after the injury trying to recover, to return to my NHL career, which basically consisted of me going around to see any and every doctor I could find that I thought was a leader in this area and who might be able to help me. After about five years of doing that, I was told I had made remarkable progress, but I still won't be medically cleared to return to play. That was a very difficult time for me. I spent my whole life, from the time I was two and a half years old, dreaming of playing in the NHL. Despite being off for that long, it still was very difficult for me to accept. At the same time, I didn't want those experiences over those few years to go to waste. It was very important for me to do something to help the players that were actually continuing to get injured, not in the same way, but have injuries that could benefit from my experiences over those years. Pretty much, those experiences were happening on an almost nightly basis, amongst my colleagues, not just in the NHL, but also in professional sports. At every level of sports, those things were happening. With the support of many of those leading doctors, I began work on the foundation at about that time."

When I asked whether he had contact with the Avalanche, Moore said: *"I obviously think fondly of my time with the Avalanche, and I obviously feel very connected to the people of Denver and the state of Colorado, who have been incredibly supportive of me, obviously from the moment the incident happened, even through today. I feel a special connection to those people and to the team. At the same time, I haven't had much contact with the team, and I do look forward to, if they feel it's appropriate for them, I would obviously love to have them be a part of the foundation. However they feel comfortable."*

My story prompted considerable reaction from Colorado readers, who again demonstrated that their memory about Moore was longer than that of the Avalanche organization. To be fair, it was obvious that the NHL wouldn't have been thrilled with the Avalanche doing something along the lines of holding a Steve Moore Night among its Alumni Nights, but it also would have been the right thing to do.

At another point during that conference call, Moore was asked if the game had become too fast to be able to expect players to make instant decisions about avoiding contact that could lead to concussions.

"I do think that's an important question," Moore said. *"It's something that a lot of people who haven't played the game at that speed don't realize, that things happen so quickly. It's not like you're making like a calculated decision in most instances. You're reacting . . . The speed of the game has increased significantly over the years for a variety of reasons, so it's something that needs to be taken into consideration; whether we make rule changes, or equipment changes, or all these things, that's certainly a major factor. At times, the speed of the game does require that players are not going to be able to perhaps understand the effects of a body check they're making in a split second."*

Moore didn't even know it, but there was some irony to that question and response in this sense: Brad Malone, the Avalanche forward who

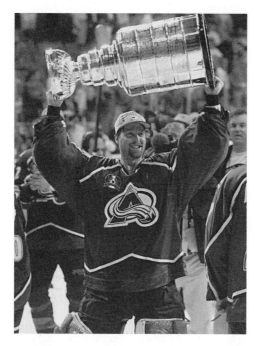

Patrick Roy's third Stanley Cup championship as a player came in 1996 with the Avalanche. He had just stopped all 63 shots he faced from the Florida Panthers in Game 4 as Colorado completed the four-game sweep with a 1–0 victory in triple overtime. AP Photo/Hans Deryk

As a player, Patrick Roy was known as the best "money"—or clutch game—goaltender of all time. Here, he celebrates another win with teammate Peter Forsberg, destined to become a fellow Hall of Famer. Jerry Mellman

When the Avalanche elevated Joe Sakic to the top of the hockey front-office hierarchy, they were hoping for a repeat of this scene. Here, Sakic, the Avalanche captain, hoists the Stanley Cup in front of celebrating multitudes at the Denver Civic Center in 2001. Ray Bourque and coach Bob Hartley flank him. Jerry Mellman

At the May 2013 news conference, Patrick Roy was introduced as the Avalanche's new coach by team president Josh Kroenke and executive vice president of hockey operations Joe Sakic. AP Photo/Brennan Linsley

Patrick Roy behind the Avalanche bench. Jerry Mellman

Patrick Roy directs winger Cody McLeod at a March practice in Montreal. AP
Photo/The Canadian Press, Paul Chiasson

Patrick Roy had tried to land Nathan MacKinnon for the Quebec Remparts when
MacKinnon was only 15. By the time MacKinnon was 18, he was skating as an
electrifying NHL rookie for the Roy-coached Avalanche. Jerry Mellman

Matt Duchene cried when the Avalanche lost and screamed at the top of his lungs when the Avalanche won. That was when he was a kid in Ontario. As an "adult" Avalanche star, he handled the ups and downs more professionally. (That's his story, and we'll allow him to stick to it.) Jerry Mellman

Swede Gabriel Landeskog was only 19 when he became the Avalanche captain, serving so eloquently as their locker room spokesman in his second language, most listening forgot—or never even realized—he wasn't raised in North America. After thinking it through, Patrick Roy decided to leave the "C" on Landeskog's chest in 2013–14. Jerry Mellman

Even as a youngster in Russia, Semyon Varlamov revered Patrick Roy. Here, Varlamov is in the crease for the Roy-coached Avalanche against the Minnesota Wild as his top defenseman, Minnesota-born Erik Johnson (6), tends to business behind the net. Jerry Mellman

Avalanche center Paul Stastny is the son of a Hall of Famer who played for Czechoslovakia against the Americans' Miracle on Ice team before defecting in the final days of the Cold War. Paul was born in Canada and played for the United States in Olympic competition, including in 2014. Jerry Mellman

Patrick Roy had the nerve to move Ryan O'Reilly, the Avalanche's crafty young center, to left wing. And it worked better than anyone could have imagined. Jerry Mellman

was recalled from Lake Erie on November 18, was involved in that sort of hit on University of Denver center Jesse Martin in October 2010, when Malone was playing for North Dakota. Colorado already had drafted Malone in the fourth round of the 2007 draft, and the Atlanta Thrashers had selected Martin in the seventh round in 2006.

As Martin tried to collect the puck in the game at Grand Forks, Malone hit him, leading with his right elbow. His right shoulder hit the side of Martin's head. In the immediate aftermath, Martin was diagnosed as having fractured vertebrae, and because of the pressure on the spine and other issues, the trauma briefly was considered potentially fatal. Even if Martin survived, the fear was that he would be paralyzed. Airlifted to the Twin Cities area, Martin soon was out of danger in a Minneapolis hospital, and at one point was scheduled to undergo surgery to fuse C-1 and C-2 vertebrae, which would have left him with limited neck movement. Conferring with other doctors, the Martin family made the decision to have him moved to a St. Paul hospital. The surgery there instead involved aligning the vertebrae fractures and installing a screw. That surgery was successful, but Jesse was through playing hockey. His road back to normal was long and arduous, but he managed to obtain his DU degree in 2011 and returned home to Edmonton, where he began a job at a local bank in November 2011. He continued to suffer effects from the concussion, and never was going to recover a full range of motion or be 100 percent physically. Mike Chambers and I collaborated on a series of stories chronicling Jesse's injury and recovery that the Denver Post *nominated for the Pulitzer Prize.*

That's included here not to pick on Malone, but to note that his hit on Martin—unnecessary but obviously not calculated to injure—was more typical of the dangers in the sport than Bertuzzi's attack on Moore.

With the Avalanche, Malone played 22 games in the 2011–12 and 2012–13 seasons while spending most of the time with Lake Erie. After his November recall this time, Malone played five games while Jamie McGinn was out with a knee injury, then became a nightly healthy scratch and extra body. On a two-way contract, he was making $735,000 on a prorated basis when in the NHL. It was obvious, though, that he had earned Roy's trust as a player at least capable of short-term tenancy on the NHL roster in times of injuries.

THURSDAY, DECEMBER 19, AT DENVER: AVALANCHE 4, OILERS 2. RECORD: 23–10–1

The Oilers again were struggling, but they had young number one over-all draft choices Ryan Nugent-Hopkins and Taylor Hall on the roster. "I think both teams have a great future," Roy said after the win at home. "There's no doubt in my mind. Both teams—we just need to learn to be more mature and learn, getting experience."

The Avalanche recovered from the beat-down at Edmonton two weeks earlier, and the Pepsi Center crowd was treated to a good show—and a preview of coming attractions in the league. Hall and Nugent-Hopkins had the Edmonton goals, and Ryan O'Reilly and Matt Duchene (empty-netter) were among the Colorado scorers. Duchene also had the second assist on O'Reilly's goal, which came on a nice tic-tac-toe passing play that started when he slid the puck to Nathan Mac-Kinnon. "In the past, I think he would have tried to do everything on his own," Roy said. "There, he passed the puck to MacKinnon, and it ended up on the stick of O'Reilly on the other side. I think Matt's playing really well offensively and defensively, and that's the thing I like about his game. You can have players who play really well offensively, but if they aren't capable of playing good defensively, it hurts their game. And I think right now Dutchy is playing well in both zones."

The message was getting across.

DISMISSED, BUT NOT FORGOTTEN

Semyon Varlamov got good news the next day. At the request of the district attorney's office, a judge dismissed the sole remaining charge—misdemeanor assault—against him. Prosecutors said their investigation convinced them they wouldn't be able to prove the case beyond a reasonable doubt. Most significantly, the spokeswoman for the DA's office also acknowledged that stories from the principals changed during the process. Finally, media reports sufficiently acknowledged that the woman who acted as an interpreter for Evgeniya Vavrinyuk during her news conference also was a key witness in the case and the fiancée of Vavrinyuk's lawyer.

※ ※ ※

On the Avalanche's chartered flight to Los Angeles, the boys settled in for their regular card game: Texas hold 'em.

The most popular player in the game was a "mark" so willing that teammates suspected he considered it part of morale building. That was Matt Duchene. One teammate—who shall go nameless—labels him "the worst card player I've ever seen in my life."

When allowed to make the musical selections anywhere, Duchene's country music tastes drove everyone crazy. He was an unabashed fan of just about every major country act. At the card table, though, his theme song might have best been sung by Kenny Rogers: "You got to know when to hold 'em, know when to fold 'em."

Jean-Sebastien Giguere was hot and cold, but he was coveted as a member of the game because of his deep pockets.

If there was a first star of the poker game, it tended to be Cody McLeod. P. A. Parenteau wasn't bad either, and neither was Jamie McGinn.

After landing, the team headed for the hotel. There, the barbed humor among teammates tended to come from Parenteau, Patrick Bordeleau, Max Talbot, Gabriel Landeskog, and—surprise—Semyon Varlamov. Especially as his English improved, the goaltender was finding imaginative ways to use it.

SATURDAY, DECEMBER 21, AT LOS ANGELES: KINGS 3, AVALANCHE 2 (SO). RECORD: 23–10–2
MONDAY, DECEMBER 23, AT SAN JOSE: SHARKS 5, AVALANCHE 4 (SO). RECORD: 23–10–3

The Avalanche suddenly had lost their last three shootouts, and although that wasn't particularly alarming—as long as the trend didn't continue—it was a lost opportunity to pile up points in intra-conference play. At Los Angeles, the Avalanche recovered from a 2–0 deficit on goals from Erik Johnson and Ryan O'Reilly, but they couldn't get anything past Kings goalie Martin Jones in the shootout, and Anze Kopitar's one success on Varlamov was enough for the Kings.

After the game, Varlamov made his first public comment about the dropping of the charges against him.

"You know what? I'm excited for sure. The process is over," Varlamov said. "Like I've said before, I'm glad to be here today and just want to say thank you to my teammates, the ownership, the GM, and the Avalanche fans for supporting me."

Said Patrick Roy: "From the first day this thing came out, he had the support of his teammates. Now it's behind us. Now let's focus and play hockey."

Two days later, as the Avalanche were preparing to meet San Jose, Vavrinyuk signaled that she wouldn't quietly accept the dropping of the charges. Through a Colorado media consultant, she issued a statement saying she was "saddened" by the D.A.'s decision, and that she had severed ties with her original attorney in the case. The statement added:

"As I told police, I was badly beaten by Semyon in the early morning hours of October 29th and very scared, but decided that I had to report it as he had been abusive throughout our relationship and would not change. I left the residence that we shared with only my personal items, $10 in my pocket, and nowhere to live. I was very much vulnerable, alone and confused in a foreign country where I don't speak the language or have any family or support system. While Semyon continued to play hockey, his fans and his employer, the Colorado Avalanche, rallied to his support. Meanwhile, many people made derogatory remarks about me, and several people profited from my dire circumstances, including those whom I unfortunately trusted."

The drama was continuing.

At San Jose, in the climax to a wild and entertaining game, Nathan MacKinnon and Matt Duchene couldn't beat the Sharks' Antti Niemi on Colorado's two shootout attempts, and the Avalanche didn't get a third shot because Logan Couture and Patrick Marleau scored against Varlamov to clinch the win. Here's how wild regulation had been: Colorado trailed 3–2 going into the final two minutes, got goals from Johnson and Jamie McGinn 12 seconds apart, but then had to go to overtime because, with the San Jose net empty, Joe Pavelski scored for the Sharks with 20 seconds left in regulation.

FROM THE NOTEBOOK OF ADRIAN DATER

Predictably, the Varlamov legal issues caused some tension between Roy and me. He let me know during his postgame interview in San Jose—on the air—that he wasn't happy that I wrote a newspaper blog that afternoon, essentially getting the statement released in Vavrinyuk's name out there for the public to read. In my mind, it was responsible, nonjudgmental reporting of something newsworthy and following our pattern of dutifully passing along everything anyone connected to the case had said. I wrote the blog on my iPhone at a Chipotle on Santa Clara Street after the Avalanche morning skate, and it was simply a cut-and-paste job of the statement. I didn't think anything more of it after clicking "publish," and dived into my chicken burrito with gusto.

As I was walking to the arena for the game a few hours later, Varlamov's agent, Paul Theofanous, with whom I've had a cordial working relationship for years, texted me to let me know he thought I was out of line to post Vavrinyuk's statement. I was a bit surprised. I had thought Theofanous would understand my professional obligations. I thought: Wait a minute; all I did was what I thought any journalist would do. You cover a story, and when there's some sort of resolution of verdict, as when charges are dropped, you get the winner's side and then you get the loser's side. You're endorsing nothing. For me, that final blog was going to be the last time I ever wrote the woman's name, or so I thought.

Could I understand the Varlamov camp not liking the fact that essentially all of Vavrinyuk's accusations were aired one last time, after the case was dismissed? Could I understand Theofanous wanting to protect his client? Yes, on both. But when you watch People's Court, don't you always hear from the loser on the way out even after the judge rendered a verdict? Don't you, in fact, hear that after most any public court case?

The more I thought about it, I realized that although I disagreed with his opinion, I should just accept his right to have his say, too, and forget it.

After the game, though, Roy let me know he shared Theofanous's opinion, and he did so when I asked a fairly routine question about his reaction to the shootout loss. On TV, he got in his dig on me about Varlamov not being happy "about that blog you wrote today."

As Roy walked back to the visiting coach's office, I walked after him and said, "Patrick, would you like to talk more about that blog?"

He said no.

Well, he said it differently than that, but this was a coach who had just suffered a tough loss, and like Theofanous, believed he was standing up for Varlamov.

I had covered Roy the player for eight years. One thing I always knew about Roy was that while he doesn't forget a slight and usually finds a way to get even somehow, he also usually won't hold a grudge too long in media dealings. Usually, you have your argument with him, and it's over the next day.

Being the type that also cannot forget a slight, always wanting either to even the score or at least resolve it, I texted Roy from my hotel room the next morning before heading home to Denver for Christmas.

I pointed out to him that a blog a couple weeks prior about Vavrinyuk, about her asking for payment for any interview the press wanted with her, was considered very damaging to her case by a couple people I knew in law enforcement—and certainly by the public. So, if I had always been out to get Varlamov, well, that blog wouldn't seem to support that theory much.

Although Roy reiterated that he thought the blog was unnecessary because the case had been closed already, the heat from the previous night was long gone. Roy even signed off with this text: "I wish you a merry Christmas!"

That's hockey for you: swearing and hairy eyeballs one night, Christmas greetings the next.

❈ ❈ ❈

The NHL's television contracts aren't nearly as lucrative as those of the NBA, and basketball is quite willing to do the bidding of the networks and pack Christmas with games from morning to night.

Hockey does it differently, and it does it right. The collective bargaining agreement dictates that the league is completely shut down after games on December 23, and teams can't reconvene until the morning of December 27, with games resuming that night. So the Avalanche went their separate ways for the Christmas break, which also meant in many cases that families traveled to Denver.

FRIDAY, DECEMBER 27, AT CHICAGO: BLACKHAWKS 7, AVALANCHE 2. RECORD: 23–11–3

After the three-day holiday break, the Avalanche convened at the Denver airport, took the chartered flight to Chicago, went to a hotel for a nap, then went to the United Center for the game—and, predictably, got waxed. Patrick Sharp had a hat trick, and Jonathan Toews had two goals for the defending Stanley Cup champions. Jean-Sebastien Giguere gave up all seven goals before Varlamov took over for the third period.

"We didn't have our 'A' game and when we don't have that, we're going to come up short against a team like this," Roy said.

Giguere gave up the seven goals on only 24 shots. Nobody was stupid enough to blame him for this one. The defense was horrible in front of him, and Johnson and Jan Hejda had an off night. Yet the whispers were beginning in the organization. Because of the team's success and Varlamov's strong work on most nights as the regular, it was a bit under the radar that Giguere hadn't been nearly as good in his occasional work in recent weeks as in his first four starts of the season, when he allowed only three goals. The concerns were that after the Olympic break, the Avalanche would play 24 games in 47 nights, and Varlamov—almost certainly ticketed to play for Russia in the Olympics, too—likely would need considerable backup help during the stretch that would determine if Colorado made the playoffs. Despite some ridiculous media overreaction and talk early in the season that Giguere had earned consideration for the number one job, it was obvious that at the very least, physically he wasn't up to playing that much.

For the first time, there were doubts about Giguere.

* * *

The Olympic selections for various countries were due to be announced during the Avalanche's seven-game home stand. Colorado was likely to have at least four, possibly as many as six players heading to Sochi. So after it was noted that Roy played in the first Olympics with full NHL participation during an in-season league shutdown, the Avalanche coach was asked at the morning skate before the December 29 Winnipeg game if he wanted as many representatives off his roster as possible, or if he had mixed feelings.

Once again, Roy demonstrated his thoughtfulness and premeditation, and his artfulness in finding a way to make a point he wanted to make.

"It depends," Roy said. "It probably has changed a lot since I retired. It's a lot different than it was. In my years, if I was there, I was happy; if I was not there, I was happy. Now the players want to be part of it. It seems to me that the players have a lot of pride to play in that. On my side, it was tough for me to be at a high level at that time of the year [for the Olympics] and then do it again at playoff time. That's my only question. Can you get two highs in the same season? Maybe yes, maybe no. I don't know."

The backstory there was that after Roy and Joe Sakic played for Canada in those '98 Games, the Avalanche blew the 3–1 lead in the first round of the playoffs against Edmonton and lost the series.

Clearly, Roy's message to his Olympic players was—and was going to be—to remember not to leave everything under the Olympic flame.

SUNDAY, DECEMBER 29, AT DENVER: JETS 2, AVALANCHE 1 (OT). RECORD: 23–11–4

Suddenly, the Avalanche had lost four straight, but they had gotten points in three of the four. This time, Winnipeg's Blake Wheeler scored with 1.5 seconds left in overtime to end it.

P. A. Parenteau got tangled up with a Jet in the neutral zone in the second period, crashed to the ice, and needed to be helped to the dressing room. After the game, Roy said Parenteau would undergo an MRI the next day and he would know more then.

Briefly lost in the wild finish was that the Jets' Dustin Byfuglien gave Varlamov two short shoves/punches to the mask right after the goal was scored, and as he skated away, Varlamov took a swing in his direction with his stick that didn't connect. Although video was passed around quickly on social media, most comments would have to wait until the next day. Nathan MacKinnon had his ninth goal for the Avalanche.

"I'm very happy in some ways because we had 19 [consecutive] games against our conference," Roy said. "We finished it with nine wins, six losses, and four overtime and shootout losses. In my opinion, it was a tough stretch and an important one, and I thought we did a good job. We picked up 22 points."

After the Avalanche practice the next afternoon, Roy said the news about Parenteau wasn't as bad as feared. He had suffered a sprained medial collateral ligament and would be out about six weeks. Because that would take him right up to the Olympic break, in theory he would have another two weeks to recover and conceivably could be back in the lineup when NHL games resumed in late February.

"We haven't been hit too much by injuries," Roy said. "From my standpoint, we've been more lucky than anything else."

By then, Roy had seen footage of the Byfuglien swipes at Varlamov and the goalie's stick swing in response.

"For me, it's classless, but I am not going to make a big story of this," Roy said. "It was unnecessary. I don't think he had to do that. At the same time, it's positive. It starts to show that Varly gets under other teams' skins. They knew they had to go under him if they wanted to win the game. The more Varly is going to play like this, the more you're going to see an incident like that, which is great in some ways."

Roy said that as a player, opponents had reacted that way to him "many, many times. I loved it. I loved it. That means you're under their skin. They're mad at you. You're a problem to them. Hey, Varly is a problem to them right now. He should be flattered. If nobody touches you, it's because you're not doing much on the ice. Even the same thing for a forward. When a forward starts scoring, what the coach does is send an instigator after him, give a glove in the face or go after the whistle and try to get you off your game. It's the next step. Varly is playing so well, teams are going to try to get in his face a little bit more. I love it."

TUESDAY, DECEMBER 31, AT DENVER: AVALANCHE 5, BLUE JACKETS 3. RECORD: 24–11–4

The power-play problems were over, at least for the time being. The Avalanche rallied from a 1–0 deficit and was three-for-three with the manpower advantage against the Blue Jackets. Ryan O'Reilly's power-play goal late in the second period broke a 2–2 tie and put Colorado ahead for good.

The Avalanche were outshot, 38–23, with Varlamov having another good night. "We didn't have our legs at the start of the game," Roy said. "We didn't have the start we expected. But the quality teams find ways to win hockey games, and that's what we did."

As he was about to step away from the podium, Roy closed with: "Before leaving, I would like to wish a Happy New Year to all our fans."

He was always thinking.

SELECTED AND SNUBBED

The U.S. Olympic team selections were unveiled after the Maple Leafs-Red Wings Outdoor Classic game on New Year's Day in Ann Arbor.

Only one of the two Avalanche veterans of the 2010 team was picked.

Going in, Paul Stastny was a longer shot to make the team than Erik Johnson, due to the abundance of American talent at center and his lackluster play for stretches of the 2013–14 season as team GM David Poile, the highly respected GM of the Nashville Predators, and others involved with the Olympic team watched.

Stastny made the team.

Johnson didn't.

The choices on defense made it clear that the team management was determined to begin a new era in the national program at the position with younger, smaller, and generally more mobile players. Johnson wasn't the only veteran of the 2010 Games spurned. Jack Johnson of Columbus, Erik's frequent defensive partner in international play, didn't make the team, either. The other glaring omission on the blue line was Phoenix's Keith Yandle. What added to the disappointment for Erik Johnson was that one of the choices was Kevin Shattenkirk, the former Colorado first-round pick who went to St. Louis with Chris Stewart in the deal for Johnson.

"I didn't expect to make it at the beginning of the year," Johnson said. "But how well I've played these last three months, I was back in the mix. So that's probably the hardest part, knowing that I couldn't have done any more as far as my play to make it. You know, I played fantastic these first three months, so it's disappointing, but my focus is on this team now. I'll use that two-week break to recharge and get ready for the playoffs."

Patrick Roy wouldn't admit it publicly, but he didn't mind that Johnson was omitted. Unless he was added as an injury replacement, Johnson would get that chance to recharge both physically and mentally for the stretch run and then perhaps the playoffs.

THURSDAY, JANUARY 2, AT DENVER: AVALANCHE 2, FLYERS 1. RECORD: 25–11–4

In his 29-save night, one of the several Flyers that Semyon Varlamov robbed was Steve Downie, his former teammate, with a pad save on a second period power play. "Downie almost got me with the backhand," said. "He has great skill. I was lucky on that one."

Ryan O'Reilly and Jamie McGinn had the Avalanche goals.

FROM THE NOTEBOOK OF TERRY FREI

The Avalanche, of course, weren't operating in a Colorado professional sports vacuum. As the rarity who had covered all four major-league sports as a beat writer and columnist, I long had been aware of hockey's unique status. In late 2013, I was writing and talking about the Avalanche, Nuggets, and Broncos (and more) in my work at the paper; and also as a radio cohost on weekends and in spot duty during the week. I often caught myself shaking my head about how relatively underplayed the hockey team's remarkable turnaround was in the Denver media.

Now, don't get me wrong; the Avalanche weren't ignored, and were getting more coverage than in a typical early season in recent years because of the success and the presence of the celebrity head coach. Since the team's arrival in Denver nearly 20 years earlier, the Denver Post *had given many Avalanche stories significant play. But there were times, especially early in the season when editors' preferences for not just the Broncos, but also the Nuggets and the NBA, seemed obvious* issues in the decisions. Plus, there especially was a void in commentary on the Avalanche. So I used many of my commentary slots to attempt to fill it—as I did with other off-the-beaten-track sports subjects on the Colorado scene (i.e., anything other than the Broncos).

We fully realized that the way it worked, the bandwagon and the press box both would get crowded after the end of the Bronco season, especially if the Avalanche made the playoffs and the Nuggets didn't. We also knew some of us would have to point out to our compatriots which guy was Jan Hejda.

Roy did a weekly show on Denver's 104.3FM, The Fan Morning Show, with Mike Evans, Vic Lombardi, and Nate Lundy, and got considerable exposure there. But even on sports talk radio—and, yes, I was part of it—the ratings-driven strategy was all Broncos all the time. My belief remained that it became a self-fulfilling prophecy, with discerning sports fans who appreciated an across-the-spectrum approach tuning out when they heard the 723rd discussion of the week about Peyton Manning's proficiency passing in cold weather. After nearly 20 years of the Avalanche's presence in Denver, with two Stanley Cup championships and even after 11 years of alleged sellouts, I had come to accept and understand the hockey team's second-tier status in town among the mass general sports fan constituency . . . and members of the media.

By the New Year, the Avalanche were half of an almost bizarre transformation of the Kroenkes' franchises.

With Josh Kroenke as team president, the hockey team was winning considerable praise in the Colorado market, and nationally and internationally, showing that decisive moves and a perfect storm of circumstances—young players maturing, better coaching, sharper vision in the front office—could lead to a stunning turnaround in the NHL.

With Josh Kroenke as team president, the basketball Nuggets were imploding and crumbling. This, after a 57-win season that earned George Karl coach of the year honors but wasn't enough to save his job after the Golden State Warriors ousted the Nuggets in the first round of the playoffs. General manager Masai Ujiri, the NBA's executive of the year, who felt unappreciated after protracted negotiations on a new contract, bailed to go to the Toronto Raptors. The Nuggets hired Tim Connelly—the epitome of the young, earnest, new-wave basketball man who bought into "analytics" as more appropriate than the eye test— from the New Orleans front office to replace Ujiri; and brought in Brian

Shaw—the former journeyman guard and longtime NBA assistant coach—to replace Karl. The message was that Karl's coaching was fool's gold, leading to regular-season success with a style of game that wasn't suited for the tighter postseason, where the half-court game was more important. Yes, the Nuggets were going to take a step or two back in the regular season to nurture young talent and develop the kind of game and collective personality more appropriate for the playoffs!

Yet, in the first days of 2014, the Nuggets were 14–17, mired in an eight-game losing streak and booed off the floor at home, where they had lost only three times the previous season under Karl. They had significant injuries, most notably to enigmatic center JaVale McGee and forward Danilo Gallinari, but that didn't explain it all.

Even worse, veteran guard Andre Miller—not known as a malcontent—hollered at Shaw during a time-out of the January 1 home-court loss to the awful Philadelphia 76ers. Miller had figured out he was destined for the first DNP-CD (Did Not Play-Coach's Decision) of his Denver stay, ending a long iron-man streak (a streak Shaw later admitted he wasn't aware of), and wasn't happy about it. The argument carried over to the dressing room, but it wasn't only Miller involved in the heated discussions between players and coaches. A full-fledged revolt seemed possible. Initially, Miller was suspended without pay for two games, but that had to be rescinded—in the wake of protests from his agent and also likely feedback from the league and players' union. Instead, he was told to just stay away from the team. The day after the incident, the Nuggets held individual meetings with players, again trying to close ranks. Miller sat out and continued to collect on his $5-million annual salary, and the Nuggets looked ridiculous. The weird part, though, was that the fixation on the Broncos led to a surprising lack of critical examination of the Nuggets' follies from the mainstream media theoretically expected to stay in touch with the entire Colorado sports scene.

The Kroenke operation had spun 180 degrees on its axis in Denver.

Suddenly, Josh Kroenke was doing a masterful job of directing the Avalanche and getting considerable praise from the hockey-first constituency—the same folks who for years had accused him and his father of being inept, uncaring, and even cheap on the hockey side of the operation.

*Suddenly, Josh Kroene was doing an inept job of directing the Nug-
gets and getting considerable criticism from the basketball-first constituency—the same folks who for years had generally conceded that the
Kroenkes, as former basketball players themselves, at least were committed to putting a winning team on the floor.*

*The Broncos had finished the regular season 13–3, won the AFC
West and the home-field advantage through the AFC playoffs, and
needed only two home wins to advance to the Super Bowl.*

SATURDAY, JANUARY 4, AT DENVER: AVALANCHE 4, SHARKS 3. RECORD: 26–11–4

The Avalanche reached the halfway point of the season on a 112-point
pace, a stunning start on an amazing turnaround. They almost let this
one get away, taking a 4–0 lead, largely on the strength of Nathan
MacKinnon's first two-goal game, and then hanging on.

After the fourth goal, San Jose's Andrew Desjardins speared the
Avalanche's John Mitchell in what amounted to a "cup check" at the
next face-off, and Colorado was upset that the move wasn't penalized.
"We kind of lost our focus for a bit," Roy said. "But it's a team concept
here. Everybody is pushing hard; everybody wants to make the playoffs.
The way we're playing in this stretch, we're giving ourselves a chance
right now. There's a long way to go, and the second half will be another
good challenge for us. But I'm very happy with our team."

MacKinnon took the NHL rookie scoring lead with his big game.
"[Pucks] are starting to go in a little more than they did at the beginning
of the year, which is nice," he said. "I'm a little bit more relaxed. Hopefully, it continues. It's night and day since the beginning of the year; I
feel a lot more comfortable out there."

Among the eye-popping aspects of the turnaround was that at the
halfway point, the Avalanche already had 17 points more than they had
in the entire 48-game previous season.

Roy was getting much of the credit, of course.

"The coaching staff that I have, we're having fun, and they do a
tremendous job," he said. "And I'm really happy with how the players
have respected the teaching that we've been doing, how they've been
willing to try things that we've been bringing up. I've said all along that

I was there to be their partner, and I just feel that I have a great partnership with the players.

"I think that's the one thing that I'm probably most proud of. I didn't know what to expect, but when I looked at our roster, I thought we had a really good team. I'm not here to talk about what happened in the past, but the first day we got on the ice I saw how receptive the guys were and how hard they were ready to work, and I thought it could be a good mix between them and the coaching staff."

MONDAY, JANUARY 6, AT DENVER: FLAMES 4, AVALANCHE 3. RECORD: 26–12–4

Bob Hartley's Flames came in with only one goal in their previous four games, yet they managed the four goals in the victory over Jean-Sebastien Giguere and the Avalanche, who wasted another two-goal night from MacKinnon. None of that thrilled Roy, but then he also got wind of what Giguere had said in a live postgame interview on the Avalanche's Altitude network.

Giguere said the Flames "are a team that prides themselves on working hard, and sometimes hard work will beat you, because if you are not willing to match their intensity, you know it's going to cause a surprise. Tonight I think they were maybe, they were a little hungrier in front of the net, both nets. They were hungrier, you know. They got some, some would say lucky bounces, but they created those bounces by going to the net, by creating traffic, and that's how you score a goal in this game, in this league. I'm not sure we were willing to do that in front of their net."

A few minutes later, when he met with the media, Roy went off on Giguere. It started out fairly innocently. "I thought tonight that was a game that should finish 2–1 for us," Roy said. "We shouldn't have given up more than one goal tonight here." Discussing the Flames' second-period goals, he said, "They just put pucks at the net, and they went through. I mean, to me, they were not dangerous shots. I think Jiggy should have played better tonight. We're not going to look at our team. We might not have had the jump that we should have, but Jiggy needed to be better. He hasn't played well in the last four or five games, and he should stand up and say, 'I'm not playing up to what I should.' He did not. He needs to be better, and we need to have him playing better, period."

What most missed in all of this was that this hadn't come out of nowhere. It was the result of building concern about Giguere's capability as a Varlamov backup.

Plus, as a rookie NHL head coach, Roy was as much, or more, about being a former major junior coach, but in this instance he definitely was responding as a former NHL goaltender. Whether the Avalanche had played well around the net was almost beside the point. Roy, the goalie, sometimes could be guilty of denial about letting in soft goals or not playing well in general. Yet the one thing he did was generally bite his tongue when his teammates had let him down. That doesn't mean the discerning couldn't infer that he was steamed at his defensemen, or anyone else. He would be terse, clipped, mad. But you had to read between the lines. In general, he didn't try to transfer the blame for his bad games. There were nights when he seemed to say every goal had been a fluke or the product of a bad bounce, and not his fault, but he never said his team was soft around him. That's what Giguere seemed to be saying, and it bothered Roy that he said it.

Also indicative of the way the night went, Ryan O'Reilly suffered a shoulder injury—in the group celebration of one of the Avalanche goals.

❁ ❁ ❁

The next day at practice, Roy didn't retract those comments about Giguere—but he wouldn't be drawn into amplifying on them. He said, "My job after a game is to analyze games to our fans, and you know me, I'll always be truthful in my comments, and that's all I have to say."

Giguere, meanwhile, said he hadn't read or even heard of the comments. (The good, old *I don't read the newspaper* gambit . . .) "At the end of the day, I have not been playing my best," he acknowledged. "My job isn't that difficult to assess. I've got to go in there, give [Semyon Varlamov] a rest, and make it so they want to play me again. In goaltending, I firmly believe you make your own luck by working hard at practice and having a good attitude, and it's up to me to maybe up my practice level to the level that it should be, so when I do get to play, I'm sharper. It's hard, with the schedule this year, to get a lot of practice and get some momentum, but you've got to take what you get and make the best out of it."

There was other news to steer the conversations away from the potential controversy. That day, the official word came that three more Avalanche players were headed to Sochi—Matt Duchene with Canada, Gabriel Landeskog with Sweden, and Varlamov with Russia.

Duchene was the most giddy, talking about getting up early to watch the 1998 Canadian team's games in Nagano live, and wearing his Joe Sakic 2002 Olympic jersey once a week to school. "Other than getting drafted by the Avalanche, I think it's the biggest accomplishment in my career, and it feels awesome," he said. "I feel honored and humbled to be picked for that hockey team."

Duchene said he had taken his dog outside that morning, and when he came back in his house, he discovered he had missed a call from a Boston number. He hoped it was Bruins' GM Peter Chiarelli, part of the Team Canada staff. "I called back, and he gave me the good news," Duchene said.

Given his own youthful fascination with his nation's previous Olympic teams, it seemed a good guess that Duchene would grasp the tremendous pressure the 2014 team would be under. "I'm excited for that," he said. "It's daunting, it's little bit scary, but I have a month and a little bit to get ready."

After Varlamov's eventful first half of the season—on and off the ice—his expected selection was a relief. "Believe me, I was nervous," he said. "You never know until they say you're going or you're not going. There's always lots of questions. Right now, I read in the Russian news that I'm going to the Olympics." He laughed and added, "That's how I found out this morning." He even added that he hoped it wasn't a hoax.

The Swedes had done it a little differently. Landeskog admitted that he had gotten word of his selection from a member of the Sweden coaching staff about a week earlier, but he had been told to keep it quiet.

The trash-talking started.

"I told Varly I'm coming high glove on him, and we'll see if he bites," Landeskog said.

For his part, Roy repeated his message, publicly saying he congratulated the players chosen, but reminded them of their day jobs, so to speak.

Jan Hejda wasn't selected for the Czech Republic team, mainly because he hadn't even tried to hide his contempt for the national team coach. So the Avalanche's top defensive pairing—both considered likely choices at the start of the season to represent their countries in Sochi—were shut out of Olympics participation. Again, given that testing post-Olympic schedule, deep down Roy probably didn't mind that.

WEDNESDAY, JANUARY 8, AT DENVER: AVALANCHE 4, SENATORS 3 (OT). RECORD: 27–12–4

Tyson Barrie had been productive since his mid-November recall from Lake Erie. He seemed both more assertive and comfortable by the New Year, and against the Senators, he had an assist on Paul Stastny's game-tying goal with 2:20 left in regulation and scored the goal that ended the game in overtime. Four-on-four, with its open ice, was made for him.

"I know they've been wanting to see a little more out of me in that area, the offensive stuff, and that's my game," Barrie said. "In the third there, when we were down a goal, I just kind of said, 'I'm going for it.'"

THOSE DARNED RINGS

Former Blackhawks star turned NBC studio analyst Jeremy Roenick was at the Avalanche practice facility the next morning, taping segments for future broadcasts. That summoned memories of his famous verbal jousting with Patrick Roy during Colorado's best-ever playoff series—the 1996 Western Conference semifinals, which the Avalanche won in six games but easily could have lost if they hadn't pulled out Game 4 in overtime in Chicago to even the series. The catch there? Veteran referee Andy Van Hellemond swallowed his whistle and didn't call anything on Sandis Ozolinsh for hauling down Roenick from behind in overtime. At the very least, it should have been a minor for tripping or, more appropriately, led to a penalty shot being awarded to Roenick. Roy subsequently said he would have stopped the shot anyway; Roenick countered that he had scored on Roy in Game 3 and asked where Roy was then. "Probably getting his jock out of the rafters of the United Center," Roenick said. The next day in Denver, Roy came back with: "I can't hear Jeremy because I've got my two Stanley Cup rings plugging my ears."

Nearly eighteen years later, Roy was asked if, with two more rings to use as earplugs, he heard anything Roenick said during the visit. Roy laughed and said, "I had the other two rings in my mouth. I couldn't say anything to him."

FRIDAY, JANUARY 10, AT DENVER: ISLANDERS 2, AVALANCHE 1 (OT). RECORD: 27–12–5

Nathan MacKinnon had the only Colorado goal, getting to 15 for the season, but Michael Grabner's overtime score for the Islanders prevented the Avalanche from closing out the seven-game home stand with two points for a win. Roy said he was satisfied with getting ten points of the possible 14 on the seven-game home stand, and it was reasonable to argue that it was good enough to cement the Avalanche's status as a likely playoff team.

SATURDAY, JANUARY 11, AT ST. PAUL: AVALANCHE 4, WILD 2. RECORD: 28–12–5

Ryan O'Reilly returned to the lineup in style, scoring twice for the Avalanche—and being careful of his shoulder in the celebrations. It also was an important victory, given Colorado's hope to stay ahead of the Wild for the third and final guaranteed playoff spot out of the Central Division, and given that the Avalanche had traveled after playing the night before—often an itinerary for disaster. O'Reilly's second goal broke a 2–2 tie with 7:16 left, when he took a pass from Matt Duchene and went top shelf from a tough angle against Niklas Backstrom.

O'Reilly had 16 goals for the season, tying him with Duchene for the team lead. After the Avalanche had signed Duchene and Gabe Landeskog to extensions in the offseason, the fact that O'Reilly's and Semyon Varlamov's contracts were going to expire after the season seemed glaring. Wasn't it time to get them locked up, too? With Varlamov's agent, Paul Theofanous, hanging around Denver a lot, the assumption was that he was not only shepherding the goalie through his legal issues, he was talking with the Avalanche about a new deal. But nothing was going on with O'Reilly.

FROM THE NOTEBOOK OF ADRIAN DATER

If there was one story that made me feel paranoid as a reporter later on, it was the 2013 O'Reilly saga. When O'Reilly still was unsigned after the lockout ended on January 6, he went to the Kontinental Hockey League to play with his brother, Cal. O'Reilly's relationship with Colorado management became so bad that his agents, Pat Morris and Mark Guy of Ontario's Newport Sports—a high-powered firm started by longtime agent Don Meehan—strongly indicated that if the Avs didn't sign him or trade him, O'Reilly might just play in Russia for the next three years, then become an unrestricted free agent in the NHL.

Although the Avs would later claim they wanted O'Reilly back all along, the truth is there were no talks between the team and O'Reilly's when, out of the blue, the Flames swooped in with that two-year, $10-million offer sheet, which the Avalanche matched.

The story was a nightmare to cover, and as the calendar flipped into January 2014, I started thinking more about O'Reilly's contract status again. Under terms of the offer sheet, the Avs couldn't trade O'Reilly for one calendar year, which would be February 28.

After O'Reilly's two-goal game against the Wild, I started playing GM and wrote a blog saying the Avs should re-sign him to an extension as soon as possible, that trading him or letting things drag on again into next year would be, well, stupid.

Two days later, after the Avalanche practice at Johnny's Ice House on Chicago's Madison Street, near the United Center, I got the hairy eyeball from Roy.

"Are you his agent? Are you getting a cut of his next deal?," Roy sniped at me in passing, on the way to the team bus. "We should just sign him to a 25-year contract, yes?"

OK, so he didn't like the blog.

Neither did Joe Sakic, when I reached him on the cell phone later that night.

"Why are you trying to stir things up?," Sakic asked, more than a little irritated.

Well, I said, because the year before, the O'Reilly contract situation was partially responsible for the season being a disaster.

"Last year was last year," Sakic shot back, becoming even more irritated. "Things are good. And while I wouldn't normally say this, but since you just MUST know, we've agreed to play out the year and talk in the summer. You're making something out of nothing and calling us stupid!"

Hmm. When it came from the temperamental Roy, I wasn't much fazed by his sarcasm in his reaction to the blog. With this coming from the more even-tempered Mr. Classy Sakic, I started rethinking things.

Maybe I was guilty of putting the cart before the horse, to borrow a favored hockey cliché. O'Reilly could simply be retained by a qualifying offer in July if he went that far still unsigned. Only if the Avs decided to trade him was there any realistic way he wouldn't still be with the team for two more years because of his age and experience.

I told Sakic that the following day's paper—in which I expanded on the blog with a look at O'Reilly's great night in Minnesota and touched on the contract stuff again—would be the last I wrote of the contract until July.

I don't think he believed me at all, but Sakic parted on good terms with me on the phone as I walked from dinner at the Drake Hotel (classy, elegant, historic, and expensive) to the Marriott Residence Inn on Dearborn Street ($74 a night AND free breakfast).

Sports writers have budgets to keep in mind, too.

❈ ❈ ❈

On the flight from the Twin Cities to Chicago, much of the teasing focused on what kind of bill the Avalanche players were going to run up for poor Nathan MacKinnon and the other first-year NHL players at the annual "rookie" dinner. By then, his teammates still thought of MacKinnon as both a "kid" and a proven teammate. They were aware of the bushels of fan mail the team was receiving for him, plenty from teenaged girls hoping to command his attention. And they knew he was handling the fame well, though not being a choirboy, either. Giguere's house rule, especially because he and his wife had three young children, was that MacKinnon wasn't allowed to have overnight female guests.

The boys came hungry. At the team dinner on January 13 in Chicago, MacKinnon's share was just short of $5,000.

"He got off light," said one veteran Avalanche player. "My day, it was triple that, easy."

These kids nowadays . . .

TUESDAY, JANUARY 14, AT CHICAGO: AVALANCHE 3, BLACKHAWKS 2 (OT). RECORD: 29–12–5

Blown out less than three weeks earlier in the same building, the Avalanche knocked off the defending Stanley Cup champions when Tyson Barrie's second goal of the game—yes, with 50.7 seconds left in overtime, his specialty—ended things. Notably, the young defenseman who hadn't scored a goal for Colorado until December 16 suddenly had five and seemed to have earned Roy's trust.

O'Reilly had the other goal. But the big star—and the first star—was Varlamov, who had 46 saves. Perhaps as significant, the Avalanche were shorthanded because Paul Stastny was scratched with a leg injury; and then defenseman Cory Sarich, listed in the lineup, couldn't play because of a back issue. Finally, then Erik Johnson wrenched his back when knocked into the boards in the second period and couldn't play in the third. So Colorado finished the game with only 16 skaters.

"We were missing some players against a very good team, so I knew I had to play well," Varlamov said.

It didn't come into play, but Jean-Sebastien Giguere was fighting back pain, and Sami Aittokallio was recalled from Lake Erie to back up Varlamov for the night.

✿ ✿ ✿

Twice in the next four weeks, the Avalanche were going to play the team that had been the opposition in the biggest single professional sports game ever played in Denver. The team was the New Jersey Devils, and the game was Game 7 of the 2001 Stanley Cup finals. There were a couple of side stories to spice it up: for one, older hockey fans in Colorado still remembered that the Devils were the infamous Colorado Rockies from 1976 to 1982, before the move to New Jersey.

And Martin Brodeur, who had been in the Devils' net in 2001 and eight years later broke Roy's record for career wins, still was playing at age 41. His father had been the Canadiens' team photographer during Roy's days with Montreal; Brodeur idolized Roy then, but there had been tension between the two when they became NHL goaltending contemporaries. Nothing scandalous was involved, unless you count Brodeur's wife's alleged comment during the 2001 Cup finals. Rather,

Roy's competitiveness was the major culprit, including when they both were on the 1998 Canadian Olympic team, and Roy played every game; and in 2002, when one of several reasons Roy withdrew from Olympic team consideration was that he didn't like the idea of sharing time with Brodeur or—even worse—backing him up. Although Roy publicly handled Brodeur's breaking of his record with class, it still wasn't something he celebrated.

❂ ❂ ❂

Brodeur was sharing time in the Devils' net with Cory Schneider, and he played in what was generally considered his likely final game in his Montreal hometown the same night the Avalanche won in Chicago. The Devils won 4–1, and Brodeur had 29 saves. It seemed unlikely that he would play in Denver, but that didn't prevent Roy from being asked about Brodeur, both on the day before and the day of the game. The biggest contrast was that Roy had retired at age 37, after having two terrific statistical seasons, whereas Brodeur still was playing at 41. It also was interesting that he mentioned Brodeur's relationship with the Devils' president and general manager, which made it reasonable to wonder if he were hinting of deterioration in his relationship with Pierre Lacroix at the tail end of his own career.

"I admire what he does," Roy said of Brodeur. "It's amazing what he's been doing. I could appreciate what he's going through. The relation he has with Lou Lamoriello seems to me to be very special. There's a lot of respect between those two men. He's been loyal to this team, and this team has been loyal to him, and I think that's what carrying him on right now. He has played some great games. Last night in Montreal, he had to play well, and he played a really good game, whether it's his last game in Montreal or not, that's up to him to decide. But it's amazing what he's been doing. He's been a great goalie in our league, one of the best without a doubt."

Could Roy imagine still playing at 41?

"No, it was different," he said. "My personality is a lot different than his. I'm not saying Marty's not taking the game seriously. He has a better approach probably than I had. After a loss, I took it tough. I took it almost personal. Marty takes it more like, hey, let's go back tomorrow, and I think that helps to have a longer career, without a doubt. It's amazing what he does."

That raised eyebrows in this sense: As a coach, Roy had preached—and his players had loved—the idea of short memories and turning the page after bad nights or losses. It was pointed out that if Roy's portrayal of Brodeur was correct, Roy the coach was more like Brodeur the player.

"Maybe I am, but inside, I always want to win," he said. "Winning is not everything; it's the only thing. It matters to me, but at the same time, I understand our players are coming in and working hard, and that's the thing that we control."

Roy characterized his relationship with Brodeur as "more respect than anything else. I never hung out with Marty in the offseason or things like this."

Asked again why he had been comfortable with retiring so "soon," Roy noted he tentatively had decided long before the end of the 2002–03 season. "I called Ray Bourque one night and I said, 'Ray, when do we know it's over?' He said, 'Don't worry, you'll know.' Even if Marty's ready to retire, he's not going to say it because he's the same way I was. He doesn't want to say it because sometimes you finish the year and you think maybe I have one more year under my belt, my tank is not empty. Mine was. I was ready to move on."

When he mentioned the empty tank, was he talking mentally or physically?

"In my case, I think it was more mentally than physically, because I think physically I could have played more," he said.

At that point, too, Roy had known he had the Remparts waiting, and he was coaching them within two years, beginning the path that brought him back to Denver.

Roy had a casual conversation with Brodeur at the Colorado morning skate when the Devils' goalie came out to the visiting bench, and Roy came over. They knew the meeting wouldn't go unnoticed—cell phone pictures quickly were posted—but it was completely cordial.

THURSDAY, JANUARY 16, AT DENVER: AVALANCHE 2, DEVILS 1 (SO). RECORD: 30–12–5

As expected, Brodeur didn't play, and Ryan O'Reilly had the Avalanche's only goal on Schneider and then one of the successes in the shootout. Varlamov again was terrific, and he was becoming exasperated about being asked to discuss his play and specific saves.

"Ask Patrick Roy," he said. "I don't want to talk about myself playing bad or good. Ask Patrick. You're always asking me about this save, that save. Ask Patrick about my game. Don't ask me."

Varlamov did smile when asked if he was getting to like shootouts. "Not really," he said. "There are so many pressures on the goalies, I'd like to win games without shootouts."

The most interesting thing about Roy's postgame comments was his willingness to bring up that he was second-guessing himself for using a lineup with only 11 forwards and alternately double-shifting one of his top forwards to center the fourth line with Brad Malone and Patrick Bordeleau. The results were mixed, because Malone and Bordeleau were on for both regulation goals. Bordeleau even set up O'Reilly for the Avalanche score on a nice pass from behind the goal line—an area not exactly known as his office.

"That could be a reason we gave up a little more shots and we didn't play as well defensively, because I overplayed some of our guys," Roy said. "But at the same time, I was comfortable. I thought in the first period, that line played well, whoever I was putting with them, they did a good job, and I was very pleased with their effort. They protected the puck well. Unfortunately for them, they gave up that goal [that] tied the game at 1–1."

That was a sign, too, that Roy didn't want anyone to get too carried away with portraying the fourth line guys as the heroes of the game.

SATURDAY, JANUARY 18, AT NASHVILLE: AVALANCHE 5, PREDATORS 4. RECORD: 31–12–5

Defenseman Nick Holden had two goals as the Avalanche won in Nashville for the first time in five years. The Avalanche led 3–0 and 5–1, and then hung on.

The next day, P. A. Parenteau, who had been expected to be out until at least early February, passed all the conditioning and other tests, including a "bag" skate, and was deemed recovered from his knee injury and able to return to the lineup against Toronto. After being the Avalanche's leading goal scorer the previous season, with 18 in the 48-game schedule, he still was trying to completely win over his new coach, whose attitude about Parenteau seemed to fluctuate. Also, Alex Tanguay was getting close to being able to play again after being out of the lineup since early November. Their returns certainly would help.

FORWARDS

NO. 15, P. A. PARENTEAU, 6'0", 193 LBS., BORN MARCH 24, 1983, HULL, QUEBEC

What's a guy got to do?

It's one of the common refrains among longtime minor-league players . . . in any sport that has minor leagues. Whether it is delusion—yes, even stone-handed second basemen with career minor-league batting averages of .231 think they should have reached the majors by now—or justified by performance, athletes tend to think that all they need is a chance, and only a conspiracy has denied them that chance. It happens a lot in hockey, where especially undersized or just so-so skaters among the minor-league forwards can cleverly put up impressive numbers but have them shrugged off as irrelevant because they won't translate to the NHL.

Parenteau's three seasons of major junior with three different teams in the QMJHL came while Patrick Roy still was with the Avalanche. By 2009, the native of Hull, Quebec, adjacent to and across the provincial border from Ottawa, was 25 years old and in his seventh year in a minor-league career spent mostly in the AHL, with a brief stop with Augusta of the East Coast Hockey League (ECHL). Yes, *that* Augusta. He could have checked out the golf course where the Masters is played annually. He racked up 166 goals in the AHL, waiting for his first real chance. He played five games with the Blackhawks in the 2006–07 season but didn't have a goal and wasn't able to stick. He passed through the Anaheim and Chicago organizations, then went to the Rangers, but his 63 goals in the 2007–08 and 2008–09 seasons with Hartford in the AHL didn't earn him a ticket to the NHL, either.

What's a guy got to do?

"I always enjoyed the game," Parenteau said. "Even my years in the AHL, I was always loving the game, and that was a big part of keeping going. It was a long and tough road, but I always enjoyed playing, even if it was three-on-three on a Sunday afternoon. I always enjoyed being on the ice and scoring goals."

He got a better shot late in the 2009–10 season with the Rangers following his call-up from Hartford.

"Obviously, especially toward the end, I couldn't do anything more in the AHL than I was doing, and I was not getting the call from the Rangers," Parenteau recalled. "So I was kind of getting down, and I even thought about Europe a few times; but I knew I had my place in this league. I knew it all along, and all I needed was one shot, and a really good one. [Coaches John] Tortorella and Jim Schoenfeld gave it to me with the Rangers, and I never really looked back."

Those 22 games with the Blueshirts convinced the Islanders to sign him as an unrestricted free agent in July 2010 and install him in an NHL lineup—for good.

"It should have happened sooner," Parenteau said in a tone that didn't come close to bitterness. "I'm going to be honest with you: I needed three or four years in the AHL. I was all offense. I didn't know how to play in my own end. I never had to play in my own end in the 'Q' or when I was younger. I learned the game, I learned it a tough way, and now I'm a better player for it. But I think maybe one year in Hartford would have been enough. I played almost three, so it was a little longer than I wanted, a little longer than it should have been, I think, but like I said, it's a matter of timing, and at least I got my shot."

He had 38 goals in his two seasons with the Islanders and then hit unrestricted free agency again.

"I have mixed feelings about the Islanders," he said. "I really think they should have extended me when I was there. But maybe they didn't have the money at the time. I'm really grateful for the chance they gave me. Jack Capuano, the head coach there, always believed in me. I played against him in the minors for a long time, and he knew what I was all about. As soon as he got the job, he put me on the first line, so that's the guy who changed my life and changed my career, and I'll always remember that."

He hit the free-agent market again in July 2012—and the Avalanche called.

"Right away, Joe Sakic called me," Parenteau said. (And this was still when Sakic technically was below Greg Sherman on the organization chart.) "He was the first guy, at 12:01, it was the first team, the first everything . . . and the best offer. I could sense they really wanted me."

The deal—$16 million over four years—seemed a risk for a winger who had spent much of his career in the minors. But he played well enough in the otherwise awful lockout season to make the commitment seem justified.

"I wake up in the morning and I'm, like, I'm a full-time NHLer and a pretty good one now, too," he said. "I'm enjoying it every second now. I paid my dues, maybe a little longer than I should have—six and a half years in the minors is a long time—but I stuck with it and knew what I was capable of. Now it's paying off and making it even sweeter now that I waited so long. It's just a tough league to crack with all the young guys. If you're not a first pick or a second-round pick, it's going to take you a long time. You're going to have to pay your dues. If I'm the poster guy for determination or for keeping going, for believing in yourself, so be it. If I had a message to send to all those guys, it's, 'Keep going. If you think you've got your place, keep going until they tell you, you don't.'"

After living alone downtown during his first season with the Avalanche, Parenteau moved his girlfriend, Elsa, to Denver, and they were living in the house they rented from Detroit defenseman Kyle Quincey, who had kept his home in Denver after leaving the Avalanche. In the summer of 2013, Elsa gave birth to a son, Gabriel, and she had a four-year-old daughter whom Parenteau considered his stepdaughter.

NO. 40, ALEX TANGUAY, 6'1", 194 LBS., BORN NOVEMBER 21, 1979, STE-JUSTINE, QUEBEC

In conjunction with the world-famous Quebec Pee Wee tournament, a young Tanguay and his team were selected to be on the ice with the Nordiques at the end of a practice. He and his teammates got to take penalty shots on Quebec goalie Ron Hextall and then play in a five-minute "game" against the Nordiques with Hextall as their goalie, and their goalie playing for the NHL team.

Alex found himself lined up to take a face-off against his idol—Joe Sakic.

"Joe just put the face-off through my legs and went around to score on Ronnie Hextall," Tanguay recalled with a laugh. "I knew he was good, but he didn't have to show me up!"

A few years later, Tanguay became a Sakic teammate with the Avalanche after he was the first of Colorado's four first-round draft choices in 1998, all gathered with the hope of somehow landing the top overall choice and claiming center Vincent Lecavalier. But Tampa Bay ended up with the top choice and wouldn't trade it, not even for a Colorado package featuring the multiple first-round picks. Because his agent—whom Tanguay soon fired—didn't come to terms with the Avalanche by the deadline, Tanguay played one more season with the Halifax Mooseheads before joining Colorado for the 1999–2000 season.

The pinnacle of Tanguay's first Colorado stay was the two-goal effort in Game 7 of the 2001 finals, and he had six solid seasons with the Avalanche, but he never reached the star level. His 29 goals in 2005–06 were his career high, and he was traded to Calgary after the season. That began a nomadic existence for Tanguay, who went from the Flames, to Tampa Bay, to Montreal, and back to Calgary for three seasons before the guy who stole the face-off from him traded for him and brought him back to Colorado, inheriting a contract that ran through 2015–16.

"I still feel like I have some very good years ahead of me," he said.

Tanguay was familiar with his surroundings and was even a familiar face to the Colorado media and hockey community, but it was jarring to realize that the last time through, he'd been the "kid."

"I kind of grew up in this city and became more of an adult," Tanguay said. "My wife [Helene] is from Quebec, and she lived here with me the last year I was here. Now we come back with three kids and we run around with them. It's certainly not the same lifestyle. She has family here, so that's helped the transition for her that way. For me, it's like coming home. I was a kid when I came here, and getting the nice car here, the first apartment, you get to earn some money for the first time."

Yes, he lived in Roy's basement for two seasons, when Roy's three children were young and could be playmates on computer games. Now, his guardian, so to speak, was his coach.

"I still see the fire in him, that will to win," Tanguay said. "I don't think that will ever go away from him. You watch him play, and you watch him coach, and he still wants to get the same thing accomplished at the end of the night. There's been a big learning curve for him, and he took his time in junior and learned the right way. He's been great, he's been a great influence on our team—the positiveness, and the way they've been preparing strategies and finding solutions to help our team through periods has been great. It's something that has been uplifting for all of us in here and fun to see. Because it's a different game from junior, I'm sure he's still finding sometimes where he's not set in his ways yet in the NHL, but it's been fun for me to see the player become the coach."

Tanguay's return had its ups and downs, primarily involving the knee and hip injuries. But in late January, he was about to return to the lineup, and he hoped his injury woes were behind him.

NO. 11, JAMIE MCGINN, 6'1", 210 LBS., BORN AUGUST 5, 1988, FERGUS, ONTARIO

Although Fergus has a population of only about 19,000, it's wrong to say McGinn was a small-town boy.

His family lived in the country, outside of the town that's about 20 miles north of Guelph.

"I played in Fergus for only one year and then in Guelph for one year," McGinn said. For the next eight years, his father, Bob, routinely drove him 70 miles to Toronto, where Jamie played in the Greater Toronto Hockey League programs. "We had to do a lot of traveling because of where we were located," McGinn said. "It was a tough decision at a young age, but I had to go where the compete level was a little higher and the players were a little better. I wanted to give myself a better chance of going on. We had a Dodge Caravan that had over 600,000 kilometers on it and had four transmissions or something like that. My dad was very proud that he kept it on the road."

Eventually, McGinn joined major junior's Ottawa 67s, then was San Jose's second-round draft pick in 2006. For his first three pro seasons, he split time between the AHL and the Sharks, but he had stuck with San Jose and had 12 goals in 61 games in February 2012 when he came to Colorado in a trade. The Avalanche got McGinn and two prospects for Daniel Winnik and T. J. Galiardi. Given more ice time, he came through with eight goals in 17 games for Colorado and delivered the sort of physical play the Avalanche sought.

"I'd never been traded before, so it was kind of a shock at the time," he said. "It was a great opportunity for me to play more and show I'm ready to make the jump into a higher role. Coming here, it was something special; I could see in the locker room that we were going to have a good team in the future."

In the lockout year, he had 11 goals; and from the moment Roy took the coaching job, he seemed ticketed for a significant role, as evidenced by the original plan to have McGinn on one of MacKinnon's wings on a third line. That evolved over the season, including with McGinn on one of the top two lines.

During the 2013–14 season, his younger brother, Tye, 23, who also played in the Toronto minor hockey programs for several years, was with the Flyers' AHL affiliate. Brock, 20, was playing major junior for the Guelph Storm of the Ontario Hockey League (OHL). Jamie laughed, and said his dad finally got sick of all the driving, and Brock had to make do with playing his minor hockey in Guelph before ending up with the Storm.

Jamie still was only 25 during the 2013–14 season, but depending on when the tally was taken, as many as ten players on the Colorado roster could be younger than he was.

"I feel like I act like a young guy," he said with a laugh.

NO. 7, JOHN MITCHELL, 6'1", 204 LBS., BORN JANUARY 22, 1985, OAKVILLE, ONTARIO

His teammates joked that Mitchell was the Swiss Army knife of the Avalanche—complimenting him as the versatile forward who could be plugged in virtually anywhere, from the fourth line to the first line. As the inevitable injuries struck the Avalanche, Mitchell was the guy moving around to compensate. Much of the season, he was centering the line with Max Talbot and McGinn, but that was far from written in stone.

"You always want to play a big part in any winning team, but at the same time you have to not overstep your boundaries and limits and do the little things," he said. "I know I'm not going to be a guy to go out there and score 40 goals or be on the power play every night, but I can come in and hopefully step in any situation when needed, and I'm fine with that."

Another example that the collaborative decision-making process during Greg Sherman's tenure at the top of the hockey hierarchy led to some savvy moves, Mitchell's value in the utility role validated his 2012 free-agent signing. After his OHL career with Plymouth, he spent three full seasons with the Toronto Marlies of the AHL without getting a call-up. Although he finally cracked the NHL and had played 222 games with the Maple Leafs and Rangers, he still was considered a fringe NHL player at the time of the signing after playing on the fourth line during New York's run to the Eastern Conference finals. And during the Avalanche recovery season, he was struggling to score, but still was an important cog. Cerebral by nature, he was the team's player representative and occasionally threw around three-dollar words or phrases such as, "In conjunction with our first period, we . . ." He was sometimes the subject of ire on fan message boards, where was called "Johnny Malkin" for his tendency to hold on to the puck for long stretches. But, over time, he became a key and well-respected member of the locker room.

"I wouldn't say I'm pinching myself, because I know we have a good team here, a really good squad here," he said. "We have a great bunch of guys, and we have a lot of character guys. It's a young group, too, and we have a lot of guys who have played 200 or 300 games, and they're still in their early 20s. I think that goes a long way. I think the coaching staff has done a good job at giving us the right systems every day, feeding us the right information on scouting and things like that. That certainly helps. This is only my second year here, but there are other guys who have been here a few years together, and that helps. They've got that chemistry now, and you see that, and it's contagious. Then everybody can join in, and there are no outcasts."

ON THE BLOCK

TUESDAY, JANUARY 21, AT DENVER: MAPLE LEAFS 5, AVALANCHE 2. RECORD: 31–13–5

With P. A. Parenteau playing only 12 minutes as Patrick Roy showed signs of working him back in gradually after his knee injury, the Avalanche had one of their worst games of the season. But it wasn't much noticed in the wake of the Broncos' Sunday victory over New England in the AFC championship game and Denver's imminent trip to New Jersey for the Super Bowl matchup against the Seattle Seahawks. One of the biggest cheers of the night came when Broncos starting offensive tackle Orlando Franklin, born in Jamaica and raised in Toronto, was shown on the huge scoreboard screens. It wasn't noted that Franklin, briefly a hockey winger himself in his youth, was a diehard Maple Leafs fan. After the game, he sheepishly explained that he was an Avalanche fan "on any other night."

Roy again was philosophical, even about a subpar game from Varlamov, who was yanked in the second period after giving up the first three goals. "There are nights like this as a goalie," Roy said. "Pucks find their way in. I think Varly was just a bit tired. I almost took him out after the first period. I didn't see in him the same energy he has showed since the start of the year. I let him battle through, and when he gave up that third goal, I said there's no need to push that."

FRIDAY, JANUARY 24, AT SUNRISE, FLORIDA: AVALANCHE 3, PANTHERS 2. RECORD: 32–13–5 SATURDAY, JANUARY 25, AT TAMPA: LIGHTNING 5, AVALANCHE 2. RECORD: 32–14–5

After missing 36 games with the knee and hip injuries, Alex Tanguay finally was back in the lineup against the Panthers, reunited on a line with Paul Stastny and Gabriel Landeskog. Roy declared going in that Tanguay would play Friday but not the next night against Tampa Bay. The returns led to Brad Malone's demotion to Lake Erie.

At Sunrise, Colorado was ahead 3–0 after two periods—on goals by Ryan O'Reilly, Stastny, and Jamie McGinn—and held on to beat the Panthers. The Avalanche improved to 28–0–2 in games when they led after two periods, but that didn't completely mollify Roy. "I thought that was a great test for us in some ways, because we were up by three goals, and we knew they were going to put pressure on us," he said. "I thought it was a good opportunity for us to play a strong third period in our own end, and it wasn't the case. But we were outstanding in the first two periods."

After the game, Jean-Sebastien Giguere—scheduled to play the next night at Tampa—walked out of the visitors' dressing room in Sunrise with his right hip area bandaged up. For the second time in the month, "Jiggy" was ailing.

Prior to the 2011–12 season, Giguere had surgery on his groin; and after a summer of rehab, said he felt better than he had in years. For most of the next two seasons with the Avalanche, Giguere had no health problems, and his play turned back the clock. No, not to his best days with Anaheim, but at least enough to make it clear he wasn't washed up and could at least be a competent backup, perhaps more if necessary.

But, in January, something started going wrong for Giguere again. The team said it was his back. Sami Aittokallio was recalled from Lake Erie for the game in Chicago, but after being available for a few games again, Giguere was back on the shelf.

Asked as he left the Sunrise dressing room if he was all right, Giguere responded, "Yep."

But the next day, about 180 miles north up Alligator Alley in Tampa, Giguere was too sore to make his scheduled start against the Lightning.

With Varlamov having played the night before and without much rest of late, Roy decided to give the start to the resummoned Aittokallio.

Drafted 107th overall by the Avs in 2010, Aittokallio hailed from the city of Tampere, nicknamed the "Manchester of Finland" for its industrial history. Aittokallio wasn't the first Avalanche player to have come from Tampere, however. Fan favorite Ville Nieminen, a member of Colorado's 2001 Cup team, came from there, as did other NHLers Jyrki Lumme, Teppo Numminen, and Vesa Toskala.

Aittokallio joined the Avalanche late the night before, but got in some rest during the day before facing the Lightning.

It was a mighty strange sight to see Aittokallio in the net. Varlamov and Giguere had started all but one game in their two-plus seasons together with the Avalanche. The only exception was Aittokallio's spot start late in the 2013 season at Los Angeles.

Just as in that game in Los Angeles, Aittokallio would not, ahem, Finnish it. The big Finn stopped all 11 shots he faced in the first period, but by the end of the second period, Tampa Bay had three goals, and Aittokallio had a seat on the bench and wore a baseball cap.

Aittokallio gave up three goals on seven shots. A bad period, sure, but it was still just a 3–2 game entering the third. Maybe the kid could atone with a great third period and another Avalanche win? He never got the chance. Roy pulled him, putting Varlamov back in, feeling the team's best chance for a comeback win would be with him in net. It made sense logically, but Varlamov would allow two late goals to rookie Tyler Johnson in the 5–2 loss.

Aittokallio couldn't hide his disappointment.

"Yeah, I wanted to finish," he said. "But I've got to be better. This lets me know how much I still have to do."

Sometimes, it's not the number of goals against. It can just be one really bad goal that shakes everyone's confidence around a team, and for Aittokallio that goal was Tampa Bay's second, by light-scoring defenseman Mark Barberio. Sure, the kid got a bad bounce when Barberio's shot deflected off the leg of Patrick Bordeleau. But there was still plenty of time and space for Aittokallio to readjust to the shot and stop it. Instead, it squirmed in under his right armpit. It was the type of goal where the netminder will just look up at the sky, wondering how this could have happened.

The goal was still on Aittokallio's mind well after the game as he forlornly ripped off tape and other equipment and stuffed it into a big red bag labeled "Lake Erie Monsters." Aittokallio seemed to know— even though he hadn't been told yet—that he'd blown a good chance to impress Roy and would soon be back in Lake Erie.

"I've got to stop that," Aittokallio said a couple of times quietly, his mind still clearly on that bad goal.

Aittokallio might not even have understood that at the time, Roy was disillusioned with Giguere, and not only because of his nagging injury. If the Finn had done well, Colorado might have found a way to keep him around longer. It could have been something along the lines of, "Hey, Jiggy, rest up a while . . . no hurry." Or, maybe, more than that.

Sure enough, by the next game, Aittokallio was back with the Monsters, and Giguere felt good enough to be back on the bench.

FROM THE NOTEBOOK OF ADRIAN DATER

The Avalanche moved on to Dallas, and on the day of the game against the Stars, the rumors started again. Louis Jean of Montreal's TVA Sports reported that the Avalanche had offered P. A. Parenteau to the Canadiens for winger Rene Bourque. That was hard for me to believe. He also noted that the Canadiens had turned it down, which was even harder for me to believe. It seemed unlikely that the Avalanche would offer their leading goal scorer from the previous season, the one playing under a four-year, $16-million free-agent contract, to Montreal for Bourque, considered one of the NHL's most underachieving players of the previous two or three years. That said, Louis Jean was a respected member of the Canadian hockey media. I started making calls.

Parenteau's agent, Allan Walsh, was incredulous. He immediately called the story "bogus." (Later, through my own sources, I would learn that Jean's original report had plenty of truth to it.) But Walsh was also upset at the Avalanche.

That's because on the day of the Montreal rumors, Roy told Parenteau he would be a healthy scratch that night against the Stars. That often happens in the NHL when a player is on the verge of being traded, and the team involved is trying to avoid having a deal scuttled by an injury.

A good agent stands up for his clients, and Walsh built up a solid clientele with fierce advocacy on their behalf, sometimes even on Twitter. During the 2012–13 lockout, @walsha became one of the more outspoken and entertaining Twitter accounts.

Walsh held his tongue publicly over Parenteau's benching, but he wasn't happy. Neither was Parenteau. He had worked his way back from the knee injury far earlier than expected, and now he was in street clothes as a healthy scratch in Dallas. His first three games back hadn't been impressive, but wasn't this overreaction—whether or not it was tied to a trade?

Parenteau didn't whine. Though not happy, he took the benching—it would turn out to be short-lived, but mainly because of injuries—professionally.

Once a player's name is in trade rumors, though, it usually stays in them until the trading deadline passes.

Parenteau had reason to wonder: would he still be with the Avalanche beyond March 5?

MONDAY, JANUARY 27, AT DALLAS: AVALANCHE 4, STARS 3. RECORD: 33–14–5

Yes, the Stars got three goals, but Varlamov made 41 saves. "They kind of threw the kitchen sink at us at the end," said Matt Duchene. "Varly was great for us again."

Parenteau, indeed, was a healthy scratch as Tanguay was back in the lineup. Roy portrayed it as a means of not pushing Parenteau too hard, too soon in his return from the knee injury and brought up Tanguay's situation. "We [will] have three games in four nights," Roy said. "It's a demanding schedule, so we'll do the same thing with P. A. that we did with Alex."

Duchene, still on a bit of a high as he looked forward to the Olympics, again was slumping for the Avalanche—at least in goal scoring. He assisted on Jamie McGinn's goal against the Stars, but he had had only one goal in the past 18 games. "I'm just trying to not let it get me down, and not be on that emotional roller coaster," Duchene said. "But it's crazy. I think I've hit more goalposts than I have in the last two years in this stretch. I keep getting hooked, but I'm not getting penalty shots or anything. But I've just got to keep working, and eventually it'll go in. But other guys are scoring, so just give them the puck."

❁ ❁ ❁

Back in Denver the next day, Roy said he wouldn't change the lineup for the upcoming home game against Minnesota, meaning Parenteau would sit out again. He also tried to defuse any tensions, saying, "P. A. is a good player, he's playing hard for us, and I'm sure he's going to help us in the near future." But he also made it clear he was thrilled to have Tanguay back. "He brings something so important to this team," Roy said. "When he's playing with Paulie and Landy, I want to say we're 14–1, and that speaks a lot for itself. It's always good to have a guy like Alex, who won a Stanley Cup with us, and I think he brings a lot of very good leadership to this team."

THURSDAY, JANUARY 30, AT DENVER: AVALANCHE 5, WILD 4. RECORD: 34–14–5

Things just kept getting better for Semyon Varlamov. During the day, the Avalanche announced that he had signed a five-year, $29.5-million contract extension to kick in the next season and tie him up through 2018–19. It was the result of negotiating mostly between agent Paul Theofanous and GM Greg Sherman, who still was handling the contract work for the Avalanche in the wake of Joe Sakic's elevation to the top position in the hockey operation. The trade for Varlamov and signing him to the original three-year Colorado deal was a risk for Sherman, and it seemed to have been vindicated.

Varlamov didn't have one of his better games that night against the Wild, but it was just good enough. After the game, he sounded very much like a relieved man. "Great news for me," he said. "I think [this is] one of the biggest days of my life, happiest. I'm happy. I want to say, 'Thank you,' to the whole organization, Colorado Avalanche, to give me a chance to play for this team. Thanks for my teammates. I think they play very well for me. That's why I signed the contract, because they help me."

He noted that when he first signed with Colorado, "I didn't think I played that well, that great, the first two years. Thank God the right people came to the team during the summer, Patrick and especially Francois Allaire. Those guys helped me a lot. They changed my game, so I want to say thanks to those guys and to my teammates. It's a good thing I signed a deal right now, so I don't have to worry about that. Now I can stay focused on my game. Olympics are coming, and that's a big thing, too, but I don't have to worry about my contract."

Ryan O'Reilly got his team-high 20th goal of the season, getting him to that benchmark for the first time in his five-season career as he continued to play wing on the line with Duchene and Jamie McGinn. Also, Nathan MacKinnon's near-breakaway goal with 2:25 left put the Avalanche ahead 5–3 against the Wild, and they hung on in the final meeting of the season between Colorado and Minnesota. The Avalanche ended up with nine points in the five games.

The negatives were that Tanguay again tweaked his hip and seemed likely to be out of the lineup again for a while, and Paul Stastny suffered a minor ankle injury—minor enough that it didn't seem to threaten his involvement in the Olympics.

SATURDAY, FEBRUARY 1, AT DENVER: AVALANCHE 7, SABRES 1. RECORD: 35–14–5

Gabriel Landeskog and McGinn each scored twice as the Avalanche coasted in their final home game before the Olympic break.

"Our guys were sharp. We were skating well," Roy said. "It was a beauty watching our guys." He was going against one of his most heated major junior coaching rivals, Ted Nolan, who had taken over the Sabres after the teams met in Buffalo in mid-October. The weird thing was that now, in theory, Nolan could be making decisions about Roy's son Frederick, the Sabres' farmhand.

Marc-Andre Cliche, the penalty-killing specialist, finally got his first career NHL goal. Roy smiled when asked that. "Everybody was pretty happy for him on the bench," Roy said. "He is valuable for us. He puts hard work in on the P. K., blocking shots, and it's nice to see someone rewarded."

Cliche converted a pass from Patrick Bordeleau. "It could not have been a better setup for me," Cliche said. "I just said, 'Finally, so much weight off my shoulders.' I know I'm not here to score, but when you score one like that, it feels unbelievable."

FROM THE NOTEBOOK OF ADRIAN DATER

The Avalanche landed in New Jersey soon enough for Joe Sakic and other members of the team and organization—those able to get tickets one way or another—to attend Super Bowl XLVIII at MetLife Stadium in East Rutherford. Kickoff was at 6:30 p.m., Eastern Time.

I was there, too. Because of the perfect synchronization with the Avalanche schedule, I changed my plane ticket to a Saturday departure and joined my newspaper's entourage to help out in our coverage of the game—my first Super Bowl.

I showed up.

The Broncos didn't.

Sakic was caught in an approximately 90-minute wait for a train out of the stadium area after the game, along with about 35,000 other people. Somehow, officials in charge of Super Bowl planning miscalculated the number of people who might hop the train out of East Rutherford—despite the fact that they had made it impossible to drive and park at the game as regular fans, forcing everyone to take mass transit.

Sakic had gotten a ride to the game, as one might expect, in a limo. But there were problems getting a limo after the game, so he was forced to ride the train like all the other fans. He got on the right train back to the Avalanche hotel and still got to bed before midnight. Not me.

I got on the wrong train. Instead of getting on the one that would stop at Princeton Junction, where I was staying at a nearby Residence Inn, I got on the one that went in an opposite direction. (A couple of cops on duty had told me that I would be just fine getting on the train I boarded.) Instead of getting off at Princeton at midnight or so, I wound up in Middletown, New Jersey, at approximately 2:30 a.m.—soon after the final train of the night going back in that direction had left.

I thought I would have to hunker down for the night in another Marriott in Middletown and take a train back the next morning, but there are no Marriotts in Middletown—as my Marriott smartphone app confirmed.

Luckily, I was able to call for a cab and get a driver willing to make the approximately 75-minute trip to Princeton at that late hour. The agreed-upon fare would be $100.

As if to make up for my likely reduced wholesale fare, I got a talkative cabbie who happened to be a hockey fan. Make that, a very big New York Rangers fan. For the next hour or so, I nodded in weary agreement to every Rangers superlative of the previous 50 years, from Andy Bathgate to Joe Zanussi. He was actually a really nice guy, and I was grateful when we got back to Princeton.

But the night wasn't over that easily. I couldn't find my car. For 40 minutes or so, I walked every square inch of the massive Princeton Junction parking lot, but my gray Dodge Charger just wasn't there.

I concluded that no way could I have mistaken my memory of the location this badly. The car had to have been stolen. It's New Jersey, I thought. It happens.

Another cab was idling by the train station. I decided to return to the hotel and start making calls to the local police and Budget Rental Car. One more problem, though: The cabbie was high as a kite. The smell of pot reeked throughout the cheap black vinyl interior. Not only that: he didn't speak English very well. So I had a stoned, foreign-language speaking cabdriver who didn't know where I needed him to take me.

That turned out to be about my only personal good luck on the trip. In the frustrating interim of him not being able to understand me as he started a halting drive out of the parking lot, I decided to just tell him to take me back to the entrance so I could get out and get into another cab. But a thought occurred to me: the parking lot was so massive, maybe there were parts of it I hadn't explored?

I was SURE I had taken my first right entering the lot and parked in the row closest to the road. I told the driver to "take me back to the entrance, on the road just past the Dunkin' Donuts coming in." After about the tenth time telling him this, it finally seeped into his pot-soaked brain that there was, indeed, a Dunkin' Donuts nearby, and we made our way to the entrance near there. Suddenly, things looked refreshingly different again. I hit the "unlock" button on my car-key thingy, and yellow lights in the back suddenly flashed.

Turns out, I had gone to the wrong parking lot entirely. The place was so big that there were lots on opposite sides of the tracks, but with the same common gathering place in the center, I was thrown off, left to wander aimlessly with a laptop/luggage case missing one wheel scraping forlornly into the cement.

I got to the hotel at about 4:30.

The next night, between the first and second periods of the game against the Devils in Newark, I spotted Sakic in the press box area of the Prudential Center. Knowing that he grew up near Seattle, in British Columbia, I congratulated Sakic on the Seahawks' win.

"Shhh," Sakic said, while munching on kettle chips.

I'd written about Sakic's allegiance to the Seahawks before, but he knew the Broncos' fans back home were still reeling from the blowout, and he didn't want to lose any goodwill by gloating.

Here's my favorite part of that night: Sakic dropped a couple of the chips, and to my astonishment, he got down on his hands and knees to pick them up. Shouldn't a Hall of Famer just let the cleaning staff get those? I even wrote about it in my blog that night. A day or two later, in Philly, Patrick Roy mocked my blog. "Hey Adrian, over here," Roy said from another room, as he then got on his hands and knees pretending to pick up something, which immediately busted up the entire team in laughter.

DENVER STARTS PAYING ATTENTION

MONDAY, FEBRUARY 3, AT NEWARK: AVALANCHE 2, DEVILS 1 (OT). RECORD: 36–14–5

In front of a snowstorm-lessened crowd at the Prudential Center, the Devils led 1–0 entering the final minutes, when Patrick Roy gambled and won. He pulled Jean-Sebastien Giguere with 2:33 left and watched as P. A. Parenteau tied it with 1:47 left, with a tip of Tyson Barrie's slap shot.

It would turn out to embolden Roy to defy convention more and more as the season continued, and start a league-wide trend.

"Why not?," Roy said after the game, a perfect variation of the "Why Not Us?" team motto. "Why wait? Might as well know right away. We had the line I thought would be best for us to score the goal. But I won't take credit for this. The players did it."

Ryan O'Reilly got the game winner at 28 seconds of overtime, converting Matt Duchene's setup pass. Cory Schneider again played in the net for the Devils, with Martin Brodeur watching.

TUESDAY, FEBRUARY 4, AT NEW YORK: RANGERS 5, AVALANCHE 1. RECORD: 36–15–5

Paul Stastny was back in the lineup, but that was about all that went right as the four-game winning streak ended. The Avalanche were outshot 20–4 in the first period alone and were down 2–0 on a pair of Ryan Callahan goals, and they were lucky it wasn't worse. The Duchene-centered line with O'Reilly and Jamie McGinn ended up being on the ice for all five New York goals.

"We talked a lot about how the start of the game was the key for this game," Roy said. "But the Rangers came out flying. They got the momentum from the first shift until the end of the first." Then he again wanted to make clear his goaltender hadn't been at fault. "The thing I want to say is that Varly was phenomenal in the first period. He kept the game at 0–0, and it could have been 4–0 or 5–0."

Asked about the Avalanche not taking advantage of a five-on-three power play, Roy shook his head. "If and if, my aunt would be my uncle," he said.

THURSDAY, FEBRUARY 6, AT PHILADELPHIA: FLYERS 3, AVALANCHE 1. RECORD: 36–16–5

Although they had 39 shots on Steve Mason, the Avalanche could break through only for Nathan MacKinnon's late goal, which came with 2:50 remaining—*after* Roy already had pulled Semyon Varlamov for a sixth attacker. "Offensively, we're going to have to find a way to score goals," Roy said. "On the trip so far, we have four goals in three games, and it's not enough in this league to win on the road."

It was only the third time all season the Avalanche had lost two in a row.

☼ ☼ ☼

The mood the day before the trip-closing game with the Islanders reflected the pending vacation for the Olympic shutdown. No matter what, players would get on planes for a minimum ten days of R&R. After an off-day practice at the Coliseum, players munched on catered sandwiches and made plans for dinner in the area. Almost everyone asked the former Islander, P. A. Parenteau, for recommendations.

"Lots of good old-school Italian places around here," Parenteau said. "You can't go wrong."

But most of the talk centered on players' Olympic break plans.

"Staying in Denver," the quiet defenseman, Andre Benoit, said. "Maybe go to the mountains with the wife and family. It'll be nice."

Patrick Bordeleau would go back to Quebec to visit his wife and family. "They stay there during the season," Bordeleau said, without elaborating.

For Maxime Talbot, he would head back to Denver, not sure what day he would become a father. His fiancée—the Canadian former Olympic figure skater, Cynthia Phaneuf (a fourth cousin of Toronto Maple Leafs star Dion Phaneuf)—was due to deliver a baby on or about February 5. But here it was, two days after that date, and he was still with the team in Long Island.

"I have no idea when it's coming," Talbot said with a laugh. "It hasn't happened yet though."

SATURDAY, FEBRUARY 8, AT UNIONDALE: AVALANCHE 5, ISLANDERS 2. RECORD: 37–16–5

The Avalanche nearly blew a sure thing at the decrepit Nassau Veterans Memorial Coliseum. Leading 3–0 with the clock moving under 12 minutes left in the third period, they were called for four straight minor penalties in less than four minutes. That created two separate five-on-three power plays, and even a moribund Isles team to that point couldn't help but take advantage. With more than six minutes left, the lead was cut to 3–2, and New York still had close to two minutes of power-play time left.

Finally, Colorado's defense stiffened, and Landeskog ended the drama with an empty-net goal. It was little noticed and seemed of minor importance, but at 12:09 of the third period, Erik Johnson was called for a slashing minor when he nailed the Islanders' Frans Nielsen across the hands. It turned out that Nielsen suffered a broken hand—and that Johnson a few days later was suspended for two games by the league. It would be Johnson's first suspension, and he argued he was being penalized for the effect—Nielsen's broken hand—rather than the action itself.

In the game, like much of the first two-thirds of the season, the Avalanche bent but didn't break, and now it was time to really look at the standings to realize what they'd done. That 37–16–5 record was eye popping.

"I'm very proud of our players," Roy said. "Like I said to the guys after the game, I wished good luck to the guys who are going to the Olympics. Hopefully, our [other] guys are going to have a good ten days off and be ready to work when we come back."

Landeskog was doing an interview after the win when he was interrupted not once but thrice.

"USA, USA," said Stastny, butting into the conversation.

Then came Nick Holden, who just stood next to Landeskog and stared a comical half-smile at him, the print interview version of the photo bomb.

Then came Talbot, who gripped Landeskog in one of those hip, young-guy versions of a handshake, then man-hugged him.

"Hey, good luck over there, and have a great break," Talbot told his team captain.

It was, indeed, a great way to go into the Olympic break for the Avalanche. For the first time all season, there was the unmistakable evidence of a team finally believing it had really *accomplished something*. It was simple arithmetic. After the Olympic break, the Avalanche would reassemble for the final 24 games with 79 points in the bank. That was ten points up on the fourth-place team in the Central Division, Minnesota, and 15 points on ninth-place Phoenix. No, a playoff spot wasn't guaranteed, but it was getting pretty close.

"It's hard to say we expected to be where we are," Landeskog said.

He thought it over for a second and added, "I don't think we would have."

A sense of warmth, of real togetherness, was clear in the Avalanche room. It had been that way even the day before, despite a two-game losing streak. It probably had something to do with the pending Olympic break. As much as coaches, GMs, and NHL owners fret over things such as losing "continuity" over the Olympics, the fact is the players not participating in the Games love it, too. It's a paid vacation, a time to go back home for a week to ten days, relax, and recharge.

❀ ❀ ❀

With four Avalanche players on four different teams, the Winter Games in Sochi were just about guaranteed to be a mixed bag for Colorado. And that's the way it turned out: Duchene won gold with Canada and Landeskog collected silver for Sweden; Stastny (U.S.) and Varlamov (Russia) came away without medals.

"I think I'm going to be on a high for a while," Duchene said after he rejoined the Avalanche. "It was a dream come true just to make the team, and then to win gold was unbelievable. I felt really good about what I contributed, and my performance, and got some great feedback from everybody there. There's so much experience I gained there I can bring to help this team. The feeling of the gold medal is unbelievable, and I think the only better feeling you could have is to raise the Cup over your heart. That's my next goal here."

The highlight for the Americans was when Stastny, with his father—the onetime Slovak flag carrier in the opening ceremonies and the nation's current representative in the European Parliament—watching and wearing a U.S. jersey, scored two goals in a 7–1 victory to open group play.

Finland eventually foiled both Varlamov and Stastny's medal hopes, first beating the Avalanche goalie and Russia 3–1 in the quarterfinals and then the listless Americans 5–0 in the bronze medal game. If you needed a showcase example of the effect of the frequent American sports philosophy—if you're not first, you stink—the bronze medal game was it. The Finns, including the ageless former Avalanche winger Teemu Selanne, acted as if they considered bronze medals something to be proud of, and the Americans played as if bronze medals were the equivalent of Cracker Jack toys.

In the quarterfinals, Varlamov, who also had been staunch in an earlier 1–0 shootout victory over Switzerland and had alternated with Sergei Bobrovsky of Columbus, was pulled after giving up the three goals to the Finns. But only the first was of the soft variety, and nobody in his right mind considered goaltending a major issue in the home nation's failure to at least reach the semifinals. The instant the game ended, though, and perhaps even before, speculation began in Colorado about whether Varlamov would be mentally scarred by the experience, affecting the rest of the Avalanche season.

Relentless in his zeal to build up Varlamov—both his self-esteem and his public image—Roy went on the offensive after the team's non-

Olympians resumed practice, saying on his radio show and in his press sessions that the Russians had played individual, rather than team, hockey in failing to meet their nation's expectations for the home team.

"Varly is a great person, and he wants to do well, and I have no doubt in my mind that he's not happy about the way that he played, and he's going to look at himself in the mirror—and I think that's what makes a career," Roy said. "It's not always perfect. That's the way it was for me anyway. I think that's going to make him a better hockey player. It'll prepare him even better for the next time. It's going to help him in his approach to the games he's going to play until the end of the year to the playoffs."

The only major non-Olympic news during the break involved two men who played for the 2001 Stanley Cup team. Milan Hejduk, who had been politely told he didn't fit in with the Avalanche's rebuilding plans after the previous season and hadn't caught on with anyone else, belatedly announced his retirement in an Avalanche news conference at Family Sports. There were no hard feelings, and it seemed a lock that the Czech winger's number 23 was destined soon to be in the Pepsi Center rafters as the last player from the glory years to be so honored. Also, Alex Tanguay's hope to remain healthy the rest of the season had turned out to be almost sadly mocking. He underwent hip surgery and was ruled out for the rest of the season. The immediate and obvious result was that it meant P. A. Parenteau not only would be back in the lineup, but his spot would be fairly secure.

WEDNESDAY, FEBRUARY 26, AT DENVER: KINGS 6, AVALANCHE 4. RECORD: 37–17–5

The Avalanche had been brilliant when taking a lead into the third period all season; this was the exception. After getting three power-play goals, Colorado blew a 4–2 lead in falling to the Kings. Both Olympic goalies—Varlamov and the Kings' Jonathan Quick (of the U.S.)—had the night off. Down 5–4, the Avalanche pulled Jean-Sebastien Giguere early in a power play, with more than two minutes remaining, held the puck in the zone, and had many chances on the six-on-four before the Kings finally got the puck out and got the empty-netter to make the final margin two goals.

With Johnson serving the first of his two-game suspension, the Avalanche had trouble controlling the traffic in front of the net, and Giguere would have had a stronger case in saying his defensemen had left him exposed than earlier in the season. But Giguere wasn't going to anger his coach again.

Roy said he believed all three of his Olympic skaters "played well."

Duchene had two assists. "I was really up for tonight," said Duchene. "I was absolutely exhausted this afternoon and tried to get a three-hour nap to fill the tank back up, but I couldn't sleep I was so much looking forward to this game. I'm pretty tired now, and this is a tough loss. We gave them the game."

FRIDAY, FEBRUARY 28, AT DENVER: AVALANCHE 4, COYOTES 2. RECORD: 38–17–5

The Nathan MacKinnon watch started.

In the wake of Alex Tanguay's departure from the lineup for the season, the rookie again was playing right wing on a line with Stastny and Landeskog against the Coyotes. He had two assists, and by the end of the night he had the NHL's first ten-game consecutive point streak for a rookie since Jonathan Toews did it for the Blackhawks in 2007. It also was noticed that the longest streak by an 18-year-old was 12 games, reached by Wayne Gretzky in 1979–80, the Oilers' first season in the NHL after they moved over from the WHA with Hartford, Winnipeg, and the Avalanche's Quebec predecessors.

"It's not about me. I'm playing with some great guys, and they make it a lot easier for me," MacKinnon said.

Varlamov looked unscarred by his Olympic experience, getting 40 saves in his first post-Sochi game and allowing only a pair of power-play goals.

"When I saw Varly after the Olympics, I saw a big smile on his face," Roy said. "I knew he was ready to bounce back."

WILL HE STAY OR WILL HE GO?

Despite the Avalanche's stunning turnaround, as the calendar turned to March, they still were only 22nd in home attendance in the NHL, averaging 15,978. Even Tampa Bay, often belittled as a hockey market, if a bit unfairly, was outdrawing the Avalanche as the Lightning came to Denver.

The contrast was that when Patrick Roy played for Colorado, the franchise, at least officially, never had an unsold ticket.

"Obviously, it is different," Roy said on the morning of the meeting with the Lightning. "You could not get a ticket. There is some work to be done, to bring people back. I would say something, though. From the start to now, when I walk in the street, the people are proud. People are telling me, 'Hey, great job; you guys are doing a good job,' and they're starting to follow the team more and more. I think this is a sign that we're going in the right direction. It has changed in the way that I guess people are disappointed with what happened in maybe four of the last five years, but I'm also confident our fans will come back and support this team and be proud of this team. That's the most important part. We want them to be proud of this team. We want them to come and have fun watching this team. And I think that's what this team has been doing.

"You look at the crowds at the last two game—great crowds. I want to see sellouts. That's what I want to see. But at the same time, I understand the situation, and I'm going to be very patient with it. All the fans who came the last two games, they cannot say to me that they did not enjoy themselves."

Neither Roy nor Joe Sakic were going to allow themselves to come off as if they believed the Avalanche "deserved" more support at the gate, and they understood the reality: There was a lag time before more "old" fans came back—or "new" fans climbed aboard the bandwagon. But the major issue was the revenue stream, meaning that the sooner the franchise could get back to automatic sellouts, even on Tuesdays against second-tier opponents, the sooner the team's budget and player payroll could approach the league's salary cap. At this point, despite the extensions and the prospect of climbing the payroll list soon, the Avalanche still were a team winning on a "budget."

SUNDAY, MARCH 2, AT DENVER: AVALANCHE 6, LIGHTNING 3. RECORD: 39–17–5

Nick Holden had his second two-goal game in the Avalanche's comeback win, and fellow D men Erik Johnson and Tyson Barrie also scored. That was significant because the four goals from the back line underscored just how willing, and even encouraging, Roy was for them to provide offense. No, not to the point of irresponsibility—the Johnson-Jan Hejda pairing was the complementary example—but to add second-wave support. In this instance, Colorado was down 3–2 after two periods before rallying.

"We're working as a unit of five," Roy said. "Our forwards are doing a really good job supporting our D defensively; and as coaches, we love it when our D jump into the rush. Sometimes you're going to give two-on-ones, but we're ready to live with that because we want a show. Everybody comes to this building to have a great show."

Johnson had finished serving his two-game suspension, and his eighth goal of the season gave him eight more than he had in the entire 2013 season. MacKinnon had two assists, stretching his consecutive game points streak to 11 . . . within one of Gretzky.

* * *

As the Avalanche arrived in Chicago, the other major story was Paul Stastny's situation as the March 5 trading deadline approached.

The problem with Stastny was that with his five-year deal expiring after the season, Colorado was taking a risk if they hadn't reached an agreement with him on an extension by the trading deadline and then kept him. Under that scenario, it was at least theoretically possible that the Avalanche would get nothing for him if he became an unrestricted free agent on July 1 and signed elsewhere.

Two things long had been established in the minds of the objective: First, Stastny was a strong all-around center and important to the Avalanche's success, making contributions that didn't necessarily show up in the summaries. And, second, he had been overpaid for five seasons. Now the issue was whether that $6.6-million annual salary was the starting point for negotiations, or whether Stastny and his agent, Matt Keator, would concede that he would have to take a pay cut to stay with Colorado. It was easy to say that all of the NHL knew he was overpaid, but all bets are off when a player hits the open market, because it takes only one team to buy in. In Stastny's case, that would mean not asking him to take a pay cut, or even offering a raise.

As the deadline approached, Sakic and Roy had presented Keator with a simple proposition: Either reach an agreement before the deadline, or be sure one would be reachable in the offseason before July 1; or Stastny might be traded before the deadline—either to a team that considered him a "rental" for the rest of the season, or one that would try to re-sign him. Did he want to leave the city where he had been playing since his freshman year of college, and especially now that the Avalanche had it going? Sure, he could have his choice where to go in the offseason, but there was no guarantee that any other team would see his former salary as the starting point for negotiations, either.

On the morning of the Avalanche's game at Chicago, which happened to be the day before the trading deadline, Blackhawks star Patrick Kane, who had just finished a second consecutive Olympics as a Stastny teammate, succinctly summarized the Avalanche center's value as a player. "He was one of our best players, to be honest with you," he said of Stastny at Sochi. "I know from playing with him in two Olympics, he's a really good team guy and probably one of my better friends on the team. I think he plays the game pretty simple, but very smart, too. He's a great player. I think he plays the way you would want a centerman to play. He plays two-way hockey, and it seems like he's always in the right place at the right time. He does all the little things on the ice. He's not going to flash and dash you, but at the same time, I think he has the ability to put up big numbers because of his skill set and how he plays the game."

At that point, Kane noticed a teammate arriving at the next stall and added, "He's the total opposite of Kris Versteeg."

Versteeg at least laughed.

At that point, it seemed entirely possible that the game against the Blackhawks could be Stastny's final one with the Avalanche. Those accusing the media of stirring this up were naive: Colorado explored dealing Stastny, weighing everything against the risk of tampering with chemistry in a surprising season and the countering risk of losing Stastny for nothing. Keator and Stastny stuck to the position that they wanted to wait to take care of the contract with Colorado, if they were going to take care of it at all.

Conspicuously, the Avalanche had a major front-office contingent on the trip, including Joe Sakic, assistant GM Craig Billington, GM Greg Sherman (still the numbers man), and Charlotte Graham, the vice president of hockey administration who would deal with all the red tape involved in bringing in a new player, including passport/visa/work permit issues. The four of them watched the morning skates from behind one goal, and Billington and Sakic took turns being on the phone.

They weren't ordering pizza from Gino's East. In fact, they were seeing what offers were out there for Stastny. They were also looking for a younger backup goaltender, both as insurance for the rest of the season and for down the road; Giguere's contract was expiring, he was starting to have back problems, and Roy still was a bit disenchanted with his play after his terrific start to the season. It seemed entirely possible that even if Colorado ultimately decided it could live with him as a backup for another season, he still might decide to retire. The Avalanche were working with a list of promising potential backups provided by Francois Allaire, who had worked with NHL goalies and goalies in Europe during his time as what amounted to a freelance goaltending tutor. The Avalanche were also inquiring about acquiring a veteran defenseman. Colorado didn't have a "problem" on the back line as much as it realized it was staking a lot on a group made up of several minor-league journeymen, and that adding a body there with the playoffs in mind couldn't hurt.

After the Colorado skate, Stastny said he hadn't heard anything. "I haven't talked with anyone, and I can just worry about what I can do, and that's to go out there and play, and that's the most important thing to me," he said. He emphasized that he left all the contract talk up to Keator. "That's how it's been ever since we've been together, for ten-plus years," he said.

Would he be willing to give the Avalanche organization a discount?

"Yeah, absolutely," he said. "Everyone knows how the business works. You can always go somewhere in the off-season and get more money somewhere else. But if you have something good and you want to stick with it, that hometown discount is something everyone's aware of. It is important to do because you want both sides to be happy. You don't want to screw over the team, and you want the team to be put in a position where they can compete down the road as well."

Sakic said that no trade was imminent "as of right now. There are conversations, like everybody, but nothing as of right now. Do I expect anything? I don't know. Whatever it is, it's got to make sense."

Roy said he could live with the Avalanche standing pat. "We need to be patient," Roy said. "Let's not forget. Twenty-ninth last year. We need to press on the right buttons. We have to make the right decisions. If there's something good for us, I'm sure Joe and I will look at it. If it's not, it's not, and we're very comfortable with our group."

TUESDAY, MARCH 4, AT CHICAGO: AVALANCHE 4, BLACKHAWKS 2. RECORD: 40–17–5

A Tyson Barrie goal at 12:50 of the third period gave the Avalanche a 3–2 lead, and the Blackhawks pulled goalie Corey Crawford late in the attempt to get the tying score. MacKinnon ended up making the setup pass from behind the net to Stastny, who got the clinching empty-netter with 32.6 seconds left.

The assist stretched his consecutive-game points streak to 12, tying him for the best ever by an 18-year-old with . . .

We'll let his teammates finish that sentence.

As he skated back to the bench, he heard a saluting chorus.

"Gretzky!" they yelled.

"It's pretty cool," MacKinnon said afterwards, very much sounding like a teenager. "I'm sure Gretzky had about 50 more points than me during the point streak. I'm really hanging on here. It's still pretty cool. He's called the Great One for a reason, and it's nice to have, I guess, one small stat that's similar as him."

When on the ice in the final minute, he said, "I was just making sure that they didn't tie it up. I'm very fortunate that Patty trusts me in the last minute as opposed to earlier in the season. That was the biggest thing on my mind. I wanted to block some shots. But when you have an empty net, obviously you want to finish it off."

Roy professed not to be thinking about the streak when he sent MacKinnon out with the net empty, but also with the Avalanche skaters outnumbered and vulnerable at the other end. "Not at all. I didn't even think about it. At the end, I just put him there because their line was playing some good hockey."

Nobody completely believed that the streak didn't at least enter into deploying MacKinnon with the net empty, but nobody's ever going to hold that sort of minor fudge against a coach. And it's the sort of move the players tend to appreciate.

Varlamov again was strong, with 36 saves, and Erik Johnson had three assists as the Avalanche won their 40th game at the earliest stage of the season—after 62 games—in franchise history. The lack of a shootout to prevent ties in earlier years skewed the figures, but it nonetheless was at least worth noting that the 2001 Stanley Cup champions, with Roy in net, didn't hit 40 wins until the 63rd game.

This also was stunning: With 20 games remaining, the Avalanche were within one point of the defending Stanley Cup champions in the Central Division standings. The new playoff format made it possible, and perhaps even likely, that as the No. 2 and No. 3 teams in the division (behind St. Louis), they'd meet in the first round—with the higher finisher getting the home-ice advantage.

"It is not necessarily a surprise to me, but it is to the NHL," Roy said. "If you're looking at everybody that was making predictions at the beginning of the year, I would say probably 80 percent, if not 90 percent, would have said the Avalanche will miss the playoffs. It's not something done yet, but we're certainly in good shape right now, and we're competing right now to maybe surprise the world of hockey and maybe have the home-ice advantage."

✿ ✿ ✿

After flying from Chicago to Detroit after the game, the Avalanche were scheduled to practice in Joe Louis Arena at 1:30 p.m. Eastern Time, which would have taken them right up to the 3 p.m. trading deadline. In part to reward the team for the win in Chicago and in part to recognize that Roy would be part of the management team deciding whether to make a deal, the practice was canceled, leaving the players to work out on their own at the hotel or to make it a day of rest.

Stastny went to Ash Wednesday mass at a downtown church, then returned to his room and ordered up the movie *American Hustle*. As he watched and waited, time crawled toward the 3 p.m. Eastern trading deadline. He had his phone by him, but he tried not to check it for texts . . . at least, not too often. Finally, the deadline passed, and then enough additional time to assure him that a last-second deal hadn't been made, either. Then he got confirmation: He still was with Colorado, with no contract extension. Both sides were rolling the dice, in effect . . . and trusting each other to believe the mutual assurances that the goal was to have him re-sign with the Avalanche in the off-season.

"You're happy it's over with," Stastny said. "Obviously, there's high risk, high reward if you wait it out on both sides of the equation, but for me, I was comfortable playing the season out." He said he believed "both sides are comfortable" resuming talks after the season.

"I think they know, first and foremost, that this is where I want to be. Obviously, I want to stay. We have a good group of guys here. It's more about a how-to-win culture, playing a fun style, and I think when Patty and Joe came along and got their fingerprints on the team, I think a lot of things changed. To me, this is like playing on a new team than it was the last couple of years. So to me, this is kind of a new start, and I'm excited where it was going."

And he still was willing to grant that "discount"?

Yes, said Stastny, within reason.

"What's a discount for you, what's a discount for me, what's it for another guy? I don't know. You hear different numbers. Everyone knows how it works. You go to the open market to a team that needs you more, but if you're in a good position, and the team's doing well, and you have a good group of guys, and there's chemistry, you're willing to take less. As I get older, it's about winning and finding the right pieces what whatever you can do down the road to help, you want to."

Significantly, if it had happened a year earlier, Stastny almost certainly would have been dealt: He might have been looking ahead to a fresh start with another franchise with a better chance of winning, and the Avalanche would have been willing to unload him as a rental to another team for a draft choice or two. In 2014, it wasn't surprising that Stastny stayed; what was more surprising was that he stayed without at least a public announcement of agreement on a contract extension. The thorny issue of whether a "discount" meant he would accept less from Colorado than he could get on the open market, or it meant he would accept a pay cut, remained to be resolved.

"We are very happy that Paul's still here," Sakic said. "His agent wants to deal with it, they want to deal with it, in the summer. They know we want him back. There's a risk, there's always a risk, and we understand the risk."

The Avalanche made one move at the deadline, acquiring Swiss goalie Reto Berra, 27, from Calgary. He had worked with Allaire in Europe, so his inclusion on the shopping list wasn't a shock. But the Avalanche showed considerable faith in a goalie who was in his first season in the NHL after finally coming to North America and hadn't been all that impressive for the Flames, posting a save percentage of .897, with a record of 9–17–2 and a 2.95 goals-against average. In Calgary, Flames exec Brian Burke said he wasn't looking to unload Berra, but when the Avalanche offered a second-round 2014 draft choice, Burke couldn't say no. He almost seemed to be saying that the Avalanche had overspent, but Colorado was getting to the point where draft choices—perhaps beyond the first round, at least—weren't as precious as they had been during the rebuilding process.

"We wanted to make sure that if something happens to Varly, we have a good guy there if Jiggy's back doesn't hold up," Sakic said. "We have someone we know is a very good goalie. If Varly went down, the prospects aren't ready, so we wanted to make sure we solidified that goalie situation for the next few years."

For his part, Roy said he was uneasy about Giguere's back issues, and made it clear he was disappointed with Sami Aittokallio's play in his one game at Tampa Bay. Whether or not that one game was a fair trial was irrelevant because Roy, at least, seemed to think it was. "We realized he wasn't ready to step in if something happened," Roy said.

This was left unsaid, but implied in the wake of the lack of other activity: Barring an embarrassing collapse down the stretch or an absolute disintegration in the playoffs accompanied by a loss of poise—that is, "gooning" it up—the season would go down as a success. And if Colorado got beyond the first round? Gravy. Under those circumstances, there was no need to give up much for a rental defenseman or unload anyone with an expiring contract, whether Stastny or Ryan O'Reilly or anyone else. The expenditure of a second-round pick for a backup goalie somewhat contradicted that, but the overall message was that Colorado had nothing to lose by sticking with the status quo, at least among the skaters.

"We owe it to our players to keep this team together," Sakic said. "They've done a tremendous job. They've got great chemistry on the team, and we don't want to break that up. I also believe our fans, and especially our season-ticket holders that have stuck with us, they deserve to see a run. The guys have had a great year and keep finding ways to win. Everybody deserves to see this year through."

He said he remained "confident" in the Avalanche's largely unheralded defense. "You always try to upgrade, but this D is really underrated," Sakic said. "We all had question marks at the start of the year on our back end, but as you have seen, these guys as a unit have played great. [Erik Johnson] has become the player we expected and, more important, he expected, and has had a tremendous year. Nick Holden and Nate Guenin have stepped up and really, really played well for us, playing big minutes. Tyson Barrie has elevated. You go up and down the list on the back end. Jan Hejda, too. These guys as a group have played tremendous hockey, and we're proud of what they've done as a unit."

He said potential deals for "rental" players who might leave as unrestricted free agents "are always out there, but we weren't going to do that. We weren't going for a rental. We're not in that position. We believe in this group, and we would not feel comfortable at all looking for a rental player. To me, unless there's someone out there you really believe is going to be a difference maker, I don't believe in mortgaging your future. We're not in that position right now anyway. We're still building our prospect base, and we were ready to stay status quo on that. We didn't feel we wanted or needed a rental."

One of the many "rental" players available was winger Marian Gaborik, who moved at the deadline from Columbus to Los Angeles. He was making $7.5 million in the final season of a five-year contract, so even having him on the Colorado roster for only six weeks would have significantly added to the payroll. The Kings took him on for forward Matt Frattin and second- and third-round draft choices.[1]

The twist there was that in the Avalanche glory days, Roy and Sakic often were joined at the deadline by "rentals" who, in some cases, eventually re-signed with Colorado. Most notably, the potential rentals included Ray Bourque and Rob Blake. Another, Theo Fleury, wasn't brought back—mainly because of his personal demons and off-ice problems.

So, with the exception of the addition of a third goaltender, the Avalanche roster was unchanged for the stretch run. Among other things, that meant Colorado was going to live with—and show faith in— the three defensemen who not long ago had seemed stuck in the AHL. An indication of the Avalanche's plans for both Holden and Guenin after their signings had been that they were listed in the "Avalanche System" section of the media guide. Instead, they had stuck with the NHL team and played major minutes.

---

1.   Gaborik would go on to score 11 goals in his 12 regular-season games with the Kings.

ON DEFENSE: OFF THE SCRAP HEAP

NO. 2, NICK HOLDEN, 6'4", 207 LBS., BORN MAY 15, 1987, ST. ALBERT, ALBERTA

Another Western Hockey League product, with the Chilliwack Bruins, Holden spent five seasons in the AHL while playing seven games for Columbus in brief call-ups. When the Avalanche signed him as a free agent on July 5, 2013, it was treated—even by the team—as a move to shore up the Lake Erie Monsters.

It became more than that.

Although he stuck with the Avalanche at the start of the season, he was an extra body and healthy scratch. He didn't even play in a game until November 1 and suited up for a total of only 13 in the 2013 calendar year, but he settled in as a regular among the top six after the New Year, mainly getting his chance because of Cory Sarich's back problems.

"I just wanted to come in and have a good showing in training camp, but I thought I was going to be down in Lake Erie this year, maybe be a call-up sometimes," Holden said. "I thought, 'Maybe next year, take a roster spot.' But, luckily, I had a good camp, and Patrick kept me up. We played so well at the start that I didn't play for the first month, but that didn't discourage me at all."

Once in the lineup, Holden had his ups and downs, but he displayed the offensive ability that had enabled him to lead WHL defensemen in goals with Chilliwack, 22 in 2007–08.

On the ice, Holden became more and more of a revelation, even when his mischievousness became something of a pain in the neck to some teammates. Holden's locker was right next to Gabriel Landeskog's, and when the press interviewed the captain, Holden sometimes would stand behind him and either make funny faces or grab a mike himself and start asking off-the-wall questions. By late in the season, Landeskog even got a little irritated by it all. "You need to grow up," the 21-year-old Landeskog barked at Holden, in a manner that seemed, at best, half-joking.

By the trading deadline, Holden had six goals and seemed capable of providing more offensive punch down the stretch.

NO. 5, NATE GUENIN, 6'3", 207 LBS., BORN DECEMBER 10, 1982, ALIQUIPPA, PENNSYLVANIA

Patrick Roy recruited Guenin, calling him before he signed with Colorado and promising that if he had a good camp and played well at Lake Erie, he would have a shot to be the first call-up at right defense.

It never came to that.

From the Pittsburgh area, Guenin had been raised a Penguins fan and played two seasons for the Green Bay Gamblers of the USHL. The Rangers claimed him after his second season there, in the fourth round of the 2002 draft, and he went on to play four seasons at Ohio State. Eventually signing with the Flyers, he was typecast as an organizational defenseman, and he began bouncing around in that role, also playing for the AHL affiliates of the Penguins, Blue Jackets, and Ducks and getting in 31 NHL games during call-ups. When the Avalanche signed him, he was 31 years old and had been "stuck" in the minors for seven years. But he always could think back to his grandfather, who worked 40 years in a steel mill. Compared to that, he had it pretty good.

After he came to camp, Colorado saw something in him, and rather than heading for Cleveland, perhaps to serve as the Monsters' captain, he stuck with the Avalanche. It was a nice touch when Roy told him to find a place to live in Denver as the Avalanche was about to face the Penguins on the road early in the season. No more living out of a hotel room. For the foreseeable future, he had an NHL roster spot. And he played well enough that the Avalanche demonstrated additional faith in him in mid-January, signing him to a two-year contract extension that took him through 2015–16.

"I've said all along as a player, all you can ask for is an opportunity," Guenin said. "They gave me one, and from there, it's the player's job to make the most of it. I couldn't be more thankful to Joe and Patrick and the scouting staff that scouted me and brought me in here. It's an unbelievable feeling. I come into every camp with the same mind-set, but talking to Patrick this summer, he said, 'If you come in and play hard, you're going to get an opportunity,' and they've stuck to their word. From day one, I've just worked as hard as I can. I know my role on this team, and every day, just try to perform that to my best. If you had told me this summer that I would have played as many games as I did and signed an extension in January, I probably would have laughed at you. But I knew all along that I felt I could play here, and it's just nice to see that come to fruition."

NO. 61, ANDRE BENOIT, 5'11", 191 LBS., BORN JANUARY 6, 1984, ST. ALBERT, ONTARIO

Benoit's knockabout credentials not only featured just 41 games in the NHL, all with Ottawa, but also stints with teams in Finland, Sweden, and Russia. He had played the start of the lockout season in the AHL, then joined the Senators for 33 games. He also was the franchise nominee for the Bill Masterton Trophy, which goes to the player judged to personify perseverance, sportsmanship, and dedication to hockey. He got a chance and more attention in the wake of Erik Karlsson's injury, and he even spent time in the top pairing with Chris Phillips.

When Colorado signed him, he was envisioned as the replacement for the bought-out Greg Zanon. Bigger than Tyson Barrie, but nonetheless "undersized," he wasn't flashy, but he was a hybrid-type defenseman counted on to jump into the play at times—including in overtime.

"WHAT'S MADE 'EM SO GOOD . . ."

The game in Detroit was the second and final meeting of the season between the onetime bitter rivals. There wasn't as much talk about the rivalry in Detroit as there had been in Denver in conjunction with the early season meeting, partly because the Red Wings were going to honor longtime defenseman Nick Lidstrom before the game, retiring his number.

After the morning skate, Patrick Roy diplomatically parried a question about whether Lidstrom was the best defenseman of all time, noting that any former goalie is going to be partial to the great defensemen who played in front of him, then also praising Lidstrom. When he was asked whether he felt like "Public Enemy No. 1" in Detroit, Roy joked that after his ten-year absence from the NHL, Joe Louis Arena was one place where he could be blindfolded and still find the visiting dressing room. That was it. He didn't rise to the bait.

THURSDAY, MARCH 6, AT DETROIT: AVALANCHE 3, RED WINGS 2 (OT). RECORD: 41–17–5

The prolonged Lidstrom ceremony delayed the puck drop to 8:28 p.m.

Giguere—the goalie who was on his way out, one way or another—played well as the Avalanche won. In overtime, Nathan MacKinnon, until then pointless, made a pass across the slot to an onrushing Andre Benoit, whose terrific shot made it over Jimmy Howard's shoulder and into the net to end the game. So not only had the Avalanche beaten the Red Wings on the road, MacKinnon had passed Gretzky on the list of 18-year-olds in his 13th consecutive game with a point.

"It's pretty cool that we could win like that," said MacKinnon. "Wings-Avs—I'm not sure there is a better rivalry in hockey, and it's exciting for our team. To be part of the overtime is pretty cool and, yeah, for the points streak, it's definitely nice as well to continue it."

For his part, Giguere said after the game that he wasn't offended by the Avalanche's acquisition of Berra, who wasn't going to join the team until after it arrived back in Denver.

"This doesn't change anything for me," said Giguere. "My only job is to go in there and try to give Varly a good rest and make sure I try to leave a good impression for the coach for the next game."

Roy agreed, though, that Giguere seemed to respond to a challenge.

"It's what I said when I met him," Roy said. "I said, 'You're allowed to change our plans.' If Jiggy plays like he did tonight, it helps his cause, for sure."

Those were complications the Avalanche could live with.

The Wings' Todd Bertuzzi played his 519th regular-season game since his attack on Steve Moore in Vancouver.

FROM THE NOTEBOOK OF TERRY FREI

I had covered the trip to Chicago and Detroit, and I admit I mainly was shocked that the Avalanche hadn't acquired a defenseman. But by being on the road at the deadline, I had a better chance to see this chemistry at work. Since the arrival of the Avalanche, I'd never really encountered that kind of us-against-the-world feeling so often summoned in other sports, often to contrived degrees. Previously, when the Avalanche were doing well, it was an atmosphere of cockiness, of knowing the world knew they were that good. Now Roy was cultivating that "shock the hockey world" mantra and image as much as possible, and it seemed to fit.

In Detroit, I also encountered the most direct expression of what seemed to be a common league-wide sentiment about Roy and the Avalanche. I went to the morning skates at Joe Louis Arena and was in the group talking with Detroit coach Mike Babcock after the Red Wings' turn on the ice. When asked about the Avalanche, he walked a tight-rope, making it clear that he believed Roy had been in the right place at the right time, but also complimenting the rookie NHL coach and his staff.

"What's made 'em so good this year is being bad long enough to get really good players," Babcock said. "I'm not trying to be a smart-ass; that's how you do it in this league now. You get bad enough so you get MacKinnon or these high, high-end players. Their top six forwards they put out on the ice are flat-out fun to watch. It's absolutely scary. Then their third line knows how to play, and then they have a fourth line that's got meat. So, to me, they've got a good group, and I think they've done a really good job giving that team structure; the goaltending plays well, and their back end on the right side is very active. So, all in all, they've been a real good team, and they're fast. You might have 40 shots, and they might have 12, but they only need about 12. They can score. It just flat-out goes in the net for them."

Asked specifically about Roy's impact, he said: "You know, every-thing about coaching is you have to arrive at the right time—let's not kid ourselves. So you arrive when the players arrive and are coming of age, that helps you a lot. But they're structured, they play hard, they play right, and they keep people accountable. The goalie stops the puck. [Roy] has brought a lot. But once again, I'd say to you, it's important as a coach to pick your spots, too."

Babcock was mostly right, and he had given the coaching staff credit. But completely buying into the idea that this was a team stacked with talent after getting high draft choices was a bit unfair, given the sprink-ling of unheralded journeymen through the Colorado roster.

Finally, I asked Babcock about coaching Matt Duchene with the Canadian Olympic team. "He's a great kid," Babcock said. "High-end skill. Initially at the Olympics, he was deferring to the other players. You look around the room and go, 'There's Toews, and there's Crosby,' and so he's giving the puck to everybody else instead of just playing. Once we got him just playing, I thought he was really good. He's in a competitive program that now demands you play a certain way, and then, so when you come to a program that demands you play a certain way, you're able to do it. A great kid, obviously huge skill, a powerful skater, and he's going to be a good pro for a long time. And he really appears that he wants to be, and that's the biggest battle of all."

I had been seeing the mention of Gretzky's point streak as an 18-year-old in the press notes each night as MacKinnon chased that mark, then passed it. I had been very careful not to label it a "record," because it really wasn't, at least not in the sense that you could open the annually published NHL Official Guide and Record Book *and find it. It was an NHL best, or the longest streak ever posted by an 18-year-old. But I also kept noticing the dates of Gretzky's 12-game streak—December 9, 1979, to January 5, 1980. I noted several times that it was the first season the Oilers, Jets, Nordiques, and Whalers had moved over from the WHA, and I also knew that was the season Don Cherry coached the Colorado Rockies. And, yes, I was covering the Rockies and Cherry then. Finally, I looked up the Oilers' schedule and figured out that Game 6 of the Gretzky streak came against the Rockies in Denver on December 21, 1979.*

I checked with Denver Post *librarian Vickie Makings. She went to the microfilm and sent me the PDFs of the clippings via e-mail attachment, and there it was: I indeed had covered that game. I wrote of Gretzky's first appearance in Denver in the advance story the day of the game, then didn't even mention him in the game story because he had only one assist in the Rockies' 5–4 victory. (Or maybe it was cut.) One of my favorite players of all time, tough winger Ron Delorme, nicknamed "Chief" because of his Metis heritage (this was before political correctness banned such references as bigoted), had two goals, and Cherry proclaimed: "Right now, Delorme is the best player on this team by a country mile."*

Gretzky's points streak ended on January 7, 1980, or 19 days before his 19th birthday. So he spent three and a half months in the NHL as an 18-year-old. MacKinnon would have a full season, since his 19th birthday would be September 1, 2014.

SATURDAY, MARCH 8, AT DENVER: BLUES 2, AVALANCHE 1. RECORD: 41–18–5

This didn't rule out the Avalanche catching the Blues and winning the Central Division title, but made it much more of a long shot. At least this time Colorado seemed to belong on the same ice with the Blues, rather than being blown away. Ryan Miller, acquired from Buffalo at the trading deadline, was in the net for the Blues and only allowed P. A. Parenteau's 15th goal of the season.

More disquieting was the fact that Stastny "tweaked" his back on his first shift and didn't return, giving Roy a short bench the rest of the game.

After MacKinnon went pointless, ending his streak, he was motionless at his stall afterwards, staring straight ahead until approached. "I never cared about the streak," he said. "It's just a points streak. I want to help my team any way I can. I have to do a better job."

Despite being kept off the score sheet against the Blues, he still was a runaway leader in rookie scoring, with 22 goals and 51 points.

Roy and Ken Hitchcock hadn't gone out to dinner the night before, but they didn't toss verbal darts, either.

MONDAY, MARCH 10, AT DENVER: AVALANCHE 3, JETS 2 (OT). RECORD: 42–18–5

Duchene got the game-ender in overtime, but the downside was Parenteau suffering another medial collateral ligament knee sprain in the first period. Although he came back on the ice to try it again on a power play, he realized that wasn't wise and was done for the night—and perhaps for the season. "P. A. is a great team guy, and he wanted to give it a try," Roy said.

Those expecting Roy to be a loose cannon again were surprised—or disappointed—when the Jets again tried to play a physical game against the Avalanche, hoping to goad them off their game or into retaliation, and Roy's players kept their cool.

"It's what I said to the guys: 'We cannot end up in the penalty box,'" Roy said. "We couldn't have retaliation penalties. But that's the way we've been all year. We've been very disciplined, and we certainly want to keep it that way."

Roy used Tyson Barrie a few shifts on wing, but he also announced after the game that the Avalanche were recalling Brad Malone and former Boston College forward Paul Carey from Lake Erie.

WEDNESDAY, MARCH 12, AT DENVER: AVALANCHE 3, BLACKHAWKS 2. RECORD: 43–18–5

Ryan O'Reilly's third-period power-play goal put the Avalanche up 3–1, and Colorado held on. Notably, Roy had Nate Guenin and Nick Holden on the ice at the end, again showing faith in his AHL journeymen. Malone and Duchene had the other goals, and at the end of the night, the Avalanche were back in second in the Central Division, one point ahead of the Blackhawks. It was getting to the point where it seemed that the remainder of the season would be jockeying for home-ice advantage for a Colorado-Chicago first-round series.

With Parenteau and Alex Tanguay out, and Malone and Carey dropped onto the fourth line, it again meant the Avalanche would take on a more conventional look—two potent lines and then a defensive third line and an energy fourth line.

Could Colorado get away with that?

"Why not?," Roy asked. "We've been saying this all year. The guys have been playing hard. It doesn't matter who comes in. They just step in and perform. Why not? I have to say that in my years in Montreal when we won, we were not necessarily the best team in the NHL, but we won a lot of series and even the Stanley Cup in '93."

Roy and many others again took note that the franchise's slide, and the shrinkage of the season-ticket base made it possible for opposing team fans to buy up single-game tickets. There were so many Blackhawks fans in red at this one, they could have changed the name of Chopper Circle to Madison Street for the night. "They're all exciting games for our fans, even if I'm seeing a lot of red in the stands," Roy said.

After the game, O'Reilly was wearing the ridiculous-looking shell of a hard hat the Avalanche had started awarding among themselves to the hardest-working player of the game. O'Reilly didn't mind accepting it, but at first he was reluctant to wear it with the cameras rolling before he came around to the magnitude of the honor—and its merits in promoting team camaraderie. The hard-hat tradition began after members of the equipment staff left it at Gabriel Landeskog's locker, teasing him about his oversized head. From there, Landeskog jumped at the chance to turn it into a team tradition.

"We're having fun this year as a team," Landeskog said, "and I thought this would be something fun, too. A lot of teams do it, so why not us, too?"

Landeskog also was an enthusiastic participant in a handful of players doing a lip-sync video to the Imagine Dragons' "Radioactive." The song was familiar to NHL fans of all ages because every team in the league—apparently because it was an instruction in some manual—used it during warm-ups. A few folks had said the video seemed over the top. Landeskog was moved to defend it, saying, "There's always going to be haters out there, but we had fun with it. It's one of those things where we don't take ourselves that seriously, and some fans enjoyed it. Some fans will get pumped up for the playoffs with it, and some fans just get a laugh out of it. Either way, it was a different thing to do. I've never done something like that before, and we had a good laugh out of it."

☆ ☆ ☆

If there was any doubt about the Avalanche goaltending plans for the future, they ended when the team signed Reto Berra to a three-year, $4.35-million contract extension. The money wasn't stunning; the commitment was. That seemed a surprising amount of faith in a goalie who hadn't yet shown much in the NHL. Reading the writing on his dressing-room stall wall, Jean-Sebastien Giguere conceded that he probably would retire after the season. The Avalanche also signed John Mitchell, the Swiss-knife forward, to a three-year, $5.4-million extension. It continued a trend of tying up players with extensions and creating more financial certainty in the cap world, which made even more glaring the uncertainty surrounding Stastny and O'Reilly, whose contracts were about to expire and could be unrestricted and restricted free agents, respectively.

FRIDAY, MARCH 14, AT DENVER: DUCKS 6, AVALANCHE 4. RECORD: 43–19–5

All six Anaheim goals came in the second period, and Semyon Varlamov was pulled after the fifth. The Avalanche got to within 5–4 on goals only

33 seconds apart from Jamie McGinn and Landeskog, but Anaheim's fourth line—going against Colorado's top line—scored on Giguere before the end of the period, and there were no more goals in the third. But there were a few fireworks, befitting the new Anaheim-Colorado rivalry, with Patrick Bordeleau actually reaching over to the other bench to shove Patrick Maroon, who was yapping at Colorado players. Bordeleau drew a game misconduct. Roy hadn't shoved the partition between the benches this time, but he made it clear he wasn't happy.

Why was it getting so heated between the Ducks and Avalanche?

"Well, they seem to enjoy talking to our bench, and I guess tonight our players responded," Roy said. "I learned my lesson," he said of the fine he drew after his tirade in the opener, "and I was quiet. On a serious note, yes, there is some intensity out there, and I guess we're getting attention from other teams, which is good for our players. They deserve that. We play offense, we play intense, and we're always into those games. Even at the end, our group is fearless. We go out there, and even if we are down two goals, we don't stop, and we keep going at them."

SUNDAY, MARCH 16, AT OTTAWA: AVALANCHE 3, SENATORS 1. RECORD: 44–19–5

Andre Benoit got the Avalanche's first goal against his former team, and fellow Ontario native John Mitchell also scored, but the story of the night—again—was Varlamov's work in the net. He had 38 saves against the Senators, and it was a significant rebound in the wake of his bad game against Anaheim.

Varlamov, never exuberant when talking after games, seemed even more somber than usual—despite his strong work.

"Friday night was a nightmare for me," Varlamov said. "I should play better. I can't give up five goals in ten minutes, so I was (upset) about that game. Today was a game where you have to show the team you're ready to play better."

Benoit not only was playing against his former team, but he was about thirty miles from his hometown of St. Albert, Ontario. "It's always fun to score against an old team, and I had lots of family and friends here," he said. "Hopefully, they keep going in. It was a big game, and we were able to get a win. We have to keep this going now."

Next up was Roy's return to Montreal. Knowing what was ahead, and responding to many requests, the Avalanche had scheduled a news conference for Roy the next afternoon.

CLUB DE HOCKEY

It wasn't as big a spectacle as Patrick Roy's first time back to Montreal as a player, which came in March of 1997, about 15 months after his trade. But that did nothing to make Roy's 2014 return nothing less than a front-page, live-TV event. Probably 200 media members packed into a conference room at the Marriott Chateau Champlain to see and hear Roy.

One of Roy's big concerns throughout his first season coaching the Avs was that he might get more press attention than his players. He made it a priority not to talk about his private life all that much, or to dwell on his many past glories as a player.

But in Montreal, that wasn't realistic. Roy was, and probably always will be, the main story anytime one of his teams comes to Montreal, where he won two Stanley Cups and revolutionized the position of goalie.

Roy entered the room for the news conference from a side door and began his session with the press in French. He answered questions for about 20 minutes before granting the English-only people some time, too.

Roy tried to downplay the significance of the Montreal game—the second meeting of the season between the two teams, but the first in Montreal—but nobody was buying it.

"No, I haven't looked forward to [the Montreal] game at all," he said. "I've been talking to our players that I want a partnership with them," he said. "I want them to focus on what we have to do every night and take it one day at a time. I have to do the same thing as them. It is important to me that they are the ones in the front row."

One of the things that Roy didn't mind reminding the press that day was of a fan poll taken in *Le Journal de Montreal* in 2012. He was the landslide answer to the question: "Who would you like to see as the next Canadiens coach?"

"I truly appreciate that," Roy said. "I thought that was a great gesture from them to give me that opportunity to be on top. It made me feel good with the fans. It's not that I had doubt, but at the same time, it was nice to see the past was way behind us, and everybody had moved on. They could see me as their next coach or GM. For the ego, I have to admit, it feels good."

Roy even revealed that he'd had interest in the job and had spoken with new Montreal GM Marc Bergevin about it. Bergevin, new in his job and uncomfortable with selecting a first-time coach, too, bypassed Roy and hired the more experienced Michel Therrien on June 5, 2012—or a year before the Avalanche came after Roy.

At the news conference, Roy helpfully reminded the media that he could have been wearing the classic Habs logo on his chest again. It was classic Roy. He said it was "classy" of Bergevin to call him back and inform him of the team's intention to hire Therrien, but anyone who knew Roy at all knew he remembered any kind of rejection—no matter how politely stated—and stored it away as future motivational material.

Yet, to say Roy still held a major grudge against the Canadiens would be off the mark. In 2008, he had his number 33 retired to the rafters, as part of a touching ceremony that featured three of his Canadiens coaches—Jean Perron, Pat Burns, and Jacques Demers. Roy received several long standing ovations from fans, and one year later Roy even donned the uniform of the Canadiens again to take part in a "practice" with other Canadiens legends as part of the team's 100th anniversary celebration. He was asked at the news conference if he would look up at his number in the rafters.

"I forgot. See how focused I am for the game?" he said.

That triggered laughs.

"You know what?" he added. "I lied to you. I did it before I arrived. I just made sure it's still there. No dust on it, make sure they clean it. Perfect. They do such a great job here. This organization is a lot of class. The Hall of Fame they just built, they put a lot of pride in the past, and there's a great past in this franchise, and they're taking care of it. They certainly deserve a lot of credit for that. I learned a lot from this franchise. It helped me be the person I am but also the player I was."

Still, all around the Avs knew if there was one game Roy probably wanted to win more than any other as the regular season wound down, it was this one against Montreal. Imagined visions—"You messed up not hiring Patrick when you had the chance"—were on the minds of some, including the man himself.

TUESDAY, MARCH 18, AT MONTREAL: CANADIENS 6, AVALANCHE 3. RECORD: 44–20–5

"Two hot dogs each," Joe Sakic said, after asking Josh Kroenke if he'd ever sampled one of the between-periods frankfurters in the media lounge that have long been a staple of Canadiens home games, starting at the old Forum.

In most NHL arenas, the food for the media has long been packed away by game time. In Montreal, they're just getting started. When the horn sounds to end the first period, media and everyone else in the press box (game officials, scouts, assorted others passing through town for the night with a credential) head downstairs to begin queuing up for hot dogs sizzling on a large grill behind a counter full of condiments, cheddar cheese in plastic packets, and assorted drinks.

"*Une ou deux?*" asked the woman taking orders on how many hot dogs.

Deux is the best choice. The delicious, all-beef dogs served on skinny buns that also grill beside them go down fast, but it is perfectly acceptable to talk hockey with food in your mouth between periods in Montreal.

Sakic had long since known of the hot dog tradition in Montreal, but also from his several years playing for the Quebec Nordiques. Some say the hot dogs were even better in Quebec, because of the more buttery buns and slightly longer grilling times. (Yes, that's how intense the intra-provincial rivalry was between those franchises. It extended right down to the hot dogs.)

Sakic, Kroenke, Greg Sherman, Craig Billington, and Charlotte Grahame had flown in earlier that day on a commercial flight from Denver.

Weather delayed the flight a couple of hours, so it was close to game time when they arrived to take in Roy's first NHL game as a coach in the city that once considered him a son.

Sakic was in a good mood, and not just because of the hot dogs. His team was headed to the playoffs for sure, and the man he and Kroenke had flown to Florida several months earlier to lobby to be his first coach, Roy, was a virtual shoo-in for NHL coach of the year.

When the horn sounded to end the game, though, there was no swagger in Roy's step as he walked across the ice next to Andre Tourigny. The Canadiens won a 6–3 decision on the strength of Thomas Vanek's hat trick. The game had been 3–3 with less than seven minutes to go when Jean-Sebastien Giguere lost sight of the puck around his crease and grabbed onto the stick of Max Pacioretty. Vanek's ensuing power-play goal won it, and a downtrodden Giguere was left to explain such a poor showing on his part in a game that had lots of sentimental value to him as well.

Roy gave the Montreal native the start in net as a show of respect to a career that was almost certain to end when the season was over. Giguere, a genial man whose pride is strong and his temper sometimes stronger when he feels slighted, had come more to accept—if not endorse—Colorado's acquisition of Reto Berra. He realized this probably would have been his last year in Denver, whether he retired or tried to remain in the league. "I don't want to go out bitter and angry," he said.

In Montreal, besides the gaffe of grabbing Pacioretty's stick to draw the minor, Giguere looked slow to react on some other goals. When goalies are slow to react, the hockey saying goes, pucks "go right through them." That's how it looked on a couple of Montreal goals against the 36-year-old Giguere.

The Avs walked quietly out of the Bell Centre to a bus, which would take them to the airport and a three-hour flight to Winnipeg for a game against the Jets the next night. John Mitchell was part of the traveling party, but he lumbered in extreme pain. Mitchell had lost an edge in the second period and gone skidding into the end boards back first, hitting with so much force that his legs came up all the way to his face. Picture a guy in a mattress folding together, and that's how Mitchell's contorted body looked.

WEDNESDAY, MARCH 19, AT WINNIPEG: JETS 5, AVALANCHE 4 (OT). RECORD: 44–20–6

With the absences of Paul Stastny, held out of the back-to-back to rest his, yes, back, and Mitchell, Roy again was forced to use Tyson Barrie on the right wing. Overall, the Avs managed to score four goals. Berra looked nervous and slow in his Colorado debut. Wearing a plain, white mask, Berra finished the game flopped a few feet outside his crease, the puck in the net behind him after several patient fakes by Jets forward Blake Wheeler.

The Avs left Canada with only one of four points in their final two games; Chicago overtook them again to move into second place in the Central Division.

FRIDAY, MARCH 21, AT DENVER: BRUINS 2, AVALANCHE 0. RECORD: 44–21–6

The Avalanche lost their third straight, and it was a bit disquieting that they hadn't done well of late against good teams at home. Backup Bruins goalie Chad Johnson had the 31-save shutout, and Boston won its 11th straight.

"I thought we played an outstanding game [and] have nothing to show for it," Roy said.

Roy again was going out of his way to present a calm demeanor and quell any thoughts that the Avalanche—1–3–1 in their previous five games—were coming back to earth in an otherwise remarkable season.

TUESDAY, MARCH 25, AT NASHVILLE: AVALANCHE 5, PREDATORS 4 (SO). RECORD: 45–21–6

On the other hand, the Avalanche got away with one in Music City, playing a stinker—and winning in the shootout. Gabriel Landeskog scored twice, Cody McLeod and Nick Holden had late goals, and Ryan O'Reilly and Landeskog were successful in the shootout. Semyon Varlamov had a bad night, but he made two saves in the shootout to secure the win. "Sometimes it's nice to win a game when you're not playing well," Roy said. "That was the case tonight. I thought we deserved better against the Bruins, and tonight it was the opposite."

THURSDAY, MARCH 27, AT DENVER: AVALANCHE 3, CANUCKS 2 (OT). RECORD: 46–21–6

Tyson Barrie got his third overtime goal of the season to end it, and it was significant because of some bonding. Matt Duchene finally wearied of taking post-whistle hits from the Canucks' Ryan Kesler and reacted with a shove back, and Jamie McGinn and Landeskog both took up the case with Kesler on ensuing shifts. Kesler declined to fight with McGinn, and it all had the Avalanche belittling Kesler for picking his spots after the game. "Our players have been backing each other up pretty well," Roy said.

Barrie's winning goal came after Duchene brought the puck out of the corner, whirled, and delivered a setup pass to Barrie in front.

SATURDAY, MARCH 29, AT DENVER: AVALANCHE 3, SHARKS 2. RECORD: 47–21–6

The Avalanche reached 100 points and clinched a playoff spot with the matinee win, but both of those accomplishments had been considered inevitable for a while. So what happened on the scoreboard wasn't as significant as what happened in an on-ice collision in the opening minutes. Duchene and McGinn got tangled up just inside the San Jose zone, and Duchene—in obvious pain—struggled to get to the Colorado bench, favoring his left leg. He was done for the day. After the game, Roy's gloomy demeanor made it safe to assume he was bracing for bad news about Duchene's knee when he underwent an MRI Sunday or Monday. The Avalanche didn't make Duchene available to the media, but Roy said he had talked with him.

"Obviously, he was disappointed; he was playing so well right now," Roy said. "I'm always a positive person. I believe that he's going to be back for the playoffs. This is the way I am. But at the same time, we lost Peter Forsberg after the second round the year we won the Cup [in

2001], and a team is a team. You have to go out there and play hard and find ways to win games. That's what we're going to continue to do."

McGinn said he and Duchene "just ran into each other. We were both going for the puck. I think we both tried to get out of the way, and maybe that's what made ourselves vulnerable. It was just a freak play. I felt a tweak, but obviously not to the extent of Dutchy."

Oh, yes, there was a game, too. Varlamov had 47 saves. "We've been waiting a lot for this moment; to be in a playoff spot after four years is a great feeling for all of us," the goalie said. "It's pretty special to know you're going to fight for the Stanley Cup."

Mitchell was in the lineup after missing two games with a back injury and had a goal and an assist, and after Duchene went out, he stepped in to center Nathan MacKinnon and Ryan O'Reilly. Unspoken was the reality that if Duchene were out for the rest of the season and the playoffs, Mitchell would be among those expected to step up.

"Obviously, it's a significant loss for our team if he's out for an extended period of time," Mitchell said of Duchene. "We've had injuries during the year, and we've had plenty of guys come in and step up and fill in, and we've done OK. That's going to have to happen again, I guess."

Under different circumstances, more might have been made of this, and there might even have been a few jokes: In the Avalanche's 73rd game of the season, and his 71st, Ryan O'Reilly finally drew his first penalty of the season in the third period. He didn't hook, high stick, or elbow anyone. He didn't board anyone. He didn't even hold or interfere with anyone. He was called for playing with a broken stick. His stick snapped on a defensive zone face-off and, still holding only the shaft, O'Reilly kicked the puck over to the corner before he dropped the stick. That's verboten. O'Reilly lamented, "I need to be smarter than that."

※ ※ ※

The Avalanche didn't practice the next day, a Sunday, and the lid of secrecy was on. Duchene underwent the MRI and was determined to have a sprained medial collateral ligament, which would keep him out of the lineup for four to five weeks—in other words, at least through the first round of the playoffs. The Avalanche didn't tell anyone that, declaring there would be no additional news about Duchene until the next day, in conjunction with Monday's practice. Such secrecy cut against Duchene's grain, and he found it excruciatingly difficult to not be able to pass along the news and prognosis on Twitter.

Twitter was the modern version of Original Six players getting hammered in a bar and passing along secrets.

At practice Monday, the media mob rivaled the size of the one that came to Family Sports the day after Varlamov's arrest early in the season. At least this time, it was the result of something that had happened on the ice.

Early in the practice, the Avalanche staff texted a heads-up to the media room with the specifics of the diagnosis and prognosis—roughly, oh, 3.8 seconds before the team tweeted the summary and posted the news on its website.

Soon after, Duchene himself tweeted out (in individual tweets that have been pieced together): "Been waiting to tweet til the official release but just a few thoughts here for you guys. 100 pts & playoff bound is something all of us have been working towards for a long time. Something to be majorly proud of. Secondly, the thought of not playing in the first round for me has been devastating. We have outstanding medical and training staff that will be helping me to get healthy ASAP. I will be doing everything in my power to be ready for Game 1. And if not then, shortly after! We are a helluva team ready for the playoffs. Thanks to all of you for your thoughts and prayers they are greatly appreciated!"

On the ice, MacKinnon was centering McGinn and O'Reilly. Roy confirmed that was what he was going to try next with Duchene unavailable. "Just to give us different options," Roy said. "You can't just go 'bang' in the playoffs and try that. It's good to try different things. Our situation in the standings allows us to do this."

MacKinnon accepted moving back to center. "Hockey's hockey, and I'm sure people will think I feel pressure, but I don't," he said. "That's the least pressure situation I've been in all year, I think." He added of playing with O'Reilly and McGinn: "I'm just going to try and step in and create some chemistry with them. They'll be easy guys to play with. The way they play, they play a simple game, a give-and-go game, and that's what I like best. I like guys who move the puck quick and keep it simple. Factor [O'Reilly] has had a heck of a year, and Ginner [McGinn] is big and physical. I'm not going to replace Dutchy. That's just not going to happen. He's been one of our best players, and you can't replace him, especially at this time of year. It's going to be tough, but we're going to have to find wins without him."

Roy said Mitchell would play right wing on the Paul Stastny-centered line, also with Landeskog. The wild card was the possible return of P. A. Parenteau, who had been out three weeks because of his second MCL injury of the season. He had skated hard on his own for about 15 minutes before his teammates came on the ice. Roy said he hoped Parenteau could play in the final game of the regular season, at Anaheim on April 13.

"If not, we're pretty confident that he will be back for the first game against Chicago," Roy added.

Yes, the Avalanche still were assuming they'd be meeting the Blackhawks in the first round.

O'Reilly said that as far as he knew, no consideration had been given to moving him back to center, his natural position, in the wake of the Duchene injury. "I do love center and miss it a bit," he said. "But I like playing the wing, and I think it's good when I can be versatile like that."

TUESDAY, APRIL 1, AT COLUMBUS: AVALANCHE 3, BLUE JACKETS 2 (OT). RECORD: 48–21–6

Trailing 2–0 entering the third period, the Avalanche got goals from Brad Malone and Landeskog in the third and then the winner from Landeskog with 32.2 seconds left in overtime. Nobody wanted to brag too much about this, but Colorado was 4–0 for the season without Duchene in the lineup. But Roy did bring up how the Avalanche, with a playoff spot locked up and going against a team fighting for every point to advance to the postseason, didn't mail it in for the third period. "We changed our culture, and we never give up," Roy said.

THURSDAY, APRIL 3, AT DENVER: AVALANCHE 3, RANGERS 2 (SO). RECORD: 49–21–6

Tyson Barrie came up with late heroics again, scoring the goal with 52 seconds left in the third period that forced overtime. He fanned on his original shot from the slot, but recovered and beat Henrik Lundqvist for his 11th goal of the season. No, he didn't end it in the four-on-four this time, but got the only goal of the shootout to give the Avalanche the win and the second point. The most significant part about it was that Roy again judged the moment and, for the first time all season, included Barrie among his three overtime shooters.

"Mr. Lucky maybe," Barrie said. "I kind of whiffed on the first shot, but it just kept rolling with me, and I got a second shot at it. Just fortunate it got by him."

The injury bug struck again, though, with winger Cody McLeod suffering an ankle injury in the second period and not returning. It didn't appear serious, but as the Avalanche became thinner at forward, it raised the question of whether Colorado's third and fourth lines would be capable of pitching in with important goals in the playoffs. Those with long memories recalled that on Roy's teams during his playing days, third-line center Stephane Yelle—punchless in the regular season—had a way of contributing offensively at opportune times. That could be deflating for opponents, especially when they had invested considerable attention and energy on neutralizing Joe Sakic's and Peter Forsberg's lines.

GRIT

NO. 24, MARC-ANDRE CLICHE, 6'0", 202 LBS., BORN FEBRUARY 11, 1984, ROUYN-NORANDA, QUEBEC

When the Avalanche claimed Cliche on waivers during the preseason, it was another time that the QMJHL connections of Patrick Roy and his coaching staff came into play. In major junior, Cliche played for Lewiston, Maine, going against teams coached by Roy and two of his Avalanche assistants, Andre Tourigny and Mario Duhamel, and obviously caught their eyes. What made the pickup surprising was that the Avalanche seemed well stocked at center, and Cliche was under a one-way contract at $550,000 per season, meaning he'd collect that and be an expensive minor-leaguer if Colorado sent him down to Lake Erie.

He stuck, serving as a primary penalty killer and third- and fourthliner, and the Avalanche learned to live with what couldn't be described as anything other than offensive punchlessness. He wasn't counted on to score, of course, but this was ridiculous: He still had only one goal as the Avalanche entered the final week of the regular season. As with others, the Colorado front office backed up its faith in Cliche by signing him to a two-year, $1.4-million extension.

Cliche called the deal "unreal," and added, "Being in the American Hockey League for that long and having a one-year [contract] this year and not knowing what's going to happen next year, and finally signing an extension like this, it felt really good. Everybody is happy back home, too."

The salary was low enough that it wasn't much of a risk. Still, it was an endorsement for the idea that the Avalanche could afford to have a role-playing forward—and not an enforcer—who was no threat to score.

NO. 25, MAXIME TALBOT, 5'11", 190 LBS., BORN FEBRUARY 11, 1984, LEMOYNE, QUEBEC

When Roy announced Talbot's acquisition early in the season, he cited the veteran forward's Stanley Cup credentials. In fact, Talbot scored both of Pittsburgh's goals in a 2–1 victory over Detroit in Game 7 of the 2009 Stanley Cup finals, and had scored twice in Game 3.

"The personal achievement of that game, I feel like that might come when I retire, when I look back and think, 'That was freakin' amazing,'" Talbot said after joining the Avalanche.

His eight goals in the 2009 postseason were only four short of his regular season total. In Pittsburgh, his popularity crossed sports lines, in part because he appeared in several television commercials, including some for a car dealership that earned him the teasing nickname "Super-star." He moved on to the Flyers as an unrestricted free agent in July 2011, so he brought a five-year, $8.75-million deal with him to Colorado that ran through 2015–16.

Roy also noted that Talbot was a coveted penalty killer, so it wasn't a surprise when he settled into that role, along with Cliche, with the Avalanche. By late in the season, though, partly because he wasn't play-ing with playmakers or scorers, his seven goals for Colorado was one of the issues involved in the question of whether the Avalanche, partly due to injuries, were too reliant on role-players.

Talbot missed only one game for the Avalanche, to be with Cynthia Phaneuf, for the February 27 birth of their son, Jaxson.

By late in the season, with a playoff berth all but locked up, Talbot was looking ahead to a postseason reprise. "I still think that I could top it," he said of Game 7 five years earlier. "You dream of the overtime, Stanley Cup, game-winning goal. Looking back, you win the Cup, enjoy it for a short period of time and then you think, 'OK, we're going to win again.' You realize how tough it is to go back there. You snap your fingers, and it's over. So the goal all the time is to try to help get back to that place."

NO. 55, CODY McLEOD, 6'2", 210 LBS., BORN JUNE 26, 1984, BINSCARTH, MANITOBA

When he made it to the NHL, McLeod became the first player from the village of Binscarth—population 500—to do so. In fact, just making major junior, with the Portland Winterhawks, was a big deal; and when Cody got his first hat trick there as a 17-year-old, the next morning the town mayor called his mother, Sandra, to congratulate her.

Sandra was a caretaker for elderly patients, and Cody's father, Peter, drove a truck on long-haul trips. He was gone often, so his mother had the responsibility of driving him to Foxwarren, ten miles away, to play hockey. Eventually, he played four seasons for Portland, getting 661 penalty minutes in 257 games. The Avalanche signed him as an un-drafted free agent, and he seemed locked in as a career minor-leaguer until he ended up on a productive line with Mark Rycroft, in the twi-light of his career, and Cody McCormick at Lake Erie. He set his sights higher, and he was recalled to play the final 49 games with the Ava-lanche in 2007–08. He even had 15 goals the next season, then settled into the role of "middleweight" enforcer and energy forward. Part of the price was living with his occasional ill-advised penalties, but he even wore the "A" often as assistant captain.

NO. 58, PATRICK BORDELEAU, 6'6", 225 LBS., BORN MARCH 23, 1986, MONTREAL

Another player who went up against Roy's teams in the QMJHL, Bor-deleau was with three teams in the league over four seasons before beginning a five-year stay in the minors, including as far down as the ECHL. Eventually, he spent three full seasons and part of a fourth with Lake Erie before getting his chance with the Avalanche following the end of the lockout in early 2013. Early on, Roy seemed locked in on having Bordeleau around as his enforcer and agitator, and over the course of the season, he occasionally showed flashes of offensive touch.

It became tricky when he suffered ligament damage in his left hand in a December 5 fight against Edmonton's Luke Gazdic, but Roy asked him to keep playing—with fighting off limits—to be a physical deterrent and presence. Of course, because he couldn't announce that he couldn't fight, eyebrows occasionally were raised when he seemed to pass on chances to drop the gloves. Ultimately, though, he let the world know of the injury in mid-March, adding that it was healed—and that he would fight again if circumstances warranted. He had continued to play a physical game, and with another game against the Blues coming up, it seemed safe to assume he would kick that up a notch.

AND DOWN THE STRETCH THEY COME!

SATURDAY, APRIL 5, AT ST. LOUIS: AVALANCHE 4, BLUES 0. RECORD: 50–21–6

After looking overmatched against the Blues in the three previous meetings, Colorado not only got the shutout, it played a physical game that clearly got under the fingernails of Ken Hitchcock's team. Roy hadn't liked how the Blues had pushed his team around in the earlier meetings, and he was determined not to let it happen again.

This time, Colorado got goals from Paul Stastny, Nathan MacKinnon, Nick Holden, and Ryan O'Reilly, and romped.

In the third period, Patrick Bordeleau—playing on the third line in the wake of injuries to Matt Duchene and Cody McLeod—made a big run at Blues defenseman Kevin Shattenkirk. Just as Shattenkirk passed the puck along the glass at his own blue line, Bordeleau crushed him with a hard but legal hit. Shattenkirk's own stick nailed him in the face, and he was bloodied. Hitchcock and his players didn't consider it a clean and legal hit, and the response was to goon it up from there. Blues captain David Backes grabbed MacKinnon and threw him down to the ice.

FROM THE NOTEBOOK OF ADRIAN DATER

It was my turn to go from hearing Patrick Roy to asking Ken Hitchcock for comment.

First, some background from my perspective: There are good reasons the Blues' coach is a favorite of the media in the NHL. When asked an honest question about the game, Hitch almost always gave full and insightful answers. He also remembered reporters' names and was good about calling back even the out-of-towners. (If players and coaches only realized how much goodwill that buys with the media, how much benefit of the doubt it gives them in times of turmoil, they'd do it more often.)

But inside the game itself, plenty of people don't like him. Those critics consider the portly coach to be arrogant, condescending, pompous, self-righteous, and hypocritical. With his arms folded on the bench and the occasional sneer, Hitchcock often gives off the vibe that he's the smartest guy in the building. Thing is, that's very often the case.

Hitchcock is a hockey lifer, thoroughly consumed with the team. But he does leave time to read books on a wide variety of topics, especially the history of the Civil War. When he was a coach with Philadelphia, Hitchcock often trekked to Pennsylvania battlefields such as Gettysburg, even taking part in reenactments in full uniform of both sides.

When the Avalanche arrived in St. Louis, the Blues remained the one team in the league Roy's group hadn't beaten. Hitchcock was 3–0 against Roy, including that ugly 7–1 spanking early in the year. The Avs were a nice little story and all, but to Hitchcock they seemed inconsequential to his mighty team. But that wasn't the biggest reason Roy burned to at least get one win against Hitchcock before the playoffs.

Roy never forgets a slight. Fifteen years later, he still brings up an article I wrote for the Denver Post *about him smashing the television and VCR in the visiting coach's office in Anaheim, displaying his anger at Bob Hartley.*

I broke the story, but it was two weeks after it happened, and the Canadiens were in town when the story appeared on the top of the front page. Roy blew up at me, accusing me of purposely holding the story until his ex-team and all its media came to town so they could make the story even bigger. That's the way it played out, but it was pure coincidence that the Canadiens were there when I learned of the story.

In a newspaper war as big as ours was with the Rocky Mountain News *in those days, no way would I have held on to any story like that, for any reason. It would have been out the second I'd heard of it. (In those days, you still had to wait until the next morning's paper to get news out there.)*

A few weeks before the game at St. Louis, when the Avs were winning but not getting on the front page of the Post *sports section all that often, Roy referred to the old Anaheim story. "Maybe if I smash up a TV I can get us on the cover, no?," he asked in a media scrum.*

Do absolutely anything to tick off Roy, and he's going to file it away in his elephant-like memory and make it his life's mission to even up the score at some point. So it didn't at all surprise me when Roy clearly filed away Hitchcock's "junior hockey" comment from afar about the opening night incident in Denver, and even when he took those digs at Hitchcock after that game in Denver—leading to Hitchcock's request for Terry Frei to tell Roy "to shut the fuck up."

But Hitchcock's team won the first three games in the season series between the two teams. Roy can be a sore loser, but generally he gave the opposition credit for wins and rarely made disparaging personal remarks about other players or coaches after losses. On this warm and sunny St. Louis Saturday in early April, however, Roy was ready to get one game's worth of revenge at least against Hitchcock's team, which held the top spot in the Western Conference, seven points ahead of the Avs.

I knew this would be a good postgame interview session, and it was.

What did Roy think of Backes's actions?, I asked.

"To me, it's gutless from Backes. He showed what kind of leader he is, if you're going after an 18-year-old," Roy said. "Not very impressed, not very impressed. Gutless, in my opinion. I mean, Shattenkirk hurt himself with his own stick. His own stick hit him in the nose, and he was bleeding, and he made a pretty big act."

I couldn't run to the Blues' interview room fast enough. There, Hitchcock was addressing the assembled media.

After a couple of questions from St. Louis media, I piped up to Hitchcock.

"Patrick Roy called your captain, Backes, gutless. Do you . . ."

Hitchcock shut me off.

"Do me a favor, Adrian: Don't come in here and comment on him. I've done my commenting on him. He can say whatever he wants. He always has something to say after every game, so you guys pick up on what he wants. I'm worried about my team and the way we play."

I respected Hitchcock's space and didn't ask any follow-up questions. Hitch went off on a bit of a tangent about Bordeleau being "debris," or the kind of things he brings to a team as "debris"; and kinda/sorta wanting to call Gabe Landeskog gutless, and maybe promising to go after an Avs defender the next time they played; and, well, after that he just sort of slunk away.

Hitchcock did not come off well, and for one day anyway Roy had won all the battles against him. Hitchcock still had a claim of two playoff victories against Roy, in 1999 and 2000 as coach of Dallas—in two Western Conference finals that each finished in Game 7 Stars' wins.

In nearly 20 years as a head coach in the NHL, Hitchcock had won an awfully lot of games but still had just one Stanley Cup, with the '99 Stars. Roy could always flash his four Stanley Cup rings if he wanted, and in his first year as a head coach, he already had a 50-win season. Hitchcock went 15–23–5 his first season as an NHL coach (though it was a partial one, taking over for Bob Gainey midway through). His playoff record since going to the conference finals back-to-back with Dallas, entering the 2014 postseason, was 29–37.

As I left the Scottrade Center that day, I was overcome with one thought: Please, let these two teams meet in the playoffs someday soon. It would be a reporter's dream.

SUNDAY, APRIL 6, AT DENVER: PENGUINS 3, AVALANCHE 2 (SO). RECORD: 50–21–7

In the Penguins' only appearance of the season in Denver, Sidney Crosby was among the handful of Pittsburgh scratches. The initial instinct was to blast the Penguins for that, but Crosby had played in all 78 games up to that point, and it was hard to work up much anger over coach Dan Bylsma's decision to rest Crosby, left wing Chris Kunitz, and defensemen Brooks Orpik and Olli Maatta. All had played the night before at Minnesota.

"The only sad part is there's a lot of people coming here to see Sidney Crosby play, but that's fine," Roy said. "It's part of our business, and it's the beauty of our game, actually, because I thought it was a very entertaining game."

Ryan O'Reilly and Bordeleau had the Colorado goals before the Penguins won in the shootout, and at the end of the night, the Avalanche were four points behind St. Louis and two ahead of Chicago in the Central Division. The Avalanche finished 26–11–4 at home, and that would turn out to be the eighth-best home-ice record in the league. Also, in what had become a tradition for the franchise and for many teams, the Avalanche took off their jerseys after the game and presented them to selected fans. For the first time in four years, the ceremony didn't come as the players were preparing to bolt from Denver. Colorado was going into the season-concluding four-game road trip knowing that there would be postseason hockey in the Pepsi Center.

TUESDAY, APRIL 8, AT EDMONTON: AVALANCHE 4, OILERS 1. RECORD: 51–21–7
THURSDAY, APRIL 10, AT VANCOUVER: AVALANCHE 4, CANUCKS 2. RECORD: 52–21–7

The two road wins gave the Avalanche their longest points streak of the season, making them 8–0–1 in their last nine. That, plus the Blues' complete collapse, meant that the Avalanche suddenly had a shot—a real shot—at winning the Central Division title, which would get them out of a first-round matchup with Chicago. The wins came without four everyday forwards in the lineup, but P. A. Parenteau was on the verge of returning (again), and McLeod's ankle injury wasn't expected to keep him out much longer, either.

Roy had said up front he planned to give Semyon Varlamov some rest during the final week; he went with Jean-Sebastien Giguere in the net in Edmonton and was rewarded with a solid effort.

Two days later, Varlamov got the win at Vancouver, giving him 41 for the season and sole possession of the team record, ahead of Roy. The Avalanche coach was nice enough to avoid repeatedly pointing out that his career came before the shootout guaranteed a winner and a loser in each game. Paul Stastny had two goals against the Canucks, and by the end of the night, the Avalanche were tied with the fading Blues for first in the Central.

Although it made sense when Roy said he was going to stick to his plan to not use Varlamov at San Jose on the second night of the back-to-back, his insistence on giving Reto Berra his second start against the Sharks seemed puzzling. But Roy's occasional quirky moves had mostly worked out all season, so the reaction mostly involved affording the coach the benefit of the doubt.

After the win in Vancouver, John Mitchell—again pressed into a top two-line role because of the injuries—was on the Avalanche's postgame radio broadcast and spoke in the dressing room.

He seemed to be fine.

FROM THE NOTEBOOK OF TERRY FREI

I met the Avalanche in San Jose and covered the final two games of the trip and the regular season.

Because Colorado had played the night before and landed in the Bay Area in the middle of the night, the Avalanche didn't have a morning skate in San Jose. The Sharks, locked into second place in the Pacific and a first-round series against Los Angeles, did. So I went to the San Jose arena and was in on the formal game-morning scrum with San Jose coach Todd McLellan and spoke with him alone informally.

McLellan was a former Mike Babcock assistant at Detroit. When the Colorado job was open in 2008, I covered a Red Wings-Stars Western Conference final and asked McLellan if he was interested in the Avalanche position. He said yes, and we talked more about it. I not only put his interest on the record in a story, I suggested in a column that he would be a good hire. The Avalanche ended up re-elevating Tony Granato, and San Jose's offer to McLellan might have trumped Colorado's anyway, but it would have been interesting to see how it played out if he had ended up in Denver.

Now I was hearing McLellan assess the team I thought he should have gotten a chance to coach.

"They've obviously done remarkable things," McLellan said. "I think it started last year when Joe and Patrick came in and put their stamp on the team. They've left their mark, quite clearly. It's also a reflection on

the type of players they have there now. Some of their young players who have been high draft picks and have come into the league have really blossomed. They're a team that has done damage not only this year, but I'm sure it's going to happen for a number of years now."

It was pretty obvious he had read what his former boss, Babcock, had said the previous month and was determined to be a bit more diplomatic.

After the Avalanche arrived at the rink, because of the lack of a morning skate, Roy met with me before the game to provide pregame quotes that, with a late start on the West Coast, would make do for my early stories.

Roy said he hadn't wavered about playing Berra against the Sharks. Interestingly, he interpreted the question as wanting to know why he wasn't going with Varlamov.

"I guess because I played the position and I know how tough it is when you have a game like [Varlamov] had yesterday, coming here at three in the morning, it's short-term," Roy said. "Even if we win tonight and we don't win the first playoff game, then, what the heck. I'd rather think long-term. I believe this is about team concept. I understand Varly has a big role in our success, and he's been playing well for us from the start to the end. But this is a team, and we need Varly well-rested in the playoffs. Reto practiced well, Jiggy played a game in Edmonton, and we have to stick to the plan."

He said he hadn't decided about who would play Sunday in Anaheim. "I believe if we are in the battle, we are going to have to go with Varly," Roy said. "He's going to be well-rested."

Roy said he wasn't worrying about how the playoff pairings developed.

"I believe in destiny," he said. "If it's meant to happen, it will happen. Don't force it. Stick to what you believe. And don't have any regrets at the end after sticking to the plan."

When I asked him about his lineup in the upcoming game, he revealed that John Mitchell wouldn't play against the Sharks because he had said he was having headaches. The fear in the era of heightened awareness of concussion issues and protocols was that he had suffered a concussion. Still, I got the impression the move with Mitchell was more a precaution pending additional tests than anything else. In this world now, a player asking for aspirin can set off alarms.

FRIDAY, APRIL 11, AT SAN JOSE: SHARKS 5, AVALANCHE 1. RECORD: 52–22–7

Despite the Colorado loss, the Avalanche still were in the driver's seat in the race for the Central Division title. That was because St. Louis that night lost its fifth straight, 3–0 to Dallas, and the Avalanche and Blues remained tied at the end of the night. That meant that even if St. Louis beat Detroit on Sunday afternoon, the Avalanche could claim the divisional title with a win at Anaheim Sunday night.

But none of that was due to a Colorado goaltender's heroics.

Reto Berra was awful against the Sharks. Roy yanked the Swiss goalie after he allowed two goals on only five shots, bringing on Giguere. "It was a decision the coach made," Berra said. "I mean, I tried my best."

Said Roy: "The only reason I pulled him was just to change the momentum of the game. Obviously, right now he's probably not playing with the confidence that he probably normally has."

A more defensible move might have been to leave him in the game longer and essentially admit that the game was out of hand. But Roy never had acted as if a two-goal deficit was insurmountable, so he could make the case that he wasn't giving up. More disquieting was the fact that the goaltender the Avalanche had ticketed as Varlamov's long-range backup, and signed to a contract extension, had looked so shaky in his two starts for his new team. The other sticky point about Berra is that by having three goaltenders on the active roster down the stretch, it lessened the Avalanche options, especially as it coped with temporary injuries that didn't warrant placing players on injured reserve.[1]

The other potential problem was that Tyson Barrie was injured when hit by the Sharks' Jason Demers and didn't return. "Upper body injury," Roy said. "Obviously, closer to the playoffs, I'm going to keep it like this. We've been pretty much open to you guys all year, but right now we'll see how he goes in the next couple of days."

Barrie said later: "I think that was a clean hit. I dropped the puck to [Nathan MacKinnon], and I was looking at the puck too long."

Parenteau was back in the lineup as scheduled. And because St. Louis that night lost its fifth straight, 3–0 to Dallas, the Avalanche and Blues remained tied. That meant that even if St. Louis beat Detroit on

---

1. NHL teams can have 23 players on the active roster and 20 in the lineup each night.

Sunday afternoon, the Avalanche could claim the divisional title with a win at Anaheim Sunday night.

Roy said he would change his plans and go with Varlamov at Anaheim.

*　*　*

The Avalanche didn't practice on Saturday, so no additional word came on Barrie and Mitchell, but Colorado recalled defenseman Stefan Elliott from Lake Erie as a precaution. At least stylistically and in terms of size, he was similar to Barrie, so it wasn't inconceivable that he could end up plugged into the lineup to fill the same role.

When Anaheim had a guaranteed point because the game against the Kings went to overtime on Saturday night at the Staples Center, that ruled out Colorado catching the Ducks for the top record in the Western Conference, which would come into play to decide home-ice advantage in a Colorado-Anaheim conference final. The Ducks ended up beating the Kings 4–3 in a shootout and adding a second point.

Then on Sunday afternoon, the St. Louis collapse was complete when the Blues lost 3–0 at home to Detroit. Because Colorado owned the tiebreaker—more regulation and overtime wins—the Avalanche clinched the Central Division title while hanging around the team hotel.

After all the focus on a first-round matchup with Chicago, it now was official: The Avalanche would face Minnesota in the first round instead.

Given that nothing would be at stake in the Sunday night game (for either team, actually), word came that Roy would revert to the plan to use Giguere in the net against the Ducks. It was a classy move, of course, considering Giguere's career highlights came in his days with Anaheim. It was the second sort of gesture Roy had made to honor Giguere following his appearance at Montreal.

Because opening face-off was scheduled for 5 p.m. Pacific Time, the Avalanche didn't have a morning skate. Roy again spoke after the team arrived at the arena, in this case, the Honda Center.

He accepted congratulations for clinching the division title.

"I was watching here and there," he said of the Red Wings-Blues game. "Obviously, at the end, when it was 3–0, it was nice. But, at the same time, you always think you're going to have to come and play tonight and win the game to win the division. But here we are, and to me, this is the most surprising division championship we have had in Avalanche history. No one expected us to be where we are, and I certainly would like to give credit to our players because the players from the first day of training camp have been outstanding. You could see they wanted to see things changing, they wanted to do well, they wanted to make the playoffs. They were extremely receptive to teaching."

Did he at least give a fist pump when the Blues lost?

"It's funny how I am," he said. "I was already thinking about Minny. Yes, we're happy winning the division, but at the same time, there's a new challenge ahead of us. I always like to look more ahead than behind. I think that's what made my career, and it's the way I am. Now we know we're going to play against a very good team, and it's going to be a nice challenge for us."

Roy said Mitchell and Barrie wouldn't play against the Ducks, but he added that Barrie was being held out as a precaution and would be available to play against Minnesota.

Roy's greatness as a player was confirmed in the playoffs, so it was reasonable to ask to what extent the 2013–14 Avalanche's success would be defined in the postseason.

"I'm not going to say we have accomplished nothing," he said. "Going from second-to-last in the NHL to a playoff spot, it's pretty impressive. What's very impressive is going from second-to-last in the NHL and last in the division to win the division where you had teams like Chicago and St. Louis. But, at the same time, when the puck drops against Minny, it's a new task for us. We're still a young team, but it's a nice learning process.

"Let's not kid ourselves. Did I think we would win the division? The answer is no. Especially when 15 days or 16 days ago, we were like nine points behind the St. Louis Blues. Did I think that would happen? No. But at the same time, I was not trying to think about what would be the end of the season. I always believed we could have a very good year, and you never know where that brings you. But here we are."

He said of the matchup against Minnesota: "I think we picked up nine of ten points against these guys, and that's pretty impressive. I'm saying that we're going to have to continue to play the same kind of hockey we did against these guys. Obviously, we're going to have to look at some video and prepare ourselves. It's a team that played really well.

Everybody thought at the end they were in trouble, but this is a team that seems to find a way to come back, and they made the playoffs."

SUNDAY, APRIL 13, AT ANAHEIM: DUCKS 3, AVALANCHE 2 (OT). RECORD: 52–22–8

The framed picture in the Honda Center press box showed Ducks teammates Teemu Selanne and Jean-Sebastien Giguere (with hair) embracing and posing with the Stanley Cup after the Game 7 victory over Ottawa in 2007.

And, now, both were playing what most assumed was the final regular-season game of their long NHL careers. Selanne, the Finnish Flash, was 43 and had declared his intention to retire. Giguere was leaning that way, perhaps nudged along by the Avalanche's commitment to Berra.

The Anaheim crowd cheered Selanne on every shift as if it would be his last, which was at least a little curious given the Ducks' upcoming playoff run. During a video tribute to Giguere on the scoreboard during the first period, the fans gave him a prolonged ovation, and players from both teams tapped sticks on the ice.

Giguere made 33 saves, but the game ended when Anaheim's Nick Bonino scored at 1:33 of overtime. Selanne recruited Giguere to take a lap with him around the rink as the fans cheered.

"It's surreal a little bit," Giguere said. "I'm sure to Teemu it meant a lot more because he's meant so much to the Ducks, and people every time he was on the ice gave him a standing ovation. It's very special. For him to think of me and come and get me, it's something that is very special to me, and I'll never forget it."

Colorado finished 52–22–8 for the season, with 112 points, the third-highest total in the league behind Boston and Anaheim. Amazingly, the home and road records were identical—26–11–4. That was the best road record in the league.

The biggest compliment given to them was that expectations had been raised to the point where it seemed no big deal that this came after a 16–25–7 record and 39 points in the lockout-shortened 2012–13 season, better than only the Florida Panthers. Extrapolating, that 48-game total would have been the equivalent of 67 points in a full season.

In that sense, Colorado had made a 45-point jump in a year. That's a quantum leap.

The 52 wins tied a franchise record, joining the 2000–01 Stanley Cup champions, which went 52–10–6–4 (for 114 points) in the pre-shootout era, when games still could end in ties (and six did).

"I guess we're going to look at it at the end, when everything's going to be over, and probably realize that was a very special year," Roy said. "But right now, our focus is to prepare ourselves for Minny. I'm not looking to put things into perspective. We want to be ready for Game 1, and I thought that's great what our guys did here tonight. They could have taken it easy, but they worked hard and they played hard and certainly showed the character of our team."

Roy gave the Colorado fans a pre-playoff pep talk.

"Our fans have been one of the reasons why we had so much success, because of the support that we had, and it's going to be even more fun," he said. "The message is I'm glad that they've been patient with us, and now we hope they're going to come and cheer for us during the playoffs. We need them; they're very important to us."

The Minnesota-Colorado matchup ended up catching many by surprise, including newspaper writers who had written material for playoff previews and special sections that focused on a Chicago-Colorado first-round series. So, what did Roy have to say to the Colorado-based Chicago fans who bought tickets to the first round and had planned to show up in red at the Pepsi Center?

Smiling and beginning to walk away, Roy said over his shoulder: "Good luck on eBay."

Part III

Playoffs

IT'S MINNY

In the visiting dressing room at Anaheim, the Avalanche treated the loss to the Ducks as if it didn't matter. In fact, it didn't. So for once, conversations were audible, music was playing, and the players weren't uncomfortable looking ahead to the matchup with Minnesota and the Avalanche's first playoff series since 2010.

They noted that the Wild had been strengthened in the trading deadline deals that brought in goalie Ilya Bryzgalov and winger Matt Moulson.

"Any matchup in the West would be tough," Gabriel Landeskog said. "It'll be fun. We're excited to get going, and in the first round, it wouldn't matter who we're playing, we're going to bring the same game. Obviously, if you just look at the standings, you'd rather play Minnesota. But we know that Minnesota or Chicago or whoever it would have been would have been a tough matchup. We'll take Minnesota, and not playing until Thursday is a good thing."

Ryan O'Reilly had just finished as the Avalanche's leading goal scorer, with 28, and with just the one minor penalty, joined Butch Goring as the only NHL players ever to appear in 80 games and get two or fewer penalty minutes in a season. (Goring had two penalty minutes in 1977–78 with Los Angeles before getting zero in 1980–81, when he played in "only" 78 games with the Islanders.)

"I think no matter who you play, it's going to be tough in the first round the playoffs, everyone's so hungry," O'Reilly said. "Obviously, I think we're going to win"—he chuckled there, then continued—"but it's going to be a tough series. They have some good players we're going to have to be aware of at all times on the ice. But all in all, I think if we do the little things right, we'll come out on top."

Back in Denver, Roy gave the Avalanche Monday off.

By then, the Denver media coverage of the Avalanche had been kicked up a notch—from heightened in the wake of the Broncos' Super Bowl flop to almost Bronco-esque. Reconfiguring media areas for NBA and NHL playoffs is commonplace, but often waits until after the first round. In this instance, the Avalanche went ahead and moved the officials' and media dining area from the main pressroom to a corner of the rink level and turned the main pressroom into an interview area, complete with a raised stage and podium. No longer would a cramped room down the hall from the Avalanche dressing room have to serve as the site of postgame Roy media sessions.

FROM THE NOTEBOOK OF TERRY FREI

Noticing the headlong rush of Denver media finally finding the Avalanche late in the season, I was having fun posting "Denver media hockey bandwagon updates" on Twitter. Some misunderstood them, and it was partially my fault. They were NOT the rants of a hockey beat writer whining because "his" sport didn't get enough attention. I was not a one-sport specialist immersed in the sport's culture and arguing as an "insider."

I'm not even against bandwagons. Bandwagons are an All-American phenomenon, rewarding those who earn support and in these sorts of instances, media attention.

Here's what bothered me about the media:

First, this wasn't curling (and I meant that with all due respect to curling). It depends on perspective, because I fully admit I can't name five Major League Soccer players, and I can't defend the charge that the media in this town, including me, has "undercovered" the Rapids, for example. But I operate with the traditional assumption that the NHL and the Avalanche are among the "major four." I've never understood both the national and local approach of media members laughing off their ignorance of, or disinterest in, hockey without embarrassment.

Actually, the sport is far less complicated than football, yet many media members seem intimidated by it. (Football is much easier to bluff about, though . . . e.g., just say the third-and-eight draw is a "great call" if it works and "too conservative" when it doesn't.)

Second, the collective fixation on the Broncos by those with the power to set their own agendas and itineraries led to massive undercoverage and attention paid significant other areas of the Colorado sports scene.

Here were a few of my "bandwagon" tweets, in reverse chronological order, with some words added and edits done for reasons of context and clarity. Each followed "Denver media hockey bandwagon update."

Erik Johnson, NHL No. 1 pick, was one and done at U of Minnesota. John Calipari was not his coach.

Just think of what Nathan MacKinnon would have been like at Minnesota Duluth this season.

If the visiting team dallies, the morning skate becomes an afternoon skate.

Nathan MacKinnon was 18 at the start of the season, too.

Pulling your goalie with three minutes left is NOT normal.

I'm an open-minded, tolerant fellow, but no writer who ever has cited WAR should be allowed in a hockey press box.

You will be glared at if you call a Slovak a Czech or say a guy from BC went to BU. Those errors are equally egregious.

If a coach says they're going to take it two games at a time, you've got a scoop.

Yes, there's a reason and quite a story behind why U.S. Olympian Paul Stastny speaks Slovak.

No Avs players are expected to take a Troy Tulowitzki Scheduled Day Off.

The Avalanche didn't take a knee to get that one to overtime.

THERE ARE BAGELS AND DONUTS AT THE MORNING SKATE IN THE PLAYOFFS!

Goalie also can be the netminder, or if you really want to be cool, the padded guardian of the corded igloo.

Rockies star Lanny McDonald was better than Todd Helton, and he's already in the Hall of Fame.

After the morning skate, each coach MUST be asked if first goal is going to be big.

Avalanche captain Gabriel Landeskog is speaking to you in his second language. Honest.

1, Citizen Kane. 2, Slap Shot. 3, Casablanca. 4, The Godfather. 5, Gone with the Wind.

You must enter the winning goal pool and can't gripe if you draw Colorado's Marc-Andre Cliche or Minnesota's Clayton Stoner.

You can only do the "playoff beards" and "wacky superstitions" pieces once apiece. It's the rule.

If you can't think of anything else to write in the playoffs, just contrive something and be "controversial."

There's always the easy trash the other market because "your" mercenaries are playing "our" mercenaries.

If a guy wins four and loses three face-offs, say he "dominated, winning 57 percent."

Hey, late-arriving writers, just keep Googling and rewriting previous works of hockey scribes.

Scribes, when Patrick Roy uses your first name, he is NOT saying you're his best friend or Red Fisher.

The Minnesota Wild does not play in Minneapolis.

Your Broncos credential doesn't work.

If a hockey player is a good guy to you, it's cuz he's a hockey player. It's not because he's impressed.

It's three periods, not an ellipsis. (Or four quarters.)

The NFL draft will be during the second round of the playoffs. Oh, oh.

French-Canadian does not mean you were born in Paris.

Hockey fans might be proprietary, but they can spot the bandwagon fakers by the second paragraph.

✲ ✲ ✲

When the Avalanche reconvened for practice Tuesday, the on-ice work seemed to make it clear that, with Matt Duchene and John Mitchell out, Patrick Roy planned to stick with MacKinnon centering O'Reilly and P. A. Parenteau at the outset of the series. Mitchell wasn't skating, and it seemed safe to assume that he wouldn't play against the Wild.

"It's something we're going to star with. Is it going to stay that way? I'm not sure," Roy said. "It brings some speed in the middle, which I like. I think it's good to have that option."

A year earlier, MacKinnon was the start of the Memorial Cup spotlight, so he was accustomed to high-profile pressure.

"Obviously, with Dutchy out, it puts a lot more pressure on everybody else," MacKinnon said. "But we have tons of good forwards. It's not just going to be me that they're going to be paying attention to. I think it's good that, if they key on one guy, we'll have other guys step up. They're going to have to kind of choose who they want to pick their battles with."

Beyond Mitchell on the injury front, Jan Hejda didn't practice because of his, ahem, upper body injury, but Roy said he was expected to be able to play in Game 1. The truth was that Hejda had suffered two broken fingers, and a pin was placed in his thumb. But he indeed was going to play. And Tyson Barrie was back on the ice, underscoring that when he didn't play at Anaheim, it was a case of Roy playing it safe.

On Wednesday, alarms went off and tweets went out when Hejda wasn't out for the start of practice, but he came on the ice a little later. The Avalanche glory years were full of examples of players fighting through injuries in the postseason—including Joe Sakic with a major shoulder issue and Rob Blake with a bad wrist—so there were no guarantees that Hejda or all the other players in the lineup were going to be at 100 percent.

Joe Sakic also stepped to the podium in the media room to talk about the playoffs, and it was his first full-fledged news conference of the season. As it was about to open, he was asked if he was going to live up to his self-proclaimed image as "Quoteless Joe" in the session. He smiled and said, "Depends on what you ask!"

"It's the same feeling," Sakic said. "It's excitement. I'm excited for the players and our organization, and the fans here in Denver. There's no better playoffs than hockey playoffs, and it's great to be back. I don't have any control, I don't have to get ready for the games, so it's different that way, but the excitement's still there."

Sakic said his feelings about the 2013–14 team strengthened after the New Year. "There was not one point in the season where you thought they were getting complacent and were content with the success they were having," he said. "We knew what we had in the dressing room, but to watch the players and see how they believed in each other, that's a great team that never quits. They clinched the playoffs, and they could have taken some shortcuts after that, but they weren't satisfied. They wanted home ice against Chicago, so the confidence kept growing, and their belief and expectations kept growing, and they're here."

THURSDAY, APRIL 17, AT DENVER: AVALANCHE-WILD, GAME 1

With 3:01 left in the third period, and with the Avalanche trailing 4–3, Roy pulled Semyon Varlamov. As a rookie NHL coach, he had defied convention several times in the regular season, bringing off his goalie earlier than the usual minute or so remaining. This time, he did it with the opening game of a playoff series on the line, setting himself up for potential second-guessing . . . or ridicule.

The Avalanche couldn't get the puck past Minnesota goalie Ilya Bryzgalov.

Then, with a little more than ninety seconds remaining, Minnesota's Erik Haula lifted a backhanded clear out of the Wild zone and the puck was sliding slowly toward the Colorado net.

The empty Colorado net.

As Avalanche defenseman Erik Johnson started chasing the puck, it seemed hopeless. But wait . . .

The puck slowed.

Johnson picked up steam.

Finally, at the last second, he reached out and swatted the puck aside about six inches short of the goal line, then crashed into the post, knocking the net off its moorings. The puck had started to roll on its side and it *might* have ended up hitting the post and staying out of the net, but that question would remain unanswered. This much was indisputable: Johnson had made a terrific play, with 1:32 remaining. With the net off, the whistle blew, and Johnson and several of his teammates were angry when Minnesota's Matt Cooke, the first to the puck, shot it in the prone Johnson's direction.

The Avalanche still had a chance.

Roy called a time-out at that point and outlined more strategy. It didn't work out the way he plotted, but Paul Stastny eventually scored with 13.4 seconds remaining to make it 4–4 and send the game to overtime. Bryzgalov made the save on a Johnson shot, but the puck went to the side to Stastny, who fired it over Bryzgalov's shoulder as the "other" Russian goalie in the game tried to get over.

Then Stastny scored again at 7:27 of overtime to give the Avalanche the 5–4 victory and seemingly leave the Wild shocked and demoralized after letting the opener get away. On the game-winning play, Tyson Barrie carried the puck down the slot and was knocked down, but he managed to get it to Nathan MacKinnon, who set up Stastny. MacKinnon ended up with three assists, and by the end of the night, he was back at wing, playing with Stastny and Gabriel Landeskog.

Roy said he had considered pulling Varlamov even sooner, with four minutes remaining. "That went through our minds," he said. "At one point they had their third pairing on the ice, and we said should we give a shot at it. But I thought that was a little pushy. At the same time, you have to go with your gut feeling. This is what playoffs are."

Roy also noted that the Avalanche had worked on six-on-five every morning skate for the final month of the season. "You always hope that eventually it will pay off," he said. "You don't know when, but when it happens, you're pretty happy, and tonight could be a key moment in our playoff run."

"What a comeback!" Johnson said. "That's the kind of game you dream of winning when you're a kid."

Notably, the Avalanche had won on a night when Varlamov, who finished with 29 saves, wasn't very good; and when Johnson and Hejda struggled for most of the night in the top defensive pairing. Hejda's injury wasn't public knowledge. Colorado had come back from a 4–2 second-period deficit. Jamie McGinn's score off a rebound with 13:47 left in regulation had gotten the Avalanche within one, setting up the frantic final minutes.

"I think this win will give us some momentum going forward," Roy said. "We believe in ourselves. Sometimes you're not playing your best game, but the quality of our team is, we found a way to win this game. That's what you want in the playoffs. It was the first playoff game for a few of our guys, and I thought we did a good job."

❊ ❊ ❊

Roy's playoff pattern was going to be holding optional skates on off days when games were every other day, and his off-day media session mostly covered the issue of pulling his goalie earlier than the norm.

"It's just a feeling," he said. "I know one day it might bite us, but if we benefit, it's a long-term thing. If we do it ten times and score four goals, that's 40 percent, and it's pretty big. If you give up one goal, what the heck, let's keep doing it. I think it gives us momentum and forces them to defend. If we keep the puck in the zone, they get tired; and if it lasts, the tougher it is for them to make the right plays."

Roy said he hadn't felt strongly that he should be coming off sooner as a player.

"It was something that I started doing in junior," he said. "I remember one time pulling the goalie at 17 minutes [left] in the third period. I've done it at 12 minutes. You just look at the score. Do we need one goal, two goals, three goals; Do you need something to change the momentum? And yesterday, I thought we were playing so well in the third; we were more in their zone. I thought it was a good time."

A little later, he admitted that he pulled his goalie once in the second period when coaching in a bantam tournament. "We had a five-on-three and we were down 3–0 or 4–0, and actually we scored two goals by the end of the period and made it a 4–2 game," he said. "We lost the game, but we did it at the end of the second period."

SATURDAY, APRIL 19, AT DENVER: AVALANCHE-WILD, GAME 2

As MacKinnon sped into the zone and deked to his right, Minnesota defenseman Jared Spurgeon suddenly realized that the usual formulas of angles and speed didn't apply, tried to do a crossover—and fell down.

MacKinnon had a way of doing that to people.

Seconds later, the teenager had fired the puck past Bryzgalov to tie the game 1–1 at 6:20 of the first period.

MacKinnon ended up with a goal and three assists, giving him seven points in his first two NHL playoff games, as the Avalanche won 4–2 to retain the home-ice advantage and take a 2–0 series lead to Minnesota. The MacKinnon-Stastny-Landeskog line combined for four goals and ten points, with MacKinnon and Stastny taking turns setting up a pair of

Landeskog goals before Stastny closed out the scoring with an empty-netter. Minnesota coach Mike Yeo yanked Bryzgalov after Colorado's third goal, sending out Darcy Kuemper.

"Our line was clicking tonight, and those guys made my job easier," MacKinnon said.

Said Roy: "They had an outstanding game. They were moving the puck really well. They were skating well. I have to say one thing here: All our guys played really well. I thought that was a really good team win."

Also, Ryan O'Reilly was back at center and playing between Jamie McGinn and P. A. Parenteau.

Even without Duchene and Mitchell playing, the Avalanche seemed in control of the series. Varlamov's solid play in Game 2 was encouraging, and Roy made sure all knew that. "I didn't make too much of the first game," he said. "He played well enough to win. The goalie doesn't always need to be perfect. He needs to find a way to win. Tonight, he was rock solid. I have so much confidence in him. He has been our best player all year."

☼ ☼ ☼

The Avalanche's charter flights leave from the Signature Flight Support facility at Denver International Airport, and the day after Game 2, the team didn't practice and met there to head to the Twin Cities.

MacKinnon arrived with his landlord, Jean-Sebastien Giguere, and he conceded that the veteran goalie didn't let him drive. "I don't think he trusts me behind the wheel for more than 40 minutes," MacKinnon said, smiling. He was wearing a light blue suit and no tie, and his playoff beard was impressive for a usually baby-faced teenager.

The night before, goaltender Roberto Luongo—perhaps the NHL's most notorious gabber on Twitter—had sent out praise of MacKinnon, and his fame was spreading.

"Like you said, with the draft and the Memorial Cup, with everything last year, I think it's nothing too new," MacKinnon said. "It's magnified, it's a little bigger than I've been used to, but it's the same thing. I've never really put too much thought in this kind of stuff, and I don't think I ever will. It's nice to get some attention, but it's not very important to me."

MacKinnon said he had heard from former classmates at Shattuck-St. Mary's, and several of them would be at Game 3 in Minnesota. "I haven't seen them in a couple of years," he said. "It's pretty cool to go back there. I'll get them some tickets. There are some guys who play for the Gophers and some guys who are in Minnesota, playing somewhere else."

Also, it was striking that when Matt Duchene arrived, he hustled into the building, pulling his bag, looking like a young businessman trying to make it down a concourse on a tight connection. Roy confirmed that the plan was for Duchene to be back on skates the next morning for the first time since his injury. "We're not going to push," Roy said. "We're going to be very smart about when he comes back. He's going to want to play soon, and it's going to be up to our doctors and (trainers) to determine if he's ready to play."

MONDAY, APRIL 21, AT ST. PAUL: AVALANCHE-WILD, GAME 3
THURSDAY, APRIL 24, AT ST. PAUL: AVALANCHE-WILD, GAME 4

Ominously, the Avalanche wasted two terrific games from Varlamov in St. Paul, as Minnesota won 1–0 in overtime in Game 3 and 2–1 in Game 4 to pull even in the series. And they also lost Tyson Barrie for four to six weeks after he took a knee-on-knee hit from the notorious Matt Cooke at 2:02 of the second period in Game 3 and suffered a medial collateral ligament injury.

The loss of Barrie was wrenching, and the dirty hit from Cooke added anger to the reaction. Cooke drew a two-minute minor for kneeing. "Knee-on-knee on Tyson Barrie is without a doubt the play of the game," Roy said that night. "We lost our best offensive defenseman. I think it could have been a five-minute major. He'd be out of the game, plus I think that would have broken their momentum. We would have been on the [five-minute] power play. There are key moments in games, and now we believe the league will make the right call." Asked what that should be, he said, "I'm not working for the league. I am sure the league will make the right call."

The NHL indeed suspended Cooke for seven games two days later, but even that seemed a bit strange considering the posted video explanation showed the play several times with a narration that emphasized how dirty it was and seemed to be justifying a longer suspension. Although Cooke had been attempting to portray himself as a new man with the Wild, his track record for dirty play—dirty play that went beyond pushing-the-envelope grit—was infamous. He had been suspended five times previously. Plus, he even played a secondary role in the Steve Moore-Todd Bertuzzi mess as a member of the Canucks, because he challenged Moore to fight during the first period of the March 8, 2004, game in Vancouver. Moore obliged and held his own, and answering the call should have ended it. But it didn't, due to a combination of reasons ranging from the blowout nature of that game in the third period to the fact that Cooke hadn't beaten up Moore.

Yes, the two Avalanche losses in St. Paul were two one-goal games, but Colorado was dominated.

No, the Avalanche hadn't been as bad as some tried to make them out to be. Judging by some of the reaction, they'd gone from being the 1978 Canadiens to resembling the expansion 1993 Ottawa Senators in a span of only a few days. Yet they hadn't looked good, either. It was a major swing, but those getting carried away seemed to have forgotten or never knew that even the Colorado Stanley Cup teams played some stinkers in the postseason.

The Avalanche were outshot 46–22 in Game 3 and 32–12 (yes, 12) in Game 4, and had gone a combined zero-for-eight on the power play. The 12 shots tied the franchise playoff low, and that had come in Game 4 of the Stanley Cup finals against the New Jersey Devils. The Avs lost that game 3–2, but Roy at least could point out—if he was so inclined—that the 2001 team had managed to rebound from that embarrassment.

The only goal Kuemper allowed in the two games was O'Reilly's at 13:25 of the second period in Game 4.

The series was tied, Colorado still had home-ice advantage, but the results—and how they came about—at the very least were disquieting.

"We just need to be involved," Roy said after Game 4. "We need to make those plays. Hey, if you put a puck on net, it's possible you'll have to take a bodycheck. Our shots need to hit the net. We have to force their goalie to make the saves, and then our confidence will be coming back. Our execution is not there. We seem to be rushing plays."

Beyond that, Roy looked for the bright side.

"The way I've been all year, I've been very positive, and I'm going to continue to be today," he said. "I'm looking more at how our goaltender played. When we have the type of performance that we have from our goaltender, there's no reason for us to not believe in ourselves, coming back home. Obviously, offensively we're going to need more from some of our forwards. They're going to have to chip in and be more involved."

Although Duchene had skated in Minnesota, he still wasn't going to be cleared to play in Game 5, and John Mitchell's concussion symptoms weren't gone. Mitchell was examined a lot by Avalanche physician Andrew Parker, but the most he could do was some light stretching in the training room. Roy had plugged Ryan Wilson into the lineup as the replacement for Barrie on defense. And Colorado's 2010 first-round draft choice, diminutive center Joey Hishon, was called up from Lake Erie and played his first NHL game at an unlikely time . . . crunch time in the playoffs. His pro career had been plagued by concussions, and Roy giving him a shot in Game 4 was an admission that having so little scoring depth in the postseason was potentially fatal.

The Avalanche would have to plug on with a depleted lineup.

BALLS ON THE TABLE

Uh, what did he just say?

That was the general reaction at Patrick Roy's media session at Family Sports on the afternoon after Game 4.

What he had just said was: "Now it's our turn to—sorry for the words—put our balls on the table."

He didn't mean Titleists.

It had come up, of course, because of the Avalanche's punchlessness in the two games in St. Paul, and perhaps because of the ridiculous overreaction to the series being tied after four games. Roy correctly noted that the Colorado-Minnesota series wasn't alone in being dominated by home teams, because at that point home teams in the Western Conference were 15–1 in the postseason.

Curiously, he also seemed to go out of his way to diminish expectations. Maybe it was his attempt to take pressure off his team.

"I know we love to say we're Stanley Cup contenders, bingo, like this," he said. "Even you guys as reporters need to be positive. It's important. I know you love winning as much as I do. You know that I love winning. But we need to be patient with our group. This is a young team. This is a team that, let's not forget, finished 29th last year. These are huge steps, and this is a learning process."

He was right about one thing: Although reporters try to maintain objectivity, the fact is that it's a lot more fun to cover a winning team and be around happy athletes. In that sense, media folks—even hardened and cynical reporters—tend to root for the people they cover, rather than teams. Maybe that's splitting hairs, but it's true. If you don't believe that, check out allegedly objective media folks' Twitter feeds during games; it's obvious that for many of them, their entire perspective is based on glee when the locals win and disappointment and even anger when they lose. Also, especially during playoff series, one of the entertaining side stories almost always is the media contingents in each city accusing each other of being "homers."

Roy said the Avalanche would make some adjustments, primarily in reacting to Minnesota's approach in defensive zone coverage. And that's when he added, "Now it's our turn to—sorry for the words—put our balls on the table."

He said he still had faith in his team.

"I understand we want a fast track. I understand we want to be Stanley Cup contenders. But it's a learning process. What the Montreal Canadiens did in '86 with eight rookies [including Roy], I'm not going to tell you it's going to happen every year. Maybe it has changed."

Then he lowered his voice to a virtual whisper of emphasis. "It's tough to win the Stanley Cup," he said.

He said that when the Avalanche formulated its playoff plan, "It was not to go 16–0. How many teams have been 16–0 in the history of the NHL? Is there one? No? I'm surprised to hear that. I thought there were 100 teams. It's tough in the playoffs. The 2–2 doesn't bother me one bit. It's how we're going to bounce back that I want to see tomorrow."

He came back to the "process" of rebuilding from near-worst to contender. "Can we skip some of it?" he asked. "I hope so. But I'm very proud of what we have accomplished so far. Am I satisfied? The answer is no. But let's not forget we're playing against a good team, a team that is playing really well in their building, and their fans were outstanding. But all they did to us was what we did to them. We beat them twice here. Our fans were there. They were on their feet. Their fans were on their feet. Now we need our fans again to give that little push that our players need."

The Avalanche was one-for-15 on the power play in the postseason, last in the NHL, at 6.7 percent.

"I'd love to see our power play at 50 percent," Roy said. "But it's not going to happen in the playoffs. . . . It's not how pretty it's going to be. It's find a way to put one in."

Erik Johnson was usually an enlightening voice in these situations, because he soaked up video study and often spoke about what he and his teammates had seen—and been told.

"Probably as 'D,' I don't think we've been as clean in our exits from the D zone," he said. "I think we have to have a little more poise as a group. When we're playing well and having success, we're getting the forwards the puck in stride. We've been a little too stagnant, a little too—I don't want to say nervous; I want to say unsure to make the right play. I think we're looking a little bit too long for the perfect play. As a group of D, we have to do a much better job of making our forwards' lives a little bit easier in transition. When they get the puck, they're so dangerous."

Paul Stastny put it in perspective.

"After the last game, everyone was disappointed, but we shook it off," he said. "It's 2–2, we have home ice, and we get back to work. It almost felt like we were down 2–0 or 3–0, but we're not. We've put ourselves in good position early on, and now we've kind of stumbled a little bit, but that's all right—we're going to regroup and use that home crowd to our advantage."

It was a new series. Best-of-three. With Colorado still holding the home-ice advantage.

FROM THE NOTEBOOK OF TERRY FREI

I'm a veteran of covering many playoff series in both the NBA and NHL, and I always have been amused by the ridiculous overreactions to single games or to two games at the same site in the coverage. I've even been caught up in it myself, so I'm not claiming to be immune. In this case, at the news conference, I prefaced my question by acknowledging that Roy, as a participant in many playoff series as a player and a major junior coach, certainly understood the fluctuations in fortunes and drastic swings in evaluation—in other words, the overreactions. I noted that much of the coverage of this series would have you believe the Avalanche suddenly was overmatched and even dead, and I asked of Game 5: "Are you going to show up?"

That launched Roy into part of his filibuster, and many said later to me that it was unfortunate Roy had misunderstood me.

On the contrary, I think he completely understood me. He had become brilliant at using the media, and I mean that as high praise. Part of that is using news conferences and scrums as a means of saying what he wanted to say, getting around to it regardless of the questions, even if it took gently reworking the questions to fit his agenda. Brilliant coaches do that, and Roy had picked that up and was getting good at it, too.

But I wish I had phrased the ultimate question differently.

For several reasons, I was the only Post *representative at Family Sports that day, so I was charged with writing the quick story online and then the piece for the morning paper. As I was about to file the online story, including the "balls on the table" comment, I e-mailed editors and alerted them to Roy's words. I didn't want to try to sneak anything by and left it up to them about whether they would stay in the story. The paper tends to be conservative on such things; witness the tendency to avoid quoting anyone as using "damn" or "hell"—although all sorts of brainless ridiculousness, often of marginal taste and usually anonymous, is posted on the bottom of stories as "reader comment." (Standards are being raised on most sites . . . but not enough.)*

When my story first was posted online, the "balls on the table" comment wasn't there, pending higher editors' decision. Soon, it was added back to the story and would stay there through the rest of the online cycle and in the paper. I agreed with the decision, almost reluctantly. One, what Roy said took some interpretation to make it objectionable or in marginal taste. This wouldn't be filling in the blank and having Ken Hitchcock telling Patrick Roy "to go fuck himself" in the paper and on the newspaper site. Two, although I would have accepted leaving the words out as trying to keep standards high, it also would have been unrealistic in this instance. The comment was all over already. So, soon it was back in my story, and stayed in.

The next morning, in my weekly Saturday cohosting appearance on FM 104.3 The Fan, I repeatedly referred to the Avalanche facing a dreaded 2–2 deficit in the series. I said it that way because that was the tone of much of the roller-coaster coverage, and explained that each win drew the equivalent of, "Plan the parade, Mayor Hancock," and each loss seemed to have us reading and hearing that the Avalanche never would win again. Or, to paraphrase Dave "Tiger" Williams's famous assessment of the Penguins during a series: "Them Avalanches is done like dinner."

Judging from messages on the listener text line, some didn't "get" my irony.

Anyone who has worked in talk radio knows this: the studio text line sometimes is very, very scary.

SATURDAY, APRIL 26, AT DENVER: AVALANCHE-WILD, GAME 5

They did it again.

With Semyon Varlamov on the bench, the Colorado net empty and the Avalanche trailing by a goal, P. A. Parenteau scored with 1:14 remaining in the third period to tie the game 3–3. And Nathan MacKinnon ended it at 3:27 of overtime, converting a setup pass from Gabriel Landeskog and beating Darcy Kuemper. The Avalanche were within one win of advancing to the Western Conference semifinals.

Colorado was up 2–1 going into the third period before Minnesota scored twice to take the lead.

"After they scored two bang-bang goals like that, it sort of deflated us," Parenteau said. "But we stuck with it."

Parenteau's tying goal was his first NHL playoff point—at age 31.

"I got in the league late and played on some teams that didn't have a chance to make the playoffs," he noted. "It's never too late to make it, it's never too late to start the playoffs, and I'm feeling better and better."

His goal retroactively was controversial, because careful scrutiny of replays showed Paul Stastny was slightly offside on the play. Parenteau came on for Ryan O'Reilly in the change. "I got on the ice with a lot of speed, a lot of energy, and Pauly just fed me one in the middle, and I got my stick on it," Parenteau said.

On the Wild side, Ryan Suter whined about the missed offside the most, but Zach Parise had the right idea, noting how difficult it is for linesmen to make those instantaneous calls, in essence trying to focus on both the puck and players and their skates at the blue line. Most smart players make their point about such plays, expect the calls to even out, and even know that by not being jerks, they increase the chances of that happening.

Of his winning goal, MacKinnon said: "Landy and Pauly did a great job on the forecheck, and when Landy got the puck there I was kind of screaming for it. I didn't really pick my corner or anything; I just fired it on net, and thankfully, I managed to get it over his glove. It definitely was the most exciting goal of my career."

Actually, pulling Varlamov with slightly more than two minutes remaining might have seemed late for Roy, but his hand was forced when Landeskog drew an unsportsmanlike conduct penalty with 4:33 left for spraying ice in Kuemper's face. "It was hard to remain calm after the call," Roy said. "We had to kill that one. It was a huge kill."

The trick now was to close out the series.

"We had two looks in games over there, and we know what's going to happen over there," Roy said of the upcoming Game 6. "We're just going to have to play like we did tonight."

Had the Avalanche put their balls on the table?

"What do you think?" Roy asked his questioner. "I'm happy. We all agree on this. We did tonight. Our guys played with a lot of passion, a lot of heart. And thank you to our fans. They were on their feet when we jumped on the ice, and they were very important to our players."

The last question of the night was whether Matt Duchene was going to play in Game 6. "We're going to take a serious look at it," Roy said.

Some spirited debate already was beginning about that. One school of thought was that with the Avalanche ahead 3–2 in the series and having the Game 7 safety net at home, if necessary, why not hold Duchene out one more game? The countering view was that Duchene playing in Game 6 would provide a shot in the arm, and if it indeed came down to a Game 7 in Denver, Duchene at least wouldn't be coming in cold.

* * *

The next day in the Twin Cities, the television stations were replaying the video of Stastny being inches offside on the play that led to Parenteau's tying goal in Denver. Depending on the outlet, the stations were portraying it roughly either as the worst non-call since a missed offside as the Seattle Metropolitans won the Stanley Cup in 1917, or as the Zapruder film enhanced to conclusively show a second gunman on the grassy knoll.

✿ ✿ ✿

At the morning skate hours before Game 6, Roy said Duchene would
be a game-time decision, and Pierre LeBrun of ESPN.com brought up
that Anaheim coach Bruce Boudreau—yes, Roy's antagonist on opening
night—had said Roy's nerve to pull his goalie earlier than the norm had
caused him to rethink his own strategy. The Ducks had scored twice the
night before to tie Dallas late and went on to win in overtime.

"You start to see that more and more," Roy said. "But I'm not going
to take any credit for that. I'm going to give credit to my players. Because imagine if we get scored on pulling the goalie with three minutes
left in the game. Everybody would be going, 'Look at that stupid idiot.
He pulled the goalie with three minutes left, and he got scored on.' Our
players deserve credit. Our players are creating the trend here. Yeah,
it's the decision made by the coach to do it, but it's the players who do
the work, and they're the ones who should receive the credit for that."

MONDAY, APRIL 28, AT ST. PAUL: AVALANCHE-WILD, GAME 6

The empty-net magic ran out. This time, trailing 3–2 late, the Avalanche gave up two empty-net goals late and lost 5–2. So on the scoreboard, it was the most decisive game in the series, but that was mislead-
ing. Although the Avalanche had spotted the Wild a two-goal lead—on
Parise's power-play tip and Mikael Granlund's shot through Varlamov's
five-hole—they came back to tie it and at least make the Xcel Energy
Center fans nervous.

The first goal came after Colorado killed off the first minor in a five-
on-three disadvantage. Suter half-fanned on a shot, O'Reilly blocked it
and then controlled the puck to get it to Stastny, just out of the box. He
scored on the breakaway at 16:59 of the first. So instead of being down
3–0 at the end of one period—which easily could have happened on the
five-on-three—the Avalanche trailed 2–1 and later pulled even on Nick
Holden's goal in the second period.

Parise's second goal, though, put the Wild up late, and then came
the two empty-netters.

There were a couple of silver linings for the Avalanche. They had hung in and, despite the score, it was their best game in Minnesota in the series. "I was very happy with our team," Roy said. "Our team played really well. I thought there were a lot of positives out there."

Also, Duchene had returned to the lineup, briefly playing on the fourth line before Roy ruled he was ready to move up. "He was great tonight," Roy said. "He was flying out there. He was playing well, he was playing hard, and I had to use him. Down 2–0, you take every plan you have and you put it in the garbage can."

"It's a start, I guess," Duchene said. "You've got to learn to trust an injury like that coming back, and as the game went on, I felt more confident with it. There's still a long way to go for me. But next game is Game 7, so you lay it all on the line."

Yes, and Game 7 would be in Denver.

"You know what? We fought all year to be in that position if there was a Game 7," Roy said. "It's in our building, in front of our fans, and I think it's going to be exciting. It's great for our team, it's going to be a great experience, and I'm sure our players are excited about it. We're not happy to lose tonight, but I thought both teams played really well, and it was a great hockey game. That game could have gone either way, and it went their way tonight."

Roy said he believed that as a player, he was 0–6 on the road and 7–1 at home in those deciding games. "It is tough to win on the road in Game 7 when the home team is playing solid," he said. "I'd rather have it at home, to be honest with you."

SUDDEN DEATH . . . AND BEYOND

Patrick Roy relentlessly laid out the same agendas as Game 7 approached, both on the day between games and at the morning skate, again emphasizing that the home-ice advantage was a reward his team was going to use without apology. "How good is this?" he asked. "They're excited about it, and they should be. All year, we battled hard, we were even keel, we wanted to have that home-ice advantage, and we surprised the world of hockey by finishing first in our division, and we are receiving the benefit of it, in front of our fans. How exciting is it for Denver, not having playoff hockey for the past, what, four years, and now you're involved in a Game 7? Our fans are going to be excited; they're going to bring a lot of energy to the game."

He also noted that when involved in Game 7s as a player, he could mostly focus on getting ready personally, but it was different as a coach, assessing all the possibilities. "I'd say coaching is probably a little more demanding, but I love it."

Finally, he was asked about his final Game 7 as a player—Minnesota's overtime victory over the Avalanche in the first round in 2003, when Andrew Brunette's goal ended Roy's career.

"What I remember about that game was that we played against a team that just competed, and they were well-coached by Jacques Lemaire," Roy said. After noting that Colorado lost the final three games, he added, "I just saw a group on the other side that was resilient all year, and this was how they made the playoffs. It's a bit like we have been doing all year." He smiled wryly. "It should not have a big effect on our team because there aren't many players from then still with us."

There was only one—and that was Alex Tanguay, who was injured and not playing.

WEDNESDAY, APRIL 30, AT DENVER: AVALANCHE-WILD, GAME 7

Four times, the Avalanche took the lead, on goals from Holden, Jamie McGinn, Stastny, and Johnson.

Four times, the building erupted.

Four times, it seemed that Colorado was establishing momentum and taking control.

Four times, writers played with the parts of their stories that mentioned an upcoming Chicago series; and four times, Avalanche fans began looking forward to that delayed matchup.

Four times—the fourth when Johnson's goal made it 4–3 with 8:44 remaining in regulation—Colorado seemed on the verge of taking control.

But four times, the Wild came back to tie the game. The last time was when Jared Spurgeon patiently waited as Nathan MacKinnon went down to try to block his shot but ended up sliding harmlessly out of the way, then beat Semyon Varlamov high to the stick side to make it 4–4 with only 2:27 remaining in the third period.

Then, after the Avalanche didn't capitalize on a couple of terrific chances against Ilya Bryzgalov—who had come on for Darcy Kuemper, injured in a third-period collision—the Wild ended it at 5:02 of overtime. Nino Niederreiter scored his second goal of the game, capitalizing on a two-on-one and beating Varlamov high to the short, or glove, side from the right circle. At first, he seemed like most of the folks in the seats; he didn't know how to respond and/or didn't believe what he had just seen.

The Wild had outshot the Avalanche 35–22, but was it that Varlamov had not come up big in Game 7? Was he the sole culprit? Of course not. But with the man known as the sport's top "money" goaltender of all time watching from the bench, Varlamov wasn't good enough—not good enough to add to his reputation as a playoff goalie, and not good enough to prevent questions about whether Colorado's latest three-year commitment to him was risky and excessive.

In the Avalanche hockey operations box at the press box level, Joe Sakic and Josh Kroenke, among others, were stunned. It was over. Suddenly, when Niederreiter scored, it was over. The season and the dreams were over. Once they accepted that that was true, and that wasn't easy, they rode down the elevator together, walked down the hall, and went into the coaches' office to commiserate. There were silent stretches for a couple of minutes as all struggled to come to grips with it, but after a few minutes, the talk took a slight turn—to congratulations on a turnaround season that ultimately raised expectations to the point where making the playoffs, a reasonable goal at the start of the season, wasn't enough. This was a thunderous disappointment, but even that—that a first-round loss could be so disappointing—was a compliment.

As Roy liked to say: "Who'd have thought?"

Nobody.

But none of that lessened the sting. In the dressing room, broadcasters and media members kept trying to tell the players that they had accomplished a lot.

"It's an emptiness, and I really don't know how to handle it," said Gabriel Landeskog. "All of a sudden, it just ends. It's hard to look at that big picture right now. Maybe next week."

Said Paul Stastny: "You come into the season, you want to win the Cup. If you don't make it, you fall short of it. I don't know if you can say it tarnishes the year. I don't know if that's the right word. But tonight, what we did to teams all year kind of happened to us. Then in overtime, we had a couple of chances that were literally one inch away and could have gone our way but didn't. It's disappointing, but throughout the year, we stuck together as a team. We win as a team, and we lose as a team. We have to be proud of what these guys have done here."

At his stall, MacKinnon was staring straight ahead. A year earlier, he was celebrating a Memorial Cup championship. His spectacular rookie season had ended on a downer, and he was blaming himself for at least Spurgeon's goal. If only he'd blocked it, instead of sliding right by . . .

"It's an empty feeling," he said. "Being up by one with a couple of minutes left . . . There are going to be a lot of guys losing some sleep over some plays tonight. We definitely have some regrets going into the summer. It tarnishes the year a lot, I think. We made some huge strides, coming from second-to-last to top five in the league, whatever it was, but I think we wanted to make a run here, and we had a chance twice to win the series—once in Game 6 and obviously tonight. It's tough to describe exactly what went on. Coming back next year, it's weird to say, but we have to wait until September to get things going again, which is going to be a long summer. Especially watching the playoffs is going to be tough."

Matt Duchene noted, "I thought we had it there twice. It's heartbreaking."

Like MacKinnon, Ryan O'Reilly made no move to take off his jersey. O'Reilly outwardly took the loss the hardest of anyone still in the room. Moisture formed at the tips of his eyelids as he struggled through answers to media questions, including about the Avalanche's accomplishments. "So what?," he asked. "The only thing that matters is a Stanley Cup and winning playoff games. We failed."

P. A. Parenteau, who still wore his lucky blue and orange socks from his days with the New York Islanders as his first layer of clothing under all his Avs gear, quietly peeled them off and slumped his shoulders forward.

"Can't lose a game like that, with a lead twice in the third period," said Parenteau, always open with the media even if that meant going against the usual clichés most teammates used. "Too many easy goals we gave them tonight, and it burned us."

Across the room, Johnson, who would have been the hero had his late third-period tie-breaking goal held up, couldn't believe it was over.

"Empty. Just an empty feeling right now," Johnson said. "I really thought we had that game. It's a shock right now it didn't happen."

In the interview room, Roy was somber—but not shockingly so.

"The toughest part is to not come back tomorrow and be ready for Chicago," he said. "I'm sure tomorrow it's going to hurt more."

He admitted to having "mixed feelings. There is a side of me that is very disappointed. I thought that we could have won that game. But there is also a side of me that is extremely proud of our players. I love the way we were all year. We compete, and tonight was another good example of how hard we have been playing. I don't have enough words to say how proud I am of them. It's a process, and it's a learning process. Unfortunately, at the end, the injuries were a factor. Losing a guy like Barrie and losing a guy like Mitchell would have probably made the difference for us, and having Dutchy come in late . . . But these are not excuses we want to use. A team is a team, and we have played like this all year. We find a way to go through adversity. We got beat by a team that played really well, was well coached and deserved to win as much as we did.

"One quality we had all year: We were never satisfied. I'm certainly not going to start to be tonight. It was a great experience this year. It was fun for me to be part of it. One thing we are proud of is to see the Avs back on top, and I think that should motivate us to have another good year next year. Seeing our fans be excited about the team makes me so happy, and seeing our fans coming back to the building. It was electric out there, and I didn't want to see it ending."

He said he had "goose bumps" when the crowd cheered at the start of periods and the overtime. "I would just like to say thanks to them," he said. "The players gave everything they had, and it's a great season for us. It's hard to talk like this right now because everyone knows how much I like to win. At the same time, we have to admit that was a heck of a year."

He added, "As much as we dreamed about winning the Stanley Cup, we knew it would be tough. We aren't there yet. That hurts to say, but it's fact."

Roy said he hadn't yet been in the dressing room, and some of the preface to questions gave him additional hint that some of his players were taking it particularly hard.

"I don't want any of my players blaming themselves for the loss," he said. "We win and we lose as a team, and tonight we lost as a team."

About that time nearby, a man was hustling down the hallway, pulling a rolling computer bag. No, it wasn't a reporter. It was a member of the Wild staff, officially a hockey operations adviser. He was headed toward the Wild bus, pulled into the loading dock.

He was Andrew Brunette.

Déjà vu.

✯ ✯ ✯

Driving home, Sakic started feeling a little better. Some of the shock had worn off. "I just kept thinking about all the good things about the year, more than that last goal," he recalled later. "And I started thinking more about where we were headed. I was looking more at the big picture. Yes, we would have loved to have gone on to the next round. It didn't happen, but we like where we're going."

FROM THE NOTEBOOK OF ADRIAN DATER

Before the series, I thought matching up with the Wild, the Western Conference's seventh seed as a wild card, instead of the Blues or Black-hawks, would be a bad thing for the Avalanche.

It just never fit their "Why Not Us?" story line.

By virtue of St. Louis collapsing to lose its final six games of the season, the Avs were division winners, the "favorite" entering the playoffs.

That stripped them of their underdog identity.

The Wild still had the much higher payroll—about $11 million high-er—but it seemed as if the Avs weren't just playing with house money anymore.

Suddenly, the team that had nothing to lose all year actually did, it seemed.

There were some valid excuses as to why it all ended in seven games. The loss of Tyson Barrie in Game 3 because of Matt Cooke's cheap-shot knee, the absence of Matt Duchene for the first five games, the unavail-ability of center John Mitchell for all seven games . . . none of that did Patrick Roy's group any favors.

But finishing the story of their season with a list of excuses wouldn't be right or accurate.

Injuries or not, bad bounces or not, any NHL team should be ex-pected to win a home game in which it had the lead four times—includ-ing twice in the third period. The Wild had to play in the postseason without either of their top two goalies who started the year.

I'll admit there were times toward the end of the year when even I, the Prince of Pessimism, started to buy in to the #WhyNotUs thing. I asked myself more than once: "Maybe they're actually going to win this whole thing?" when all those supposedly impenetrable barriers (a win-ning record, a playoff berth, a division title) kept falling. All those bad Corsi and Fenwick stats? To hell with the pointy-headed numbers nerds. *I told myself:* "This team has Patrick Roy on its side, and Saint Patrick works miracles."

So in OT of that Game 7, when Gabe Landeskog and Paul Stastny came in on a two-on-one against Ryan Suter (and goalie Ilya Bryzgalov), I had long been conditioned by this team to expect the red light to come on any second, with another miracle finish in the metaphorical books and in this literal one.

Alas, the wheel finally landed on black instead of red for this team.

In the strictest sense, the Avs' season finished in disappointment. It marked the fifth time in its Denver history that the Avalanche blew at least a 3–2 lead and eventually the series. All of those series came with either Roy in goal or behind the bench.

But that's not how anyone will remember the 2013–14 Avalanche— as a bunch of chokers. That they got that far, that they finished third overall in the NHL in the regular season after a 29th-place showing, that they reestablished themselves again in a rabid but finicky sports town—that is what they'll be remembered for.

Attendance improved to 16,295, up from 15,444. They were on the front pages again, and TV media people who hadn't been within ten miles of an Avs game in years were forced to show up again.

Roy had one of the best first-year records of any coach in NHL history (52–22–8). Only Todd McLellan with San Jose (53–18–11 in 2008–09) had a better mark in recent history.

In looking back at this Avs season, Roy is the one I'll come away remembering most. Roy never wanted it to be about himself, but in the end, what Roy did has to go down as the main story line.

Just as he did in 1995 as a player, Roy journeyed from Quebec to show a Denver team what it takes to be a real winner.

In the coming years, Colorado's core of young, talented players will grab more of the spotlight, as they should. Future books no doubt might be written about Nathan MacKinnon or Matt Duchene, Gabe Landeskog or Ryan O'Reilly.

This one, for me, was about a coach who did a remarkable thing. In the face of numerous skeptics, Roy took a team in disarray and put the pieces back in order. If a book isn't written someday about this group winning a Stanley Cup, with Roy in charge, that will be a true disappointment.

FROM THE NOTEBOOK OF TERRY FREI

I agree with Adrian. (Yes, occasionally that happens.)

To reemphasize and bring this full circle: Way back in October, when we committed to doing this book, we had no idea how the season would turn out. This never was based on an assumption that we would be chronicling a championship team or season. As the season continued, and the surprises kept piling up, I was as astounded as anyone. Instead of coming back to earth after a fast start, the Avalanche plowed on. In fact, we probably didn't make enough of the amazing consistency involved in posting not just the exact same records at home and on the road (26–11–4), but also the exact same records in the first and second halves of the season (yes, also 26–11–4). All of that defies both odds and logic. They did it all with young talent, yes, but also a roster that, as we have tried to point out, didn't awe anyone with its depth, especially in the wake of the inevitable injuries.

The difference was coaching. At his introductory news conference, remember, Patrick Roy had gone out of his way to point out that 100 percent of all NHL head coaches—successful or otherwise—once were rookie head coaches. Yes, he was coaching some tremendous young talent. But with a less-than-juggernaut roster, he did the best job I've ever seen of regular-season coaching in the NHL . . . as a rookie head coach.

Roy, as you've seen, repeatedly emphasized his "partnership" with all involved—starting with the players, but also with his staff, with ownership and management, and the fans. But we're not fooling ourselves: we wouldn't have been doing this book if the Avalanche had hired a journeyman, albeit a respected journeyman, coach; and we wouldn't even have later scrambled to do this book as a "quickie" if the Avalanche had put together this kind of a season under that journeyman coach.

Ultimately, as Adrian noted, the Avalanche were "victims" of their own relentlessness and consistency—which raised expectations. In looking back over the material about Roy's feud with Ken Hitchcock, I was struck that, in a sense, "Hitch" unintentionally got his revenge, because a Colorado first-round loss to the playoff-tested defending Stanley Cup champion Blackhawks wouldn't have been "failure." Disappointment? Maybe. Failure? No way. And given the mysteries of matchups, there's even a chance the Avalanche could have knocked off the Hawks and moved on.

But as Roy was wont to say: "If and if, my aunt would be my uncle."

The question, of course, was where the Avalanche would go from there, with Roy filing away the rookie coach lessons, with Joe Sakic getting traction while running the front office, and with Josh Kroenke overseeing the family sports empire, trying to deal with the Nuggets' disintegration, and likely realizing that the NHL team was in good hands.

This book is ending.

The story continues.

UPDATES

At the 2014 NHL Awards ceremony in Las Vegas on June 24, **Patrick Roy** was named winner of the Jack Adams Award as coach of the year; **Nathan MacKinnon** accepted the Calder Trophy as rookie of the year; and **Ryan O'Reilly** was awarded the Lady Byng Trophy for sportsmanship and gentlemanly play combined with ability.

On June 30, the Avalanche traded **P. A. Parenteau** and a fifth-round draft choice to the Montreal Canadiens for veteran winger Danny Briere.

Paul Stastny became an unrestricted free agent on July 1 and signed a four-year, $28-million contract with St. Louis. The Avalanche's most significant unrestricted free-agent signings were winger Jarome Iginla (three years, $16 million) and center Jesse Winchester (two years, $1.8 million), and Colorado also sent second- and sixth-round draft choices to San Jose for defenseman Brad Stuart.

Among the players Colorado didn't attempt to bring back, **Andre Benoit** signed with Buffalo and **Brad Malone** signed with Carolina. **Cory Sarich** was unsigned on July 21, when he suffered serious injuries when a car struck his bicycle as he was on a training ride in British Columbia. He was released from a hospital within a week, but given his age, free-agent status and injuries, his return to the NHL was a longshot.

Moments before arbitration proceedings were to begin in Toronto on July 23, O'Reilly agreed to a two-year, $12-million deal with Colorado.

Jean-Sebastien Giguere announced his retirement on August 21.

STATS AND STANDINGS

Avalanche Regular-Season Statistics

Skaters	GP	G	A	PTS	+/−	PIM	ATOI
Matt Duchene	71	23	47	70	8	19	18:30
Gabriel Landeskog	81	26	39	65	21	71	18:41
Ryan O'Reilly	80	28	36	64	−1	2	19:49
Nathan MacKinnon	82	24	39	63	20	26	17:21
Paul Stastny	71	25	35	60	9	22	18:24
Erik Johnson	80	9	30	39	5	61	23:00
Jamie McGinn	79	19	19	38	−3	30	15:47
Tyson Barrie	64	13	25	38	17	20	18:33
P. A. Parenteau	55	14	19	33	3	30	16:57
John Mitchell	75	11	21	32	13	36	16:16
Andre Benoit	79	7	21	28	2	26	20:13
Maxime Talbot	70	7	18	25	4	43	16:19
Nick Holden	54	10	15	25	12	22	18:41
Jan Hejda	78	6	11	17	8	40	22:20
Cody McLeod	71	5	8	13	2	122	10:20
Alex Tanguay	16	4	7	11	7	4	17:17
Patrick Bordeleau	82	6	5	11	−1	115	6:53
Cory Sarich	54	1	9	10	7	38	17:05
Nate Guenin	68	1	8	9	3	46	17:17
Marc-Andre Cliche	76	1	6	7	−11	17	10:34
Steve Downie	11	1	6	7	4	36	16:43
Ryan Wilson	28	0	6	6	1	12	14:40
Brad Malone	32	3	2	5	−4	23	6:46
Stefan Elliott	1	1	0	1	0	0	16:51
Matt Hunwick	1	0	0	0	0	0	17:27
David Van der Gulik	2	0	0	0	0	0	5:41
Paul Carey	12	0	0	0	2	0	6:26
Karl Stollery	2	0	0	0	1	2	6:31

Goaltenders	GP	W	L	OTL	GAA	SV%	
Semyon Varlamov	63	41	14	6	2.41	.927	
Jean-Sebastien Giguere	22	11	6	1	2.62	.913	
Sami Aittokallio	1	0	1	0	4.50	.833	
Reto Berra	2	0	1	1	5.85	.781	

Avalanche Playoff Statistics

Skaters	GP	G	A	PTS	+/−	PIM	ATOI
Paul Stastny	7	5	5	10	−1	4	22:13
Nathan MacKinnon	7	2	8	10	2	4	20:34
Ryan O'Reilly	7	2	4	6	3	0	22:21
Jamie McGinn	7	2	3	5	−1	2	17:18
Nick Holden	7	3	1	4	2	8	22:09
Gabriel Landeskog	7	3	1	4	−2	8	21:12
Matt Duchene	2	0	3	3	−1	2	20:15
P. A. Parenteau	7	1	2	3	0	2	17:53
Tyson Barrie	3	0	2	2	3	0	18:17
Ryan Wilson	4	0	2	2	−1	2	15:27
Erik Johnson	7	1	1	2	−6	2	26:13
Joey Hishon	3	0	1	1	0	2	6:12
Andre Benoit	7	0	1	1	3	6	21:17
Cody McLeod	7	1	0	1	−1	22	10:50
Nate Guenin	7	0	1	1	1	4	16:00
Marc-Andre Cliche	7	0	0	0	−3	2	14:20
Jan Hejda	7	0	0	0	−6	6	21:38
Maxime Talbot	7	0	0	0	−3	4	17:08
Brad Malone	6	0	0	0	−1	2	5:53
Paul Carey	3	0	0	0	−1	0	3:46
Patrick Bordeleau	7	0	0	0	−1	10	5:43

Goaltender	P	W	L	GAA	SV%		
Semyon Varlamov	7	3	4	2.77	.913		

Eastern Conference Regular-Season Standings

Atlantic	GP	W	L	OTL	PTS	ROW	SOW	SOL	HOME	ROAD	GF	GA
Boston	82	54	19	9	117	51	3	6	31-7-3	23-12-6	261	177
Tampa Bay	82	46	27	9	101	38	8	6	25-10-6	21-17-3	240	215
Montreal	82	46	28	8	100	40	6	3	23-13-5	23-15-3	215	204
Detroit	82	39	28	15	93	34	5	9	18-13-10	21-15-5	222	230
Ottawa	82	37	31	14	88	30	7	7	18-17-6	19-14-8	236	265
Toronto	82	38	36	8	84	29	9	4	24-16-1	14-20-7	231	256
Florida	82	29	45	8	66	21	8	6	16-20-5	13-25-3	196	268
Buffalo	82	21	51	10	52	14	7	5	13-21-7	8-30-3	157	248
Metropolitan	**GP**	**W**	**L**	**OTL**	**PTS**	**ROW**	**SOW**	**SOL**	**HOME**	**ROAD**	**GF**	**GA**
Pittsburgh	82	51	24	7	109	44	7	3	28-9-4	23-15-3	249	207
NY Rangers	82	45	31	6	96	41	4	3	20-17-4	25-14-2	218	193
Philadelphia	82	42	30	10	94	39	3	8	24-14-3	18-16-7	236	235
Columbus	82	43	32	7	93	38	5	2	22-15-4	21-17-3	231	216
Washington	82	38	30	14	90	28	10	11	21-13-7	17-17-7	235	240
New Jersey	82	35	29	18	88	35	0	13	21-11-9	14-18-9	197	208
Carolina	82	36	35	11	83	34	2	4	18-17-6	18-18-5	207	230
NY Islanders	82	34	37	11	79	25	9	6	13-19-9	21-18-2	225	267

Western Conference Regular-Season Standings

Central	GP	W	L	OTL	PTS	ROW	SOW	SOL	HOME	ROAD	GF	GA
Colorado	82	52	22	8	112	47	5	4	26-11-4	26-11-4	250	220
St. Louis	82	52	23	7	111	43	9	3	28-9-4	24-14-3	248	191
Chicago	82	46	21	15	107	40	6	8	27-7-7	19-14-8	267	220
Minnesota	82	43	27	12	98	35	8	8	26-10-5	17-17-7	207	206
Dallas	82	40	31	11	91	36	4	5	23-11-7	17-20-4	235	228
Nashville	82	38	32	12	88	36	2	9	19-17-5	19-15-7	216	242
Winnipeg	82	37	35	10	84	29	8	6	18-17-6	19-18-4	227	237
Pacific	**GP**	**W**	**L**	**OTL**	**PTS**	**ROW**	**SOW**	**SOL**	**HOME**	**ROAD**	**GF**	**GA**
Anaheim	82	54	20	8	116	51	3	6	29-8-4	25-12-4	266	209
San Jose	82	51	22	9	111	41	10	7	29-7-5	22-15-4	249	200
Los Angeles	82	46	28	8	100	38	8	6	23-14-4	23-14-4	206	174
Phoenix	82	37	30	15	89	31	6	7	22-14-5	15-16-10	216	231
Vancouver	82	36	35	11	83	31	5	7	20-15-6	16-20-5	196	223
Calgary	82	35	40	7	77	28	7	3	19-19-3	16-21-4	209	241
Edmonton	82	29	44	9	67	25	4	3	16-22-3	13-22-6	203	270